KEVIN
M^CCLOUD'S
DECOR-
ATING
B·O·O·K

KEVIN McCLOUD'S DECOR-ATING B·O·O·K

PHOTOGRAPHY BY
Michael Crockett

DORLING KINDERSLEY · LONDON

For Katy and Hugo
with thanks to Deirdre

Project editor **Rosie Ford**
Art editor **Steven Wooster**
Editor **Mark Ronan**
Designer **Sarah Ponder**

First published in Great Britain in 1990 by Dorling Kindersley
Limited, 9 Henrietta Street, London WC2E 8PS

British Library Cataloguing in Publication Data

McCloud, Kevin 1959–
    Kevin McCloud's decorating book.
    1. Residences. Decorating
    I. Title
    698

    ISBN 0-86318-422-7

Typeset by Tradespools, Somerset, UK.
Colour reproduction by Bright Arts, Hong Kong
Printed and bound in Italy by A. Mondadori Editore, Verona

CONTENTS

TOOLS
MATERIALS &
TECHNIQUES

DECORATOR'S
REFERENCE

FOCUSING YOUR EFFORTS

The art of using enriched decoration has been too long forgotten and in its place rooms have been crammed with a confusion of all-over pattern. By concentrating your decorative energies on just one area of wall (in this case I chose a stick-on frieze) you can combine texture and colour to create a stunning focal point and transform the most ordinary room into something special.

INTRODUCTION

The story of decorating is one of changing tastes, which ebb and flow, and sometimes turn full cycle. Until recently, the level of fashionable decoration has been relatively austere, and black ash and chrome furniture has vied for our attention in the high street with stripped pine and floral wallpaper. As decorating "looks" these have run their course and in their place comes a new awareness of good design, a renewed confidence in handling rich and complex-looking decoration and a greater interest in a wide variety of different historical and regional styles. This is being reflected in the diversification by manufacturers who, in the field of textiles alone, are producing everything from medieval reproduction damasks and eighteenth-century brocades to Victorian Arts and Crafts designs and ethnic weaves. And the same is true for furniture, accessories and fittings. Here, I make full use of what is available today in forty "slices" of rooms, which are my interpretations of period and regional settings. Each is expressed on a plain "slice" of wall, using old and new languages of decoration, based on enriched detailing, texture, pattern and paint finishes.

Buy ornamental details as a short cut to
enriched decoration.

This book shows you how to tread your own path using these languages confidently, with an armoury of decorating principles, techniques, and special tips at your disposal.

*D*ecoration is a superficial activity – literally, only surface deep, often intended to last only a few years and not essential to our existence. But it can give a great deal of pleasure, so why not learn to appreciate good decoration just as you appreciate good food? Transforming a room with materials like paint and simple components like wood mouldings is, on the whole, inexpensive and quick, precisely because it is only surface deep. And though you will need to spend a little more time than with basic decorating, the sophisticated effects you create will more than repay your efforts. Another joy of working with paint and "stick-on" components is that nothing is irreversible: you can always "unpick" and

REAPING THE BENEFIT

Just a few simple steps, and the most basic of materials will create an atmospheric and original scheme of decoration, the rewards of which far outstrip the little extra time spent.

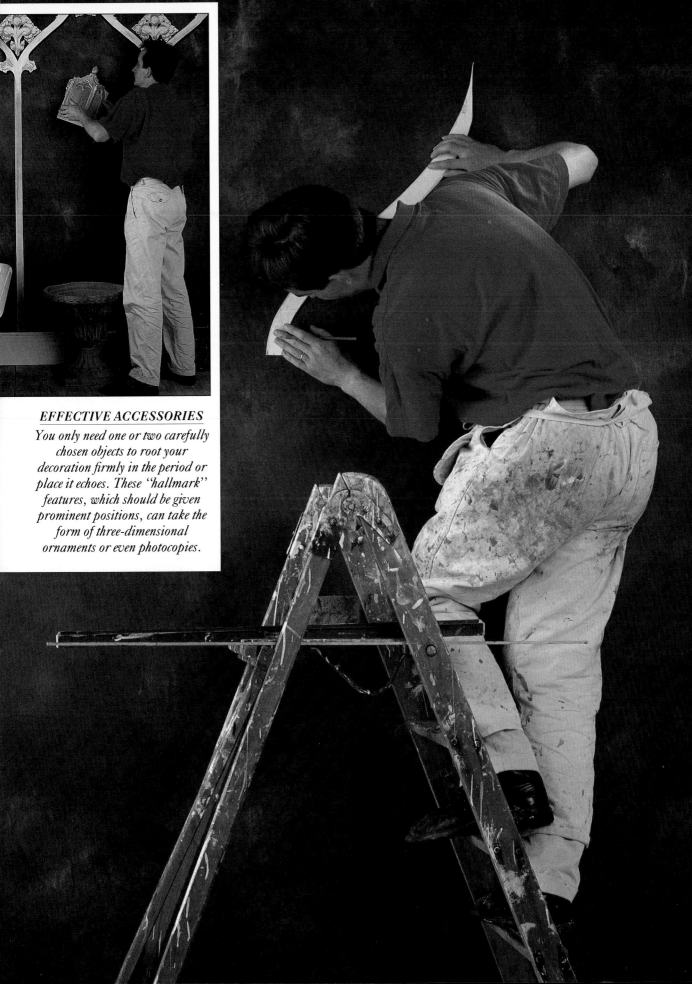

EFFECTIVE ACCESSORIES

You only need one or two carefully chosen objects to root your decoration firmly in the period or place it echoes. These "hallmark" features, which should be given prominent positions, can take the form of three-dimensional ornaments or even photocopies.

Why not use marbled wrapping paper to make a frieze?

readjust parts of a scheme, or a few years on start from scratch. The history of decoration is full of imitation and derivation. For centuries, decorators have cheated the eye, simulating expensive materials, like marble, with paint and imitating hand-painted details with paper cutouts. Decoration that relies heavily on special effects and unexpected materials to convey a strong sense of period or place is pure pastiche — this is something to celebrate because decorating should be fun!

My views on decoration are close to those of William Morris, the Victorian designer and writer, who wrote that good decoration "has the impress of imagination strong on it" and is "something which can be done by a great many people and without too much difficulty and with pleasure". In decorating you have free rein to exercise your whims and fancies. The enjoyment you get every time you walk into a room might come from the satisfaction of knowing that it quietly conveys the atmosphere of a favourite historical period, or that it is flamboyant and theatrical (and why not, say, in a dining room or sitting room where guests are entertained?). This sort of decorating does, in terms of taste, expose your soft underbelly, but it does not matter in the least since

Patterns and devices are often common to different periods.

USING PAINT

Paint techniques and the occasional special tool can perform magic in a room by giving plain surfaces unexpected finishes. Walls can be given the dusty appearance of terracotta, plastic ornament the glow of faded gold and lightweight resin the visual weight of ancient stone. This paint-effect grey stone moulding picks up on the sixteenth-century Italian flavour of a modern lamp and a pasted-up photocopy of an old Florentine inlay, which were put together in decoration for a hallway.

Plaster castings were invented to imitate hand-carved work.

decorating is not a public art like architecture, rather it is a private affair, so decorate for your own pleasure, not the approval of the outside world.

This book is decorating's equivalent of a cookery book. In it is all you need to know about the ingredients, the tools and the techniques that were used to create forty full-scale "meals", shown in the form of room "slices". And just as a good cookery book inspires you to experiment, so this book encourages you to develop your own ideas for decoration.

PRINCIPLES
OF DECORATION

GETTING IDEAS

SINCE EVERY room is different, each has its own starting point for decorating ideas. The quality of light varies from room to room, for reasons like the ceiling height and the number of windows. Some rooms may contain furnishings that you cannot fit anywhere else.

All these limiting factors are in fact departure points for creating a scheme. In the Style Directory you will see rooms that are in turn cluttered, sparsely furnished and that appear small and large. Each one makes a strong visual statement, which can sometimes mask a problem, or sometimes make a virtue out of necessity.

Transforming a room

I created a new decorative scheme for the sitting room in a late nineteenth-century house, shown in the snapshot below. In the bottom right-hand corner of the facing page you can see how the style of this room was reinterpreted in the flavour of the Arts and Crafts movement of the time, taking into account some of the inspirational materials on these pages.

Collecting reference

Inspiration for a decorating scheme can come from many sources: magazines, books, paintings, or even a piece of pottery. Hunt through old books, collecting images that take your fancy, and colour schemes that you admire, always bearing in mind the size of your room and the period of your house. You could also collect objects you particularly like, either for their colour or their shape, as well as paint-colour swatches and samples of papers, fabrics and flooring. As you build your little collection, so the identity of the room should become clearer.

Starting afresh

To help resolve the problem of how to decorate a room, it is useful to take a snapshot of the room and keep it for reference as you collect cuttings and other items of inspiration. Having a colour photograph in front of you helps to make problems seem a little more abstract; and by using felt-tip pens, you can draw suggested changes to the room directly on to the photograph before you actually begin decorating.

Snapshot of room before decoration

Magazine cuttings

Paint-colour swatches

Fabric with period design and colours

Inspirational objects, flooring and wall coverings

Stone for hearth

Stencil idea
for fireplace

Sample
wallpaper

Paint finish
for panelling

Colour
swatches
to match
wallpaper

Sample board of
limed floor

Final ideas

As you gather inspiration, you should begin to think about the relationships that are going to spring up in the room when you put your component elements together. Think about how the colours will work together. Consider using natural surfaces such as plaster and wood together, or combining slick finishes such as polished wood and marble. You may want to have a "user-friendly" finish to your painted surfaces, so think about ageing or antiquing them slightly. When putting surfaces together, it is always a good idea to make sample boards of the finishes you intend to use before starting.

For the decoration below I combined a nineteenth-century Arts and Crafts wallpaper with high panelling of colourwashed wood. The result is a modest room in light-reflective colours, in which the natural qualities of wood are exploited to establish a relaxed, homely feeling.

HISTORICAL COLOURS

WHEN YOU ARE choosing a scheme to decorate, you may want to use period colours. Several companies produce special ranges of paints in "historical" colours but these are not always accurate. The manufacturers usually rely on analyses of paint scrapings, which can be misleading because over time pigments can change colour. And, until this century, painters had no standard formulations for making up colours, and shades of a colour often varied depending on the local materials used. So trying to match

the *exact* subtle shade of what you think is an authentic colour might well be a fruitless task! Instead, it is better to think of approximations and, as I often do in choosing paints, of colours that simply suggest a period. Here is some source material for historical colours (cuttings, reproduction fabric and wallpaper) along with standard modern paint swatches in similar colours.

Pale neo-Classical colours
As neo-Classicism became the rage in mid-eighteenth-century England, so the preferred colours of its innovator, Robert Adam, became popular. Usually placed against white, his muted tones of colours varied from intense and muddied greens and reddish purples, through to pastel combinations of exquisite subtlety. Look at architectural reference books for more of his ideas on colour combinations.

Eighteenth-century
English neo-Classical colours

Frieze painted in neo-Classical colours

Taste of the early 1800s
Early nineteenth-century French and English watercolours show a taste for strong, bright and somewhat unsubtle colours. Napoleon introduced the colours of Egypt – acid yellow and rich earth colours – to France and they were soon adopted into Empire taste. Deep pinks and mauves, however, were carried over from the previous century and they were translated, along with emerald green, into the English Regency stripe colours.

French colours
*In France during the mid-eighteenth century, a taste for intense chalky-looking colours, particularly blues, greens and pinks, developed.
To get as close a match as possible to the colours in the magazine cutting, above right, I laid cut-up paint swatches on top of the picture.*

Swatches of some early nineteenth-century colours

Swatches of mid-eighteenth-century French colours

Colours from fabrics
Original period fabrics that have been well preserved out of the light, or reproductions of period designs, are often a reasonably accurate source for historical colour. The fabric shown, right, is a modern version of an early American stencilled fabric notable for its ochre brown and glorious cranberry red.

Colour swatches that match stencilled fabric

Magazine cutting of an eighteenth-century frescoed room

Nineteenth-century wallpaper

Colours from wallpapers
The early nineteenth-century Gothic design, above, is still being made according to the designer's specifications, giving an accurate indication of the colour preferences of the period.

Colour swatches to match wallpaper

Ultramarine blue similar to artists' oil paint colour

Looking at pigments
The colours of the artist's basic palette, unchanged for hundreds of years, were often those used by decorators. So I continue to use ancient palette colours in the form of powder colours and proprietary paints like emulsion.

Sample board for Rococo decor

Swatch of modern paint colours

Ultramarine powder colour

Ultramarine artists' oil paint (an ancient palette colour)

Colours from magazines
Matching colours to magazine cuttings is an inexact science, but with care you can succeed in conveying the spirit of the age. The colours for the Rococo Dining Room on page 75 were copied from a cutting of a frescoed room, above, dating from the right period, and are shown on the painted sample board beneath the magazine cutting.

19

DIVIDING WALL SPACE

ONCE SOME of the ideas for decorating your room have come together – maybe a period atmosphere you want to convey, the level of formality you require, or a completed colour scheme – start thinking about how you are going to articulate the wall space that you have before you.

A wall is like an empty canvas, which can be treated in any number of ways for different effects. Even though walls are flat, and the most usual treatment of them is two-dimensional, the overall effect of the wall decoration is much more powerful than that of floors or ceilings. This is because walls wrap around a room, enclosing the space between them. By manipulating the wall space, using division, colour and line as your tools, you can alter the character of a room.

Historically, walls have been subject to a number of horizontal divisions such as cornices and dado rails. These can be used separately or together, in similar or complementary colours to the wall, for different effects. The dado (the area between a skirting board and dado rail) is the place to make grand statements by using colours, textures and patterns that are different to the upper wall.

Floors and ceilings

When planning how to decorate the walls, think also about the floor and ceiling. The floor colour can work in tandem with the wall colour, either complementing or strengthening its effect, or it can be an entirely different colour, and act independently in the scheme.

Ceilings can also "float" independently from other structures in a room, although the colour of a ceiling can affect both the room's apparent height and lightness.

DADO EFFECTS

HORIZONTAL MOVEMENT

In this slice of wall taken from the English Baroque Parlour on page 67, the dark panelled dado is slung very low above a pale floor. The resulting effect is of a slender green band, which serves to lead the eye horizontally around a room. This sets up a feeling of movement, which is then given a rhythm by the tassels and ropes at cornice height.

FORMAL DIVISIONS

Ebonized mouldings sharply delineate the divisions on the wall: the maroon frieze, the upper wall and wallpapered dado. The principal players here are the frieze and high skirting board that counterbalance each other at the top and bottom of the wall. This vertical relationship of all the parts is more important than any horizontal movement, and so the resulting atmosphere of the scheme is very formal and upright.

CRADLE OF COLOUR

In this nineteenth-century setting, the high dado of wooden panelling and the parquet-effect wood floor combine to make a cradle of colour that occupies the lower half of the setting and makes for a supportive, secure and friendly environment. The feeling of calm and stillness that this structure conveys can also be seen in settings of completely different periods: the Venetian Studio on page 145 and the Miami Deco Living Room on page 197.

BALANCE OF COLOURS

Here I used a high dado of pale plaster, topped with a rust-effect rail, to "fight off" a heavy blue wall. If the dado were any lower, it would have appeared crushed by the weight of the blue. As it is, it forms something resembling a wall, beyond which is the night sky. This is an example of how you can use the height of your dado to control the balance of colours in a room.

EFFECTS OF CEILING COLOUR

Brightening effect *By carrying the bright yellow of the dado up on to the ceiling, the effect is to open out the space and apparently raise the height of the ceiling. As a rule, light-reflective colours, like this yellow, are safest.*

Darkening effect *This blue ceiling echoes the colour of the wall, so pushing down on the yellow dado and seeming to lower the height of the setting. Dark ceiling colours should only be considered for strongly coloured rooms.*

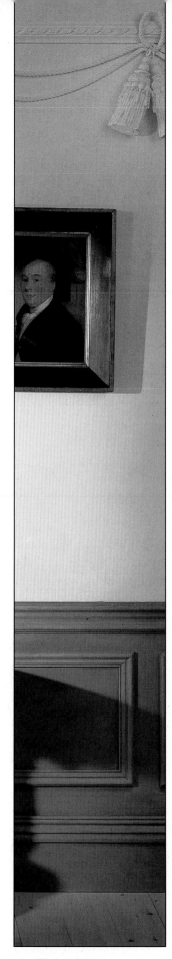

Horizontal movement

Formal divisions

Cradle of colour

Balance of colours

STRUCTURAL FEATURES

PERIOD MOULDINGS help to structure a wall and enrich the decoration of a room. If you have a home in which cornices, friezes, dado rails or skirting boards have been partly ripped out during modernization, then a local timber mill will often match your existing mouldings and make up an exact quantity of "specials" for you.

Starting afresh

If your home has no authentic features left to restore (or they are beyond repair), simply use mouldings that are commercially available, where necessary combining them to imitate more complicated period mouldings. Not only is this cheaper than having specials run up, it can also be just as effective.

All the room slices in the Style Directory were put together using materials and mouldings that were currently available from timber and plaster suppliers.

Historically, there has been a finite number of moulding patterns used in Western interior decoration. These have changed only in their scale and combination from one period to the next.

Modern manufacturers produce most standard period mouldings in many different sizes, which allows you to choose elements to suit your room. Some mouldings, with cross-sections, are shown here.

Shaker style

The American Shakers took great care over every single detail of their lives. Their rooms were not decorated for show and any detailing was there for practical reasons only. In the Shaker interior on page 107 I reproduced the mouldings found inside Shaker houses by carefully combining some commercially available mouldings. The pegboard is made from a simple plank, as is the deep dado rail (to prevent the backs of chairs scraping against the wall) but with the addition of an ogee panel moulding. I made the skirting from a plank with a rounded front edge and added beading along the top to prevent dust from settling, and pinned a small quadrant section at floor level to stop chair legs hitting the board.

Tudor decoration

In this Tudor setting, the principal wall decoration was composed of paint-textured hardboard panels and a painted frieze. But the walls needed a stronger structure to control these elements. I used a timeless dentilled cornice, a simple panel moulding to make dado-level rectangles and a modestly profiled board for the skirting.

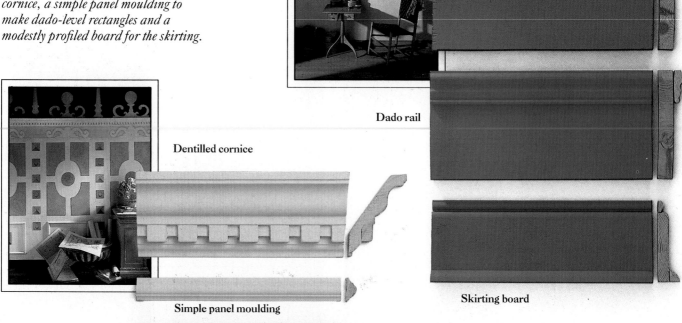

Pegboard

Dado rail

Dentilled cornice

Simple panel moulding

Skirting board

Profiled skirting board

Neo-Classical interior

The architecture of Robert Adam shows a rare sensitivity for the combined use of mouldings, enriched decoration and colour. His interiors were decorated in a variety of different materials, such as composition or fibrous plaster, painted wood, and papier-mâché. Similarly, the interior I put together makes use of mouldings produced in different media. The frieze is lincrusta, a nineteenth-century invention, finished with a plastic picture rail beneath. There is a plaster dado rail, then a skirting board made from a plank of wood topped with a machine-made moulding.

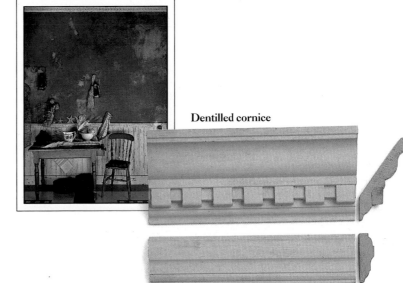

Dentilled cornice

Dado rail

Tongue-and-groove matchboarding

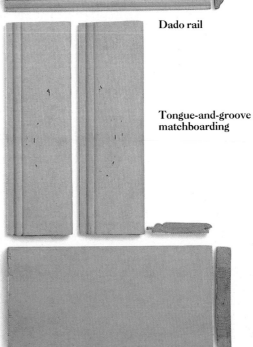

Skirting board

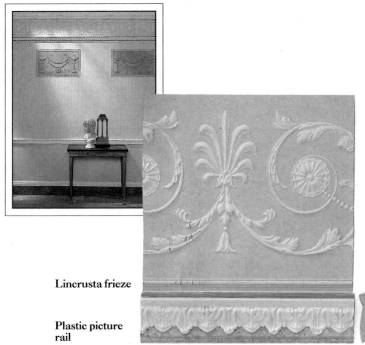

Lincrusta frieze

Plastic picture rail

Plaster dado rail

Machine-made moulding

Base for skirting board

Caribbean setting

In this Caribbean setting I captured a little of the atmosphere of the region, and the result was a mixture of ethnic functionalism with a little touch of the Colonial. The same dentilled moulding as I used in the Tudor setting proved an accurate copy of a Jamaican Colonial cornice, and works surprisingly well in combination with the simple painted matchboarding (topped with a dado rail) beneath it. Continuing the use of basic materials, you will notice how the skirting board is just a simple plank of wood, painted with emulsion.

USING RHYTHM

THE MOST underrated technical effect available when decorating, is visual rhythm, which can bounce some life into a room. Its use provides a rich vein to be tapped, and one that has been neglected too long, since enriched decoration fell from grace in the early part of the twentieth century.

At its simplest, rhythmic decoration can be two symmetrically placed windows in a room, which you decide to dress up and show off, or it might be two matching mirrors placed in a prominent and symmetrical position. This has a visually satisfying effect because it defines and emphasizes the space between and on either side of the two features.

Repeated images

At its most complicated and diffused, rhythm can be seen in wallpapers and fabrics, sending off little repeats in all directions.

Images or motifs, repeated so that they pulse around a room, set up an obvious rhythm and act as a meter by which all the components of the room can be judged. The strength of its impact depends on the scale of the images you use and the number of repeats in relation to the size of the room.

Horizontal rhythms

Sometimes, as in the examples opposite, the most obvious and exciting rhythms are those that run in just one direction, horizontally around the room. Their energies are not dissipated and they follow the architecture of the room. They are also all placed at cornice height so the repeated motifs can be clearly seen and do not become confused with any other decoration in the room. It is important that furniture, wallhangings and people do not get in the way of the flow of the pattern, or the rhythm will cease.

EFFECTS OF PATTERNS

SUBTLE MOVEMENT

This Classical lincrusta frieze has a complex design that is repeated every half a metre. Because it is low relief and painted in restrained colours, the potential rhythmic impact is reduced.

SWINGING RHYTHM

A repeat of tassels and rope can be left unfettered by background or frame. The images are large and simple and the repeat is bold and swinging. This waveform repeat will add life to a room.

RHYTHMIC IMAGERY

To pick up on the imagery of a balloon chandelier, I pasted equally-spaced colour photocopies high on to the wall. The chandelier helps identify what the image is: a sedate rhythm made up of separate beats, to give focus to the central balloon.

MULTIPLE PATTERNING

This pattern is so complicated that any energy in the repeat is dissipated. The wave pattern of the rope is complicated by the frequency of its repeat, by the brightly painted moulding, and by the vertical stripes on the wall. Yet the combination, although lacking in rhythmic power, is rich and decorative.

BALANCED COMPOSITION

A principal repeat of the bird strikes an obvious rhythm here, linked and balanced by a chain of tiny details. The zig-zag above serves as an angular wave-form, setting up a more frequent repeat. Strong rhythms within rhythms set up the visual equivalent of the resonance of sound.

GENTLE WAVES

The wave shape is a simple rhythmic device, and can be in the form of a rope, a swag, a garland or, as here, a chain. These materials come in flexible lengths, so you can adjust the distance between the "waves" until you have the right repeat for the room.

Repeated studs
These gilded studs were attached to the wall in the Victorian scheme on page 163. The idea of using relief decoration was to assert the repeats in a very strong fashion. The studs are widely spaced and give a healthy rhythmic feel to the decoration of the room.

Rhythmic panelling
In this example of all-over rhythmic wall decor, different rhythms run in varying directions all at once. However, the divisions in the main wall panelling do correspond to the simpler repeated rhythm shown above it, and work in a strictly geometrical pattern.

STYLES OF LIGHTING

THERE ARE two ways in which you can make artificial lighting work for you. The first is to double up on light sources, by fitting, for example, wall lights *and* table lamps – as many as possible. The second is to fit several separate circuits in a room so that, at the most, only two lamps occupy a single circuit. For simplicity, all the lights should be controllable from a wall-mounted panel and each circuit fitted with a dimmer switch, so you can choose where and exactly by how much to illuminate your room.

You can also experiment with ways of adapting natural light, for example by partially covering a window with muslin or oiled paper to screen bright sunlight, or soften harsh winter light.

Types of artificial light
The range of electric lighting available for the domestic market is enormous. Traditional, incandescent bulbs are now making way for all kinds of new and small fluorescent bulbs and "daylight" quality tubes. Your choice of artificial light can affect the colour of your room. Standard tungsten bulbs, for example, cast a warm yellowish light, while "daylight" bulbs cast a harder, colder light.

Electric lamps
Ideally you should arrange your electric lighting so that you can have a choice in each room between more than one light source, with a central light pendant being the last choice of all – bright, central all-over lighting tends to kill atmosphere. To direct the spread of light use translucent or completely opaque shades. Or use uplighter bowls, hung either as central pendants or as wall lamps, to throw a gentle light on to the ceiling, making an ideal background light, as seen right.

Table lamp with Kashmiri base in *papier-mâché*

Patinated metal electric wall sconce

Eighteenth-century carved wooden chandelier

Natural light

Natural light changes from season to season, in different weathers and according to the time of day. There are times when you need to modify it with curtains or blinds. But you can also adapt the quality of light and even change its colour by fitting stained glass panels to your windows (see the effect on the wall, right). Dyed muslin curtains or a sheet of muslin fitted over a window will cast soft colours in a room. Likewise, paper (even brown paper) that has been stretched on a frame and oiled (see p.332), will throw a gentle, warm light.

Steel candle lamp

Unoiled
tissue paper

Oiled
tissue
paper

Muslin for curtains

Brown paper

Candlelight

The most romantic and atmospheric lighting for interiors is without doubt that from natural flames, particularly in a dining room setting, and there are some decorative and unusual candlesticks available. However, do bear in mind the fire risk of candles, and avoid using cheap ones that burn with a lot of waste, looking instead for beeswax-based brands.

South American
metal candlestick

Seventeenth-century-
style wooden candlesticks

LIGHTING, COLOUR & MOOD

THE MOST common assumptions made about the colours of rooms are misleading. For example, the most light-reflective and cheerful colours are not just pale peach and apricot, as is popularly believed, but also bright yellow and lavender blue. If you try to modulate the atmosphere of a scheme simply by lightening its colour, you run the risk of introducing more light at the expense of the setting's character.

Before choosing a colour, consider whether you spend more time in a room by day or in the evenings. Most colour schemes look good under artificial lighting. If your problem is a dingy room by day, try adding mirrors and complementary colours (see p.336) before you consider using a pale colour scheme.

In the setting shown on these pages, the brown version (below) is most arcane and interesting. By day it is less light-reflective (bottom), but the colour responds well to daylight and makes the room seem warm and inviting. The pale scheme (right and far right), on the other hand, is less appealing by day, when it seems relatively cold and lifeless, but at night, by candlelight, it becomes magical.

Effects of colours
To demonstrate the effects of colours I repainted the same wood-panelled wall in two different colours. First of all I colourwashed it in white over blue stained wood (above and right). It was then stripped and colourwashed in a soft brown (below and left). In both instances it was possible to use the wood's texture to add interest to the painted surface, and by comparing the two photographs taken in daylight, you can immediately see that this surface interest has more influence than the colour of the paint on the setting's character. Although the brown-coloured wall darkens the room, it conveys more atmosphere than the colder blue.

WHOLE HOUSE TREATMENTS

DECORATING should be fun and enjoyable. It does not always involve major restructuring, nor should it, since in every sense of the word it is a superficial activity. All the room sets in this book are broad interpretations of styles from different countries and periods. They are not historical documents, and each one could look at home in half a dozen different types of house of different ages. If you decorate with a sense of fun, you will appreciate this.

Developing a theme

But how can you take an idea that you like for one room, and then decorate the whole house? What will give your home an identity that can assume different guises in different rooms?

The need for this variation is obvious, since we are different people when we are entertaining, to when we are in private rooms such as the bathroom or bedroom, to when we come home from work: and accordingly we make different demands on our environment. But equally, homes are single dwelling units, and far too many people decorate their homes as though the rooms were hermetically sealed and independent of each other.

On these pages are shown the three thematic principles to bear in mind when decorating a whole house, namely colour, materials and period. Using just one of them as a criterion will help you formulate a look for the inside of your house that should have some integrity. If you are able to use all three together, and make all the rooms conform by colour, materials and period, your home will grow in character even more.

Period homes

Decorating a period house can be fraught with crises of conscience. Is what you are doing right for the period of the building? Are you using the correct materials and colours? Or if what you are doing is not authentic, only interpretive, does it respect the fabric and character of the building?

How to decide

These questions are valid to some extent, particularly in valuable old houses. But decorating is a private activity and its aim is personal enjoyment; it has always reflected the tastes of individuals, not public bodies, and it should remain so. The most important consideration facing anyone decorating a period home is not what should or should not be added, but what should or should not be taken away.

The answer is to remove as little as possible of the original structure because whatever is added to a building in terms of mouldings and paint is reversible, but original features, once ripped out, cannot easily be replaced. The domestic vandalism of many nineteenth-century homes during the 1960s has meant that what is now being replaced and restored is often inaccurate and out of tune with what was probably there originally.

Choosing by colour
One of the simplest ways of carrying a theme through your whole house is by following a common colour scheme throughout. This does not mean that you should use exactly the same colour in every room, rather it is a question of choosing a colour palette and working around those colours. In the choice below, I combined colours from the orange/red end of the spectrum, which were used in Victorian, Oriental and Spanish-style settings. Each of the settings has different finishes and surface qualities. The Victorian wall is painted a deep red and spattered with paint and glaze (p.163); the panel of softened glazework is in saffron red (p.193) and the wall from the Moorish bedroom has been given a dusty terracotta finish (p.37).

Red background spattered with glaze and paint

Saffron-red softened glazework, above

Wall with terracotta paint finish, left

Choosing by materials

By adopting one principal material as your decorative linking component, you can experiment with using a wide range of colours. Here I chose textured plaster as a wall finish that you could use all over the house. The schemes illustrated here have a French/Hispanic theme. Although each was designed for a specific room in a house (a bedroom, a kitchen and a living room) they could be adapted to work equally well in other rooms.

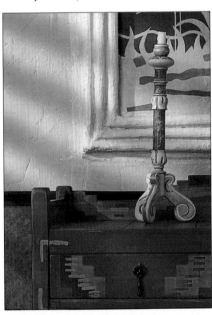

Stencilled plaster for a French kitchen scheme

Whitewashed plaster wall in a seventeenth-century Spanish bedroom setting, left

Painted plaster in a twentieth-century scheme, below

Colour, material and period

The strongest link between rooms is formed when you contrive to link them in more than one way. The sequence here shows rooms linked by a colour palette of greens, a common material of painted wood, and a common root in their styles; the English setting is based on the simple seventeenth-century style of interior that influenced early American interiors.

New England interior

Seventeenth-century English setting

American Colonial setting

CHOOSING & ENJOYING DECORATION

I HOPE THAT you find the Style Directory to be a useful source of inspiration for rich and exciting decorative treatments. All the components of each treatment are analyzed so you can select either the complete scheme or particular features of it for your own room. I suggest various ways to style the look and show how optional colourways will look for walls, floors, furniture and fabrics.

Decorating for yourself

A great deal of satisfaction can be drawn from learning the decorating skills necessary to complete your own scheme. You will find them all in the second half of the book where there is detailed coverage of every technique used as well as the tools and materials you will need.

For quick reference, there are tables on pages 324–31 which show you the composition, properties and uses of the various types of paint, varnish and pigment used in the book. Some techniques require you to mix your own paints (or adapt manufactured ones), and recipes are given on pages 332–3. This is followed by advice on buying and storing materials, and tips on calculating quantities. Terms used in the book are briefly explained on pages 336–9 and finally there is a list of useful suppliers of tools and accessories.

Styling decisions By giving examples of different types of ornamentation and furnishing I show each style's range of possibilities and demonstrate how you can tailor it to suit your room.

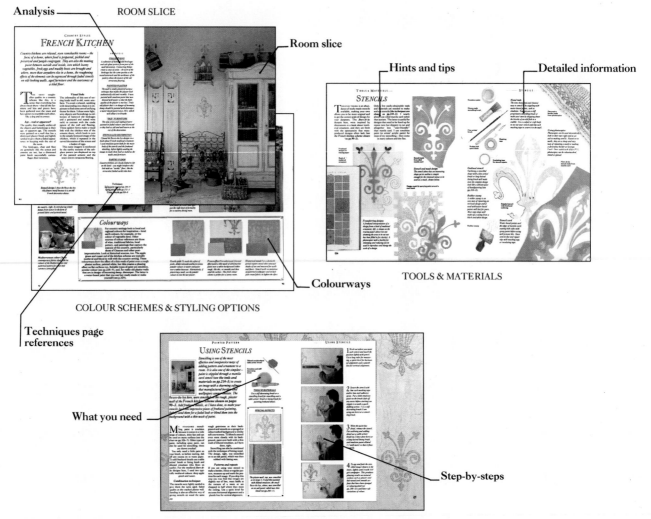

STYLE
DIRECTORY

MEDITERRANEAN STYLES

Rifle through old holiday albums and guidebooks to discover the essential elements of a Mediterranean setting: hot, yellow sunlight; warm colours; bold patterns; dusty terracotta; pale wood; plasterwork; and everywhere the evidence of a rich cultural legacy left by the ancient civilizations of the region.

We all come away from holiday feeling satisfied that we have "got to know" somewhere and are taking with us a sense of its identity. Often this identity is summed up in terms of architecture, colour, pattern and local materials, so if you want to recreate the spirit of a place, start research among old guidebooks and postcards. There you will see the key decorating elements, and find your inspiration.

Warmth and light
One essential quality of any Mediterranean setting is the light. In northern climes, where natural daylight is cold and blue, we feel more comfortable with soft colours that modulate the harshness of the light. Mediterranean sunlight is strongly yellow and its visual effect is to heat even the coolest white wall. For that reason, only one of my Mediterranean interiors has a typically white wall; the rest rely on colour, pattern and texture to suggest a sense of place.

Ancient history
Another inescapable feature of the Mediterranean landscape is its history. Some of the most sophisticated of ancient civilizations developed here and their archaeological remains provide rich inspirational pickings for the decorator. The Roman mosaic from Turkey, shown on a postcard, below right on the terracotta tile, the Classical Roman frieze that has been translated into a paper border, right, and the sample of green lincrusta, left, the pattern of which was taken from a Classical arabesque design, are all examples.

Throughout history, these early civilizations have influenced other cultures profoundly. The Italian Renaissance, for

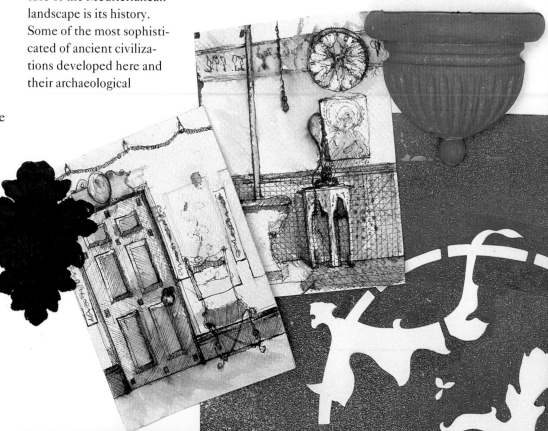

example, was founded on the traditions of Byzantine art. So it is quite legitimate to mix imagery from all of these periods.

Choice of materials is important: terracotta, plaster and pale woods, such as the pickled (limed) pine mirror above, all broadly suggest the Mediterranean. The colours and textures can provide a cheap foil against which to range the objects that will place a room in context.

MOORISH BEDROOM

The Moors, who were of Arabic and Berber descent, came from Africa and established a kingdom in southern Spain. In this Moorish scheme strong colours suggest the heat of the Mediterranean and rich drapes, "magic" carpets and burnished copper, the mystery and romance of the Arabian Nights. A bedroom is the perfect place in which to indulge your sense of luxury by surrounding yourself with fabrics and colours that provide an atmosphere of warmth. It need not be expensive – this scheme costs surprisingly little to put together, relying for effect largely on the evocative texture and colour of a terracotta paint finish and the muslin drapes above the bed, which conjure up images of a Moorish palace or Bedouin tent.

IN THE fourteenth-century Moorish palace, the Alhambra, every surface is covered with exuberant geometrical patterns. It is a rich source of inspiration, but to copy the decoration would be too time-consuming. Instead, I made an impressionistic interpretation, using strong Mediterranean colours, painted Moorish arches and Arabic furnishings: a picture, exotic fabrics and tassels.

Colour and light

The dominant feature here, is the colour of the wall. With emulsion paint and a sponge I imitated dusty terracotta, a material strongly associated with Mediterranean clay tiles and plant pots. Imitation terracotta floor tiles blend in with the rest of the colour scheme.

The quality of natural light is also an important feature. To cast a pattern on the wall like that of a screened Moorish window I attached a pierced screen (like the one used in the Byzantine Lavatory on p.49) to the window. The muslin draped over the bed diffuses the light further.

Arches and fabric swags

The horseshoe arch is a distinctive hallmark of Moorish architecture. The rhythm produced by the series of painted arches here, breaks up the wall's geometry and gives a sense of spaciousness.

The swagged fabric, tassels and fringing give a three-dimensional realism and create the impression of a richly furnished nomadic tent. The lustre of the copper pipe, which is used as a decorative moulding and as a support for the gold patterned fabric, adds to the luxury.

Arabic shapes *These ziggurat shapes are typically Arabic – copy them for painted wall decoration.*

ANALYSIS

PAINTED ARCHES

The horseshoe arch is one of the most distinctive characteristics of Moorish architecture. I cut an arch shape from a piece of card and drew round it to make a pencil guide for painting. I used deep red emulsion, dividing the arches into large stone-shaped slabs with blue lines, also of emulsion. Sanding the arches gave them the same worn, dusty appearance as the wall and a rough, stone-like texture.

TERRACOTTA WALL

The colour of dusty terracotta conjures up images of the Mediterranean, so I chose a terracotta-effect paint finish.

RICH FABRICS

In a small space a few fabrics with rich textures and colours will help create an air of luxury. The fabric printed with gold is an inexpensive modern design using the ancient images of stars and moons. The swags are interrupted by a heavy Arabian tassel. Rugs and cushions are piled on the bed.

BURNISHED COPPER

Copper plumbing pipe assumes a decorative role as a support for the fabric swags and the muslin canopy – the lustre of burnished metal adds to the sumptuousness of the setting.

SINGLE PAINTING

A picture is an effective way of making a statement of place or period. This print of an Eastern potentate puts all the other furnishings firmly into historical and geographical context.

SKIRTING BOARD & FLOOR

To continue the theme of Mediterranean terracotta I gave the skirting board the same finish as the wall and chose terracotta-effect floor tiles.

Techniques
Terracotta pp.284–5

STYLING DECISIONS

THE PRINCIPAL quality of the wall in the bedroom setting is its dustiness, which makes an earthy contrast with the luxury of the fabrics.

For an altogether more extravagant room treatment paint the walls (using the terracotta technique on p.285) in rich tomato red and then spatter them with gold paint and black glaze as I did on the wall of the Victorian room on page 163 (see pp.262–3 for the technique). For an even more palatial effect add some gold stencilling.

Consider adding items in contemporary Spanish taste, such as modern steel furniture and ceramics. In fact any craft works from around the Mediterranean will fit here, since such traditions were absorbed and used by the Moors.

Traditional pattern

If you want to introduce some complicated Moorish patterns, build up colour and pattern just as the architects of the Alhambra did. Look for fabrics, ceramic tiles, rugs and carpets with complex geometrical shapes, and interlocking polygons woven with stylized floral patterns and arabesques.

Moorish pattern Books on ornament yield references for intricate Moorish designs that can be simplified and used as a basis for painted decoration.

Modern furnishings, *left. For a contemporary mood include pieces of modern steel furniture and some monochrome furnishings to contrast with the vivid colours of Moorish textiles.*

Moorish colours, *below left. Follow in the Moorish tradition of bright primaries, choosing vivid contemporary fabrics to bring a spark of brilliance to soft terracotta paintwork and urns.*

Private luxury *Trinkets, candlesticks and perfume jars in burnished copper and brass intimate the rituals of private ablutions; a richly-patterned North African rug adds luxury underfoot.*

Colourways

Moorish buildings in the cities of southern Spain show the popular decorating colours of Hispano-Moorish architecture. The most distinctive of these are shades of the primary colours red, yellow and blue: a deep, slightly browny red, an orange-tinted yellow ochre, a vivid pastel blue, a deep, intense blue and a deep emerald-green. These colours are all strong and are best suited to painted pattern, furnishing fabrics and details rather than large areas of floor or wall, for which pastel tints of the same colours make a less overpowering choice.

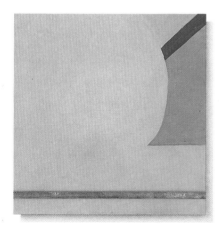

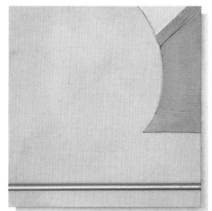

Green and beige *For a restful effect try beige, red ochre and duck-egg blue, with a verdigris finish on metalwork (see pp.286–7).*

Stone colours *Raw sienna, added to white, reproduces the colour of sandstone, against which, white and gold make neutral additions.*

Warm and cool *A grey stone-coloured background is enriched by deep terracotta, gold and copper, and is cooled by a pale grey-blue.*

GRECO-ROMAN BATHROOM

A bathroom benefits from space, either real or illusory, and a determination never to try to hide its function but rather to celebrate it. The Greco-Roman style of decoration used in this scheme takes its inspiration from the Ancient Romans and, in so doing, captures some of the more civilized attitudes towards bathing that existed then. The use of gold, antiqued plaster and sculpted and moulded decoration gives an impression of richness and luxury, which is further heightened by the strong colour scheme. The bath itself occupies centre stage and the few carefully chosen and displayed decorations serve to enhance it.

THE PLEASURES and rituals of bathing seem to have vanished in the steam of time, making today's bathroom all too often a builder's afterthought – a small room stuffed with clinical tiling and swish fitments by way of excuse. How much better to convert a larger space and put your plumbing on show as in the ancient Mediterranean. Instead of hiding pipes in ugly boxes, make them part of the decoration. In place of the ubiquitous floor-to-ceiling tiles, paint your walls to evoke the fresco work found in Classical interiors.

Special effects
The splendour of this bathroom is not the result of expensive fitments but rather creative paint finishes and the thoughtful placement of a few decorative items. The whole wall was colourwashed with a cream and then a raw sienna wash (made from water, powder colour and PVA). The dado was colourwashed again with a diluted mixture of emerald-green and white emulsion paint.

The bath as focus
The bath has been made the focus of the setting, stencilled and patinated, so that it appears verdigrised and centuries old, but with a crisp white interior. The same verdigris finish encases the joints of the pipework and wraps itself around the room in the form of a frieze.

The green dado provides a visual link with the verdigris finish on the bath and frieze, while the upper wall provides the perfect foil to the bas-relief plaster panel.

Architectural remnant *A moulded Ionic capital, painted and decorated in the Roman style, would make a very effective wall decoration.*

ANALYSIS

ARABESQUE FRIEZE
The frieze is made of lincrusta, which I cut to size and stuck on the wall. To achieve the verdigris finish, I applied green pastes over a gold basecoat and rubbed the high relief with a cloth to let the gold glint through. The studs were gilded and then stuck to the wall.

BAS-RELIEF PANEL
This new plaster moulding was given the bloom and polish of marble by using a combination of shellac and liming wax, and left unframed for an authentic, antique look.

DADO LINE
First I colourwashed the whole wall in cream and raw sienna washes. When it was dry, I stuck light-tack tape along pencil guidelines and colourwashed in green over the top.

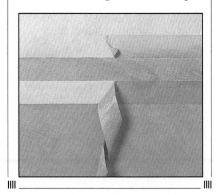

BATH & FLOORING
The bath was given a verdigris finish, decorated with a stencilled design and gilded studs, and then varnished. The slate-effect flooring is plastic tiling.

Techniques
Three-colour colourwashing
pp.250–51
Antiquing plasterwork pp.272–3
Verdigris pp.286–7
Gilding – metallic powder
pp.304–5
Stencilling pp.312–7

STYLING DECISIONS

THE KEY to styling a Greco-Roman interior, whether it be a bathroom, dining room or even a hallway, is the thoughtful choice of fittings. You do not need to have a vast array of ornamentation. Indeed quality is certainly better than quantity in this style of decoration. Space is all-important; too much clutter detracts rather than adds to the look.

Decorative elements

Concentrate on one or two decorative items and contrast their shape and texture for a bold statement. Make use of strong colours for dramatic effect, or use complementary pale colours to create a more peaceful interior. Alternatively you could soften the scheme with elegant drapes.

If, however, you like an element of surprise and want to increase the sense of ingenuity associated with the scheme, include a style twist, such as a piece of alabaster or lacquered wood.

Simply by exchanging a few decorative pieces you can alter the whole feel and mood of the scheme, whilst still retaining the overall Classical style.

Frieze finishes For different frieze effects, either pick out the pattern in verdigris colours, left, or apply a verdigris-coloured wash over a copper-coloured basecoat, right.

Simple additions You can alter the style of a room with the simplest of items; here a terracotta-coloured towel provides a strong contrast in a green scheme, which is boosted by a wooden bowl and marble sphere.

Surprise elements, *left.*
The inclusion of a black
lacquered Chinoiserie cabinet
adds a note of ingenuity to
the scheme, yet works well
with the slate-effect flooring.
The alabaster bust continues
the Roman theme of the
bathroom setting.

Fabric and flowers, *left.*
Elegantly draped green
damask and a cloud of
budding gypsophila in a vase
soften the effect of the strong
colours and forms of the
scheme whilst retaining the
original style. This styling
option is ideal if you want a
peaceful room.

Colourways

Classical interiors were usually fresco-painted in soft, pastel watercolours. Colourwashing in such colours as cream, white or pale yellow-ochre gives the soft and chalky finish so evocative of this type of decoration and could be the basis of any type of colour scheme in this style. In many Classical rooms, broad stretches of lower walls were washed a darker colour, probably to hide scuffs. Instead of a dark-green dado you could experiment with red ochre, which flatters gold paint and rust ornamentation, warm terracotta, or even black for a more esoteric, powerful effect. If you decide against a frieze consider a stencilled dado.

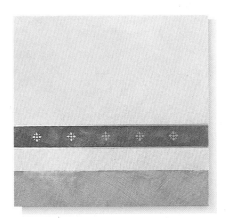

Stencilled terracotta *A terracotta band is a way of introducing a third colour in the scheme. Gold stencils can be used to mute the impact.*

Lined stencil *For a more subtle use of colour, paint stencils above the dado, and line each repeat with warm red ochre.*

Gilt edges *Delicate gold bands add to the feeling of splendour in the scheme, but be judicious and do not detail every edge in the room!*

SPANISH BAROQUE BEDROOM

The word Baroque suggests the soaring confidence of massive architecture and the rich and heavy decoration characteristic of the seventeenth and eighteenth centuries. For the decoration of a simple bedroom, draw on the ideas of this period, and place Baroque features in a diminished and modest form, in a rustic context as I have done here. My starting point for this bedroom arrangement takes its inspiration from the basic structure of a typical Mediterranean Spanish interior – whitewashed plaster walls and a terracotta floor – to which I added some Spanish Baroque details in the form of a carved bedhead, ironwork and a cherub fresco.

TRUE TO Baroque style, this Spanish bedroom is theatrical. A variety of techniques and surfaces are used for dramatic effect, just as they were in highly decorated Baroque rooms. Some features are recognizably eighteenth-century in style, like the carved bedhead and the cherub fresco, while others, like the swag and drop chains are based on old themes, which I reworked. If you use ideas like this your finished whole will suggest a time and a place that is historically recognizable.

Spanish materials

To give the setting historical authenticity I used and imitated iron, a material popular with Spanish craftsmen of this period. As large amounts of ornate cast iron ornament would overwhelm a small space, I used a variety of techniques to imitate metal on a range of different surfaces. The wooden door was painted to look like cast iron, and emulsion was dribbled down it in imitation of rust. Sand and paint were used to create the rust effect on the skirting board, the architrave and the wooden mouldings and plastic castings on and around the door. To carry the theme further, I introduced some real rust by way of the shackles and chain that perform the role of heavy swags and drops.

The limed pine bedhead, exuberantly carved and swagged in eighteenth-century style, lends further historical resonance.

Finally, I gave the aged plaster wall grandeur and depth in the form of monochrome *grisaille* framing around the door and the frescoed panel above the bed.

Delicate carving *The carving on this mirror is Baroque in style, while the soft wood is typical of European Mediterranean furniture.*

ANALYSIS

CHAIN SWAG

Rusty chains and old shackles were swagged across the wall for a lively, rhythmic effect. Iron was a material much used in the eighteenth century.

GRISAILLE

The door frame was painted in grisaille, a monochrome version of trompe l'oeil. The work was sanded to make it appear aged like the wall.

LIMED PINE

The pale colour of the bedhead was achieved by liming. In eighteenth-century fashion, it is carved, reeded, swagged, and panelled with cane.

DRESSING TABLE

Elegantly carved furniture, like this dresser, makes a delicate contribution to a solemn Baroque room. The pale wood continues the light tones of the setting.

RUSTED DOOR

The modern wood door was given visual weight using a paint technique that creates an impression of rusted iron.

Techniques

Liming wood pp.260–61
Ageing plaster walls pp.274–5
Iron & rust pp.288–9
Grisaille pp.320–21

STYLING DECISIONS

ALL THE different materials that are in the bedroom scheme are, or at least represent, natural or mineral substances: iron, rust, plaster, clay and pale wood. When it comes to styling, develop this theme by introducing other natural materials like silk, gold leaf, bronze, verdigris and *papier-mâché*. The impact of all natural materials is determined by

Fresco Natural materials should dominate in a rustic interpretation of the Baroque. This fresco, painted on to a supported plaster background, was produced with earth-colour powder colours mixed with water.

the quantity they are used in, and by the sophistication of the room's design. In the Baroque setting on the previous page man-made products like wallpaper and sophisticated paint finishes would look distinctly out of place.

Alternatively, choose Spanish mahogany or dark oak furniture to give a solemn air, and include some silver and gilt pieces or leatherwork reminiscent of the Renaissance.

Or find inspiration, as indeed Baroque art and architecture did, in images drawn from Classical sources such as ancient Greece, Rome or Pompeii.

Mediterranean mood The colour of fresh lemons excites a claret coloured, ornately patterned damask – a combination with Mediterranean exuberance.

Terracotta and verdigris Terracotta pots – a Spanish feature – look effective with verdigris (see pp.286–7). The swag on the pot is a reminder of period enrichment and the paisley fabric unites all the colours.

Religious imagery, *left.* *The religiose can be emphasized to great effect in a room with a simple white plaster wall with an ecclesiastical collection of candlesticks, devotional images, damasks and braids. Once more, natural materials like gold leaf, metal and beeswax are predominant.*

Chalk drawings *These sketches, drawn with sanguine (a hard chalk pigmented with the same red ochre that coloured the cherub fresco on the opposite page), acquire an immediacy against a whitewashed wall. Mahogany furniture lends gravity to this arrangement and blends in well with the warm tones of the images.*

Colourways

In order to retain the most basic qualities of rooms in Mediterranean countries be sure to emphasize the simplest natural finishes. White walls and a terracotta floor are ideal, but consider also using glazed tiles, faience (tin-glazed earthenware) and Moorish patterned ceramics, or using them, alternatively, as reference for your colour scheme. Earth colours are another starting point. They can be added to white paint to make tints of varying intensity, or applied one on top of another in washes (see pp.250–51 for the technique of three-colour colourwashing).

Subtle grey *Create a broken paint finish on smooth walls using simple colourwashing (see pp.248–9).*

Pale terracotta *Two layers of colour were applied and then distressed for a terracotta colour that combines effectively with verdigris.*

Metallic combination *Provide an unobtrusive background for the sharp colours of silver and rust by painting walls beige.*

BYZANTINE LAVATORY

The Byzantines considered no surface unworthy of patterned decoration. They found inspiration for their imagery in art and ornament from all over the Mediterranean and the East and expressed it in intricately patterned mosaics, tapestry, enamelwork, ceramics, painting and carving. Consequently, Byzantine and Eastern art provides a wealth of ideas for polychrome patterns and decorative motifs that can be used to transform even the smallest space into a Mediterranean sanctuary with a distinctly Eastern atmosphere. The effect here is easy to achieve: I decorated the wall and the floor using hand-printed wallpaper, stencils, spray paints, glaze and patterned wood screens.

ANALYSIS

HANDPAINTED DETAIL

I printed the peacock pattern on wallpaper with a woodblock and picked out some of the design with red ochre artists' oil paint. Horizontal lines divide the prints into rows resembling tiles.

DURING the golden age of Byzantine art (in the ninth century AD), elements of Arabian, Classical Greek and Roman, and Christian art were expressed in pattern and ornament. My sources were just as eclectic for this lavatory decoration: glazed tiles in a Turkish mosque provided the colour scheme; the gold inscription was suggested by an Arabic frieze, and the peacock pattern came from an illuminated Byzantine manuscript.

Printing and stencilling

Woodblock printing is a quick and inexpensive way of patterning a wall. The peacock design was printed on to plain blue wallpaper before it was hung (it is easier to make an impression on paper if it is not on a resilient vertical surface). I used artists' oil paints for the prints and the red freehand details.

The mosaic floor pattern was made by stippling paint through screens that were later attached to the lower wall. I stencilled all the screens with an arabesque pattern. The design is repeated, and then partly reproduced at the top of the panel; I used the same stencil, taping over the section I did not wish to repeat.

Antique finish

To soften the brightness of the freshly painted wall and create an antique appearance I applied a coat of transparent oil glaze which, having a soft surface when dry, I protected with varnish.

The inlaid table, pitcher and incense burner emphasize the Eastern provenance of the setting.

GLAZED WALLS

I toned down the colours of the paintwork with a layer of transparent oil glaze (tinted with raw umber artists' oil paint) to give the wall a warm, antique appearance. I stippled the glaze on to the mouldings and brushed it on to the walls, softening out the brushmarks with a lily-bristle softener.

STENCILLED PANELS

The pierced screens (designed for covering radiators) were painted, and then stencilled with blue, silver and brown spray paints. The source of my arabesque stencil design was the pattern on the roof of an ancient temple. The screens were fixed to the wall and divided into vertical panels with lengths of painted moulding.

PATTERNED FLOOR

Before the pierced screens were painted and attached to the wall I used it as a stencil. I stippled beige paint through the holes so as to give the impression of mosaic flooring.

Techniques

Softened glazework pp.256–7
Stencilling pp.312–7

Byzantine bird *This design is similar to the Indian woodblock I used to decorate the walls.*

STYLING DECISIONS

I F YOU like a room to be decorated with a profuse array of pattern, Byzantine art and architecture offer a wealth of source material to copy and adapt. But do not be afraid to include designs from other parts of the world, like the Mexican tiles shown on the far right, or the Indian woodblock below, used in the main scheme on the previous page.

Books about tiles and floor design are a particularly useful source of ideas for stencilling, or freehand painted patterns.

Alternative imagery

The mainspring of Byzantine art was the Christian faith combined with Greek culture; in turn, Byzantine art influenced medieval and Renaissance art, so it is quite in keeping to combine elements from all these periods.

In the style variation on the right, for example, a reproduction Greek icon is displayed against wallpaper bearing a medieval star emblem. And the sumptuous colours of the fabric are evocative of the Renaissance (see pp. 130–31). Furnishings like these will make a room more European than the lavatory scheme, which has a distinctly Eastern appearance.

Indian woodblock *The peacock is an image that crops up frequently in Byzantine art as well as that of many other cultures.*

Modern interpretation *For a less dazzling array of patterns than the main scheme, I simplified some of the designs and introduced some monochrome fabric.*

Rich impression, left. Devotional Byzantine art (which was influenced by Greek culture and Christianity) influenced medieval and Renaissance styles. For a richly-coloured Western interpretation include fabric with Renaissance colours and medieval starred wallpaper (an easy alternative to painting a pattern), combined with a solemn reproduction Greek icon for a devotional atmosphere.

Tile variation Look for tiles with patterns or colours that are akin to Byzantine designs – whatever part of the world they come from – and use them for floors or walls, alongside stencilled or handpainted patterns. These ceramic tiles are Mexican, but they look just the part.

Colourways

Glazed tiles, which were used to decorate the interior and exterior of early churches and mosques, were the inspiration for the blues, the gold and the red ochre of the lavatory setting. But darker colours need not be avoided. Experiment with a rich palette of Moroccan reds and the colours of leather for a deep and moody atmosphere. Or choose from the greens, oranges and yellows of the two colourways, below right; to tone down the colours and antique them use transparent oil glaze tinted with green or raw sienna artists' oil paints (see pp.256–7).

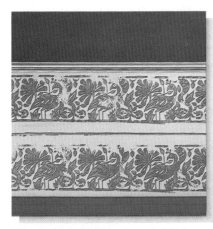

Blue and red ochre *The vivid blue of the main scheme is replaced by red ochre, which brings a restrained dignity to the colourway.*

Green and orange *A combination of refreshing mint green and warm orange, inspired by the colours of Eastern pottery.*

Bright and rich *A strong combination, best used in a small room. Orange softens the contrast between red-brown and yellow.*

CLASSICAL TOWN
STYLES

Classical imagery has never really fallen from grace. Each period in Western history has taken ancient Greek and Roman ideas and reinterpreted them to fit the spirit of the age, in the fields of interior decoration as well as architecture. The Classical town styles illustrated in this section range from the wildly extravagant and flamboyant to the more restrained and clear cut.

Classical styles suit many different types of interior. You may choose to dress a modern apartment in Classicism just for the style's theatrical bravado or you may live in a pre-1830 house that is begging for a sympathetic period feel. Though most buildings decorated in Classical style are in towns, the schemes in this section are suitable for formal country rooms.

What to look for
Architectural detailing plays an important role in Classical interiors. Hunt for mouldings, *trompe l'oeil* details in the form of paper borders or hand-tinted photocopy *découpage* and plastic

ornaments like the laurel wreath, bottom right.

When choosing soft furnishings for your scheme, try to find some that reproduce the colours and fabrics of the major European styles. Sumptuous brocades, velvets, damasks and tapestries are suitable for the grander Classical town styles, while calico and muslin look best in the simpler schemes.

Sources of ideas
When interpreting Classical ideas, it always pays dividends to examine Classical architecture, with its columns, panelling, decorative carving and entablatures. Many pattern books of the eighteenth and nineteenth centuries, now published in facsimile editions, offer pages of detailed engravings of Greek and Roman buildings. These provide good material for stencil designs and *découpage* and give you a good idea of the type of Classical motifs to look out

for on fabrics and wallpapers for your scheme.

At the grandest end of the scale is the opulent nineteenth-century French Empire style. This makes full use of brilliantly coloured silk hangings, highly polished veneers and gilt to create a sense of majesty

and splendour. English Regency interiors, which were further removed from true Classicism than Empire style, were a product of the previous century. They were lavish and frivolous, mixing striped wallpaper and loudly patterned brocades.

Rococo decoration, which originated in the

early eighteenth century, has a lighter air with its gracefully curving shapes and pale-coloured walls and furnishings.

"Quieter" Classicism
In contrast are Biedermeier and American Colonial styles, which rely on Classical simplicity for their appeal, with the emphasis being more on function and comfort than grandeur or flamboyance. There is a

lack of clutter, and any ornamentation is simple. The characteristics of Biedermeier decoration are pale wood with ebony inlay, smooth clean lines, and the minimum of carved decoration. My interpretation of Biedermeier style in a bathroom setting is on page 63.

Sometimes architects set off on grand tours of the ancient world to study Greek and Roman buildings. The capital shown on the left was made by Robert Adam who, fired with enthusiasm by his travels, created interiors in a style named neo-Classical. These interiors are characterized by a lightness of touch, with fresh colour schemes and white mouldings.

NEO-CLASSICAL HALLWAY

For the ultimate in grand statements choose an arrangement from late eighteenth-century neo-Classicism. Its elegance and scholarship, worn lightly, adapt perfectly to modern and period interiors, producing an eminently civilized living space. The style is theatrical, yet sophisticated and composed. Pastels and subtle colours assuage the grandness of the Classical forms and control the quality of natural light in subtle and complex ways.

THERE WAS a resurgence of interest in the Classical world in eighteenth-century Europe. In this spirit of rediscovery, Robert Adam set off for Italy to search for the roots of architecture in ancient Classicism. What he brought to interior decoration, both in Europe and America, was a lost sense of proportion and delicacy and a range of decorative motifs that are still emulated today world-wide.

Here I have captured some of his Classical imagery: a restrained and orderly use of decoration; clean lines; detailed enrichments on every projection; a taste for delicate colours; and a lightness achieved through the predominant use of white paint on the mouldings.

Architectural elements

Architects like Adam translated exterior architecture into interior features. Occasionally they even introduced Classical porticos and columns, but I relied on Adam's taste for a heavy cornice, a frieze and a picture rail and, below, a subtly marbled dado with enriched dado rail and skirting board. But none of these elements are expensive carvings or original eighteenth-century pieces: they are plaster and machine-cut wood mouldings, and the frieze came as a roll of lincrusta.

Colour choice

To prevent the wall looking like a pink cake decorated with white sugar-icing I selected a slightly brown and faded pink. I transformed the lincrusta frieze from a sea of foaming white into a delicately filigreed moulding by painting the background the same colour as the wall, and picking out the relief in white.

As partners to this unassuming main colour scheme I introduced a pale toffee colour for the marbled floor and the wall plaques, and by way of contrast I added a sliver of grey-green to the picture rail.

Eighteenth-century ornament *In simplified form this design would make an effective stencil, which could be used in place of a paper or lincrusta frieze.*

ANALYSIS

DECORATIVE MOULDINGS
Bringing the area of decorative moulding down to fill the upper reaches of the wall alleviates the formality of the space by reducing it to a human scale. The cornice is moulded plaster, the frieze below it is lincrusta, the leaf-patterned moulding on the picture rail is plastic and the thin beading is timber. All are painted with emulsion.

"PLASTER" PLAQUES
The plaques were made from a white lincrusta roll. I cut out the images and framed them with a border trimmed from the same roll. I then treated them in imitation of antique plasterwork.

PALE WALLS & DADO
The wall area was colourwashed with pink emulsion (as in step 3 of Three-colour colourwashing); the dado was softly marbled using pink glaze and according to the technique for Carrara marble. To give both areas the subtle, dusty quality of old distemper I gave them a thin wash of diluted white emulsion.

NEO-CLASSICAL TABLE
The table is a reproduction of a Robert Adam design at Osterley Park near London. Its clean lines contribute to the scheme's formality.

SKIRTING BOARD & FLOORING
The spattered 'porphyry' skirting board frames a hardboard floor painted to look like fossilstone marble. The paler band of marble was left when the rest of the marbled floor was glazed with transparent oil glaze tinted with brown artists' oil paint (see p.333).

STYLING DECISIONS

THE GRAND style of neo-Classicism can be interpreted in fresh and exciting ways by going back to its origins for inspiration. When planning an eighteenth-century neo-Classical scheme bear in mind the following words: restrained, sophisticated, linear, delicate and light – they should guide you in the right stylistic direction. If in doubt, aim for understatement and a minimal scheme with a frieze of Classical motifs, pale walls and perhaps some form of wall ornament, such as the elegant reproduction sconce shown on the right.

Gilt was popular during the late eighteenth century, so if you want to be a little more adventurous pick out mouldings with gold paint or stencil a frieze on the wall using a Classical motif such as an urn and add an ornamental mirror.

Ornament collections, right. The eighteenth-century aristocracy developed a taste for plundered Classical ornament – follow suit with reproduction versions.

Reinterpreting themes This ever-popular egg-and-dart pattern could be successfully incorporated into an Adam scheme as a moulded dado or picture rail.

Neo-Classical motifs

Robert Adam, who initiated this style of decoration, had favourite images such as the wheat husk, urn and gryphon. These appeared in his work on furniture, mouldings and mirror decoration. Look for paper friezes, fabrics, and plastic, lincrusta or plaster mouldings with these motifs, and reproduction Adam furniture.

Colourways

The colour schemes that were popular during the late eighteenth century were composed of pastels, both pale and intense, mixed with marble colours and the judicious use of earth tones. Gold and white were also used extensively. For a dramatic statement adopt an authentic colour scheme, which comprises shades of rich, dark grey-green heightened with antiqued gold and bronze. Or follow a gentler path with delicate tints of peach, orange, strawberry or sky blue. When using pastel colours, however, be sure to choose those containing a fair quantity of brown or grey (or mix some in yourself) to prevent them looking too florid, and consider giving them a final wash, when dry, of diluted white emulsion to produce the dusty, veiled effect of distemper. For mouldings and other enrichment apply white and add detail in the form of marbling or a little gold leaf.

Minimal approach, *left. For a controlled effect a delicate wall sconce is centred over a marble-topped table (the designs of both are attributed to Adam).*

Dominant features, *above. Gilded ornament was popular in the late eighteenth century. The imposing mirror and modern fabric with Classical designs are perfect for a large room.*

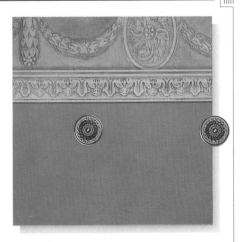

Black and white *For a formal Classical atmosphere put black detailing against a crisp white background, adding a touch of gold for warmth. Paint woodwork black using the granite technique on pages 262–3.*

Cream and peach *For a delicate, light and authentic scheme combine a yellowish cream with peach, using the latter to pick out mouldings, as well as for plain woodwork.*

Soft green *A restrained combination of grey-green (a colour much used by Adam) and dusty-looking mouldings, treated according to the technique on pages 256–7. An occasional touch of gold enlivens the overall effect.*

FRENCH EMPIRE STUDY

The style that evolved at the court of Emperor Napoleon Bonaparte (in the early nineteenth century) was one of pomp and exploit, realized in heavy Classical designs and strong colours, but also of delicacy and fineness, seen in softly draped fabrics and highly polished veneers. A quiet, private room, like a study or small sitting room, is the ideal place in which to benefit from the magical effect of dark colours and rich finishes that flash alive in flickering candlelight.

THE RICH colours of this scheme conjure up an air of grandeur. For the wall I chose an authentic Imperial purple with a dragged finish. The wall makes a dramatic foil to the glow of the gilt and the highly polished finish of the mahogany.

Classical forms of decoration were popular at the time of the French Empire. The plaster cornice (antiqued to give it a polished, waxy finish) has a Greek key pattern; the Classical theme is repeated in the (moulded plastic) Greek urn, which I treated to look like antique gilt.

Draped decoration

French Empire rooms were often lavishly draped with fabrics, sometimes like the interior of a military tent – a reflection of Napoleon's military exploits. The use of soft fabrics gave this masculine Imperial imagery gentler overtones without detracting from the essential formality of the arrangement.

Unifying themes

Decoration at floor level and on the wall plays a role in unifying various parts of the scheme. At floor level the colours of gold and ebony are echoed in the paintwork of the skirting board, a useful device for drawing the scheme together.

Colour photocopies of Montgolfier balloons (the Montgolfier brothers ascended in the first hot-air balloon in the late eighteenth century) make an inexpensive and humorous thematic contribution. Repeating an image at frieze height around all the walls will unify a room's decoration, giving it a boisterous rhythm. The balloon chandelier relates to the photocopies and adds a light touch to the otherwise sober scheme.

Montgolfier balloons *Along with the balloon-shaped chandelier, colour photocopies of balloons lighten the mood of the Empire decoration.*

ANALYSIS

CLASSICAL CORNICE

French Empire decoration drew on Classical designs; this plaster cornice, which I antiqued, is in the Classical Greek-key pattern.

HOT-AIR BALLOONS

A rusty balloon chandelier and colour photocopies of balloons add a touch of humour to the otherwise formal style of the scheme.

CANOPIED SPLENDOUR

Muslin hung from the wall on a hook, is draped either side of the bureau in a tent-like fashion. The softness of the fabric adds a delicate touch to the robust-looking decoration.

IMPERIAL PURPLE WALLS

The walls are given visual status with Imperial purple and a restrained dragged finish. I lightly dragged dark blue transparent oil glaze over a coat of deep mauve eggshell paint.

FLOOR LEVEL

An element as simple as a skirting board can be used to reinforce a colour scheme. Here the colours of gilt and ebony, seen elsewhere in the scheme, are restated in the black and gold paintwork of the skirting board.

Techniques

Dragging pp.259
Antiquing plasterwork pp.272–3
Gilding – metal leaf pp.302–3
Using photocopies pp.318–9

STYLING DECISIONS

POPULAR Empire accessories and motifs were sphinxes and pyramids (reminders of Napoleon's campaign in Egypt), urns, spheres, caryatids and laurel wreaths (Classical devices). To reinforce the Imperial grandeur of a room include Egyptian and Greek ornament, or printed fabrics and wallpapers.

Lighter interpretation

If your taste is for a gentler and less full-blooded Imperial atmosphere, make use of the Empire taste for delicate fabrics and canopies.

Gather soft fabric, such as muslin, voile or fine silk, at wide, regular intervals and hang it around your room at picture rail or cornice height. For a tented effect, drape fabric over a curtain pole and hang it above a bed. To soften a scheme further, counter the harder forms of tightly-stretched chair and bolster covers with simply draped curtains.

Much French Empire furniture was delicate and elegantly curved; day beds and chairs, for example had scrolled backs and were less robust in appearance than the furniture in the main scheme; instead of authentic Empire furniture you can include modern reproductions.

Empire ornament Marble and tortoiseshell were popular materials – instead of the real thing include stylized painted imitations.

Colourways

The colour of the wall in the main scheme is a splendid purple – a cross between mauve and ultramarine blue. The rich effect is due in part to the fact that one colour (blue, in the form of transparent oil glaze) was dragged over the top of the other (mauve, in the form of eggshell paint). The wide range of colours used in French interior decoration at the beginning of the nineteenth century was increased when the French warring gentry returned from military campaigns in Egypt, inspired by the vibrant colours of the Egyptian tombs: red ochre, rich greens, azure blue and a range of singing, acid yellows. But some delicate colours were popular too. Shades of lilac were widely used; their lightness makes them perfect for decorating a room such as a bedroom where you may want a version of Empire style that is gentler in character than the main scheme.

Gilding the laurel, *left. The laurel wreath is a potent symbol of Imperial pomp and splendour. This modern chintz fabric in gold and royal blue would look equally at home in the form of upholstery, swagged, or draped like the muslin in the main scheme.*

Classical terracotta, *right. To add warmth to a scheme introduce terracotta objects, like this reproduction neo-Classical urn and candlesticks. The relation between the colour of baked clay and purple is rich and vibrant, each colour exaggerating the intensity of the other.*

Delicate shades *Lilac colours were popular in Empire France. The powdery tones of this shade of lilac are complemented by the chalky colour of the off-white moulding. This colourway would look effective with mahogany furniture in a bedroom.*

Vibrant yellow *Choose strong yellow for a vibrant atmosphere – perhaps for a dining room. This yellow is an authentic Empire colour that looks highly effective on walls and flatters dark wood furniture.*

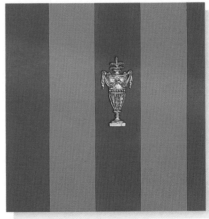

Empire greens *Broad Regency stripes in two Empire greens can be balanced by light furniture, gilt and delicate fabrics. This combination will give a bathroom a grand atmosphere.*

BIEDERMEIER BATHROOM

A room does not have to be filled with original furniture to convey the spirit of an era. By identifying key design elements and translating them into the language of decoration you can use a paintbrush and simple materials to convey a period style. The inspiration for this scheme was a style called Biedermeier (after a popular fictitious character), which was fashionable in early nineteenth-century Austria and Germany. The characteristics of Biedermeier furniture – pale wood, ebony inlay and Classical simplicity – are the theme of this elegant and delicate scheme for a bathroom.

VIENNESE craftsmen of the early nineteenth century were the innovators of Biedermeier-style furniture, which drew its inspiration directly from French Empire interior decoration (see pp.58–61), with its solidity and Classical shapes. But what made Biedermeier furniture different was the contrast between expanses of pale wood and detailed ebony inlay and the minimal amount of carved or gilded decoration. This unpretentiousness was extended to the rest of a room's decoration – floors were usually bare (floorboards or parquet) and walls painted in pale, or bright, colours.

Paint finishes

You need not buy original or even reproduction items of Biedermeier furniture to capture this style. Instead, paint simple old furniture in imitation or transfer the look on to other, less obvious, surfaces, like a bath. I stippled the bath here, with a brown glaze over a pale background to create a *clair bois* (literally pale wood) effect. To imitate ebony, I stuck a strip of waterproof tape to the bath and painted the claw and ball feet black.

As a finishing touch, I gave some plaster "tassels" the same paint treatment, and hung them from black rope against a simply colourwashed wall to give an authentic balance of detail against plain.

The use of pale woods and ebony inlay is extended to the choice of flooring. Instead of real parquet flooring I used plastic tiling, a measure which is both practical and visually effective.

Roman vase *The simplicity and clean lines of nineteenth-century Biedermeier designs were inspired by examples of Classical antiquity, like this vase.*

HANGING LIGHT SHADE

A new white plaster casting was antiqued to give it a cream-coloured waxy bloom like the Classical urn below, and used to conceal an uplighter.

DRAPES & TASSELS

Drapes and canopies were popular in nineteenth-century Europe. Here, muslin swags, pinned to ropes and tassels, form a Classical frieze against the colourwashed wall. The long drape that falls from the right-hand swag is echoed by the canopy above the bath, which is held in place by a brass rose.

SOAP BOWL

In imitation of an ancient water spout, this wooden pot was positioned above the bath to act as a soap bowl.

CLASSICAL URN

A reproduction urn gives status to the bath. The creamy colour and shallow bas-relief carving echoes the antiqued plaster casting that hangs above it.

PAINTED BATH

The bath was painted to look like clair bois *(pale wood) – a material that was used for Biedermeier furniture. Black tape was used to suggest ebony.*

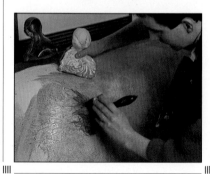

Techniques

Colourwashing pp.248–9
Antiquing plasterwork pp.272–3
Clair bois pp.296–7

STYLING DECISIONS

RESTRAINT, proportion, clarity: these are the key words that describe the style of Biedermeier furniture and decoration. Plan your room around the few carefully chosen pieces of furniture and artefacts that you want to be the focus of attention.

Always choose items of furniture that are functional and unfussy. The chair shown here, with its rounded design, is a characteristic example of Biedermeier furniture. Then consider a complementary wall finish. A possibility is to cover walls with wallpaper or fabric with broad Regency stripes or Empire motifs. Include, perhaps, some restrained wall decoration in the form of pilasters, a cornice or a frieze.

Choosing materials

Natural materials, like sandstone and plain marbles, have a simplicity that suits this style as do natural fabrics, such as muslin and calico. Introduce real sandstone and marble, discreetly, in the form of ornament, or imitate them with paint (see pp.280–81 and pp.290–95). Fresh plasterwork of any kind, including cornices and columns, can be given a delicate, polished bloom and almost marble-like finish (see the technique on pp.272–3). Make a feature of floor-boards by painting them to resemble *clair bois*.

Painted detail Clair bois *can be imitated effectively on small details, such as this finial, as well as on larger objects in a Biedermeier scheme.*

Colourways

The essential colours for any Biedermeier scheme are those of *clair bois* (pale wood) and black ebony inlay. You can introduce these in the form of furniture (either original, reproduction or painted) or small areas of paintwork, such as doors and skirting boards. Choose from the colours of any of the pale woods like cherry, ash, pear, birch and maple, and include black in the form of inlaid furniture, ornamental detail or fabric. To keep the appearance of large background areas simple, avoid complex paint finishes. Colours that give a sense of airiness and lightness are particularly effective – the soft, creamy colour of the walls in the original scheme, for example, or a pastel shade. Alternatively, consider more vibrant colours that contrast with pale wood, or tone down the colour of wood by having raw umber, drab green, or black walls.

Formal effect, *left. For a formal effect, I added bands of thinned emulsion paint, and the occasional Classical leaf.*

"Natural" materials, *right. For an elemental look, introduce a sandstone-effect dado (see pp.280–81).*

Dark and light, *below. The contrast of black silhouettes on a bright yellow wall recalls the contrast of ebony inlay and pale wood.*

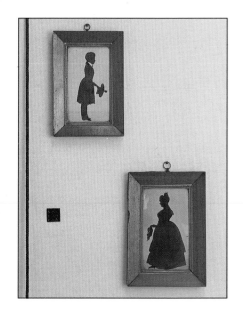

Complementary colours *A subtle beige proves a flattering and delicate complement to the hotter colours of Biedermeier furniture. Consider trying this in a bedroom, with cream muslin.*

Robust option *Flamboyant yellow makes a robust companion to the colour of pale wood; maintain a large proportion of the latter in the scheme, so that it is not dominated by the yellow.*

Unusual contrast *The most complex relationship of colours is pale wood with a blue background and a dash of calming, soft grey. Try aquamarine or turquoise as an alternative background colour for walls.*

ENGLISH BAROQUE PARLOUR

Though characterized by exuberant shapes and abundant ornamentation, the English version of seventeenth-century Baroque decoration was lighter and more restrained than its full-blown Italian counterpart. I took the most charming images of the English Baroque – swags, tassels and cherubs – and used them to ornament an otherwise minimally decorated space. This scheme has a festive mood and airy elegance that would suit any modern or period room, where you want to mix rich and plain decoration.

THE SINGLE most influential element in determining the Baroque atmosphere of the setting is the three-dimensional frieze decoration made from a plaster cornice, a moulding and tasselled swags. The flamboyant plaster cornice is a reproduction of a Baroque design; the tassels are plaster and the rope was dipped in plaster. The cherub (a common motif in Baroque decoration) is gilded.

Main structures

I decided on a low dado in order to leave plenty of empty white wall and panelled it with long rectangles that help pull the eye horizontally. The spacing of the dado panels echoes the swags above and the two combine to create a swinging musical rhythm that is in tune with the celebratory character of Baroque decorative style.

The feel of a room can be radically altered, simply by the choice of colours for the dado, the floor and the walls. In a room where the dado and floor are the same colour and finish (like the Miami Deco setting on p.197) you feel comfortably cradled as there is no visual tension between the surfaces.

But when a dado is painted in a contrasting colour (like the one here) it stands out as an independent entity, setting up visual tension, and wrapping a room with a horizontal band that creates a strong sense of movement. This "banding" effect becomes all the more obvious when you stand in the middle of a room decorated like this. The dark and oily colour used here, makes the dado appear independent of the colourwashed floor, which is almost as light as the wall.

Period features

You do not need many period items. Baroque character is impressed upon this setting using modern structural components and decorating materials. The only original Baroque elements are the framed portraits, the chair and the table.

Baroque shape *The enrichment on this design for a silver urn plays second fiddle to the rhythm of its overall shape.*

ANALYSIS

PLASTER DECORATION

Ornate plasterwork, swags, tassels and cherubs are all Baroque forms of decoration. The cornice, the tassels and the moulding are plaster; the rope was dipped in plaster. The cherub (which was gilded with metal leaf) catches the light and draws attention to the ceiling-height plasterwork.

DARK WOOD

In the spirit of the age, the portraits are framed in plain, heavy oak; the simple, dark blocks of colour balance the frothiness of the cornice and swags.

WHITE WALL

Diluted raw umber emulsion colourwashed over a basecoat of white emulsion (follow step 3 on p.251) warms and antiques the wall, emphasizing the sharp plaster decoration above.

PANELLED DADO

Seventeenth-century rooms were often panelled; I just panelled the dado, gluing simple timber mouldings straight on to the wall. To imitate the oily effect of old-fashioned oil-bound paints I painted the dado with grey-tinted mid-blue eggshell paint followed, when dry, by a coat of sage-green eggshell (diluted 1:4 with white spirit), which I softened with a dusting brush.

COLOURWASHED FLOOR

To set up a level of visual movement and tension between the different surfaces I painted the floor a different colour from the dado. The floorboards, which are nearly as light-reflective as the wall, were colourwashed with diluted emulsion paint and varnished.

Techniques
Three-colour colourwashing pp.250–51

Colourwashing wood pp.252–3

Gilding – metal leaf pp.302–3

STYLING DECISIONS

THE KEY to decorating a Baroque room is to use simple raw materials and to display various carefully chosen decorative items.

Grand materials, such as marble and ormolu, and sophisticated paint finishes like marbling and woodgraining are not of this period. Baroque craftsmen wrought beauty from simple, raw materials, like oil- and water-based paints, plaster and wood, especially hardwoods, like oak, elm and mahogany.

Furniture and floors

The open-backed chair in the main parlour scheme with its tall back, cabriole legs, carved decoration and tapestry upholstery is typical of furniture of the period. Other chairs of the period are leather-backed, or straight-backed and covered in Turkey work (a type of carpet), like those on the right.

Floorboards should be bare, and stained, colourwashed or varnished. Alternatively, lay down a Turkish carpet, leaving plenty of exposed boards.

Tapestries, in the form of curtains, hangings and heavy upholstery add an authentic warmth and a degree of texture to a Baroque style room.

Baroque cherub *The cherub was one of the most widely used Baroque motifs, so include one in your Baroque scheme in the form of plaster, plastic, wood or hand-tinted photocopy (see pp.318–9).*

Period table decoration
For a pure, ascetic look, furnish your dining room table with crisp damask linen, pewter and candlesticks. Pewter from any period will look at home in a Baroque setting as long as it is simple and solid in design. For a grander look include silver, in the form of tableware and candlesticks.

Textile warmth, *left.*
Earth-colour textiles in the
form of upholstery, wall
hangings, rugs and curtains
add comfort and warmth to
a Baroque room and
complement cool wall
colours, like white and blue.

Lighter tone, *left. You can*
completely alter the character
of a space by what you hang
on your wall. Limed oak
mirror frames (like this
reproduction of a Baroque
design) or picture frames will
bring a scrubbed freshness to
a room. To make a real
feature of the material in a
room's decoration include
limed oak furniture as well.
To lime wood follow the
technique on pages 260–61.

Colourways

Seventeenth-century Baroque paint
colours are noted for their subtlety.
Match period colours by mixing
different shades of proprietary paint.
Surfaces that were painted with
distemper had a dusty appearance and
those painted with oil-bound paints
had an oily appearance. To imitate
distemper apply diluted white
emulsion over your main colour. For an oily finish paint with
eggshell. When the first coat has dried, paint on a paler shade
of eggshell, thinned with white spirit; while the paint is still
damp, soften out the brushmarks with a dusting brush.

Cherry and pink *Make a strong*
impression in a small room with
brilliant white plasterwork and dusty
cherry and pink paintwork.

Blue and white *The woodwork,*
painted with blue eggshell and then
diluted white eggshell, makes a crisp
contrast with the white background.

Earthy pearwood *This authentic*
Baroque colour can be overpowering
in large quantities so use it for
woodwork rather than walls.

PARISIAN BEDROOM

French engravings of the eighteenth century are wonderfully inspiring if you want to create a bedroom that is Classical yet relaxed. In their decoration of private rooms, the French combined the ornate with the delicate, and Classicism with softness and warmth. I have followed their example – panelling the wall to make a strong, rhythmic background to a variety of rich fabrics and using soft lighting to create an air of intimacy. This style of scheme will lend itself perfectly to any other room that you use as a private refuge from day-to-day matters.

THIS IS a style that needs careful handling to avoid the overall effect becoming too ornate. The key to offsetting the opulence of fabrics, mirrors and plump furnishings is to make use of a simple, structured wall treatment.

The emphasis here is not on decorative paint techniques (the wall is plainly painted with emulsion paints) but on panelling, which gives the wall a rhythmic, geometric structure. The panelling, arranged in vertical strips, is made from wooden planks and edged with panel moulding. Consider panelling just one side of a room, where there is an eye-catching focal point, like the bed here. For horizontal interest add a cornice, skirting boards or dado rail.

The painted panelling makes a simple background for the elements on the wall, (two antique bell pulls and a sconce), and the plump cushions, flowing drapes and rich hangings, which help to soften the atmosphere. For a finishing touch use candlelight or subtle lighting to cast a hazy luminescence.

Colour choice

A cosy atmosphere can be created without using warm colours. I made the colours here by blending blue-green emulsion paint with blue and grey emulsion. Colours with the same sort of tonal complexity (see the *Colourways* overleaf) have a subtlety that is enhanced by soft lighting and the warm glow of gold, which you can antique to tone it down a little (see p.304). As an alternative to vertical strips of lincrusta like those on the wall (which I sprayed gold), gild a motif on the wall, or on some pieces of bedroom furniture, using metal leaf or metallic powder.

Sèvres vase This vase is in keeping with the aesthetic of the whole scheme: its surface decoration is ornate and its shape ordered.

ANALYSIS

BELL PULLS

Antique textiles have an unrivalled richness of colour; they are expensive, but small pieces can be used to great effect. Here, antique tassels and the remains of some old curtain tie backs are hung to look like bell pulls.

TOUCHES OF GOLD

Look for ways of reproducing the richness of gold details. The decorative gold strips on the wall were cut from a lincrusta frieze and sprayed with gold paint. The sconce is a reproduction of an eighteenth-century design.

PANELLING

Vertical panelling (made from planks of wood, edged with panel moulding) gives this scheme Classical symmetry and an air of restraint. The wall is painted with plain coats of emulsion paint (the colours inspired by a mid-eighteenth-century painting), which serve to emphasize the finery.

OPULENT BEDHEAD

A large piece of furniture, like this bed, makes a stunning focus of attention. The bedhead is antique – its gilt has faded naturally with age, but the fine network of cracks in the gesso are probably deliberate. This effect, known as craquelure, *was fashionable in the eighteenth century, and was probably created then. You can imitate antique gilt and create a* craquelure *effect.*

RICH FABRICS

For an atmosphere of luxury, arrange cushions and drapes that share a common colour, adding variety with patterns and textiles – use velvet, brocade, tapestry and damask.

Techniques
Craquelure pp.268–9
Gilding – metal leaf pp.302–3
Gilding – metallic powder pp.304–5

STYLING DECISIONS

THE ESSENTIAL qualities of eighteenth-century French taste are elegance and restraint. Though this period is known for some of the most luscious fabrics – damasks, velvets and brocades – and ornate furnishings – they were, and still should be, used judiciously to avoid creating an over-stuffed, cluttered look.

Grand or delicate?

A grand look can be created using reproduction damasks, tassels and mirrors. Look out for contemporary fabrics based on antique designs and those with a richness of colour and design.

The joy of working within the tight structure of panelling is that you can concentrate on the small, manageable spaces that it offers. The airy look on the right was created by using the panels as a frame for paper decoration, made from painted photocopies, and by incorporating painted furniture.

Elegance on a budget To make a headboard, cover a panel with damask and frame it with heavy picture-frame moulding. Complete the rich look with reproduction tassels and a gilt mirror.

Colourways

The inspiration for a colour scheme can come from many sources; in an eighteenth-century French scheme, where the emphasis is on fabrics, look to the muted tones of antique textiles, perhaps an old rug or bedspread. Match the colours of textiles with paint manufacturers' colour swatches, both in daylight and – particularly for a bedroom – in artificial light. Alternatively, look at mid-eighteenth-century French paintings, especially those that focus on domestic, bourgeois interiors, and arrive at an approximation of the colours used. The colours in the main scheme were matched to those in a painting by Boucher and include a green that was popular at the time (*vert de pomme*), blue and gold. Gold, in the form of gilded furniture and ornaments, and woven into fabrics was fashionable – so include a dash in your scheme too.

Dust of ages, *left. For a grand statement nothing beats antique tapestries. Make the most of small scraps of tapestry, using them to cover cushions. Tie back curtains with reproduction or antique tassels.*

Paper decorations, *far left. Pasted-up engravings are typically eighteenth-century. Imitate this fashion with photocopies taken from modern pattern books. Add colour with thinned paint and protect them with clear varnish. The ornamental photocopies here, complement the antique painted dressing table from Italy.*

Green and rose *Experiment with colours that blend and contrast. The green used in the original scheme is complemented by the rich green damask but contrasts with the delicate, burnt rose colour, which was fashionable in the mid-eighteenth century.*

Russet and white *The richness of the deep russet on this panel is offset by a chalky white (made by adding generous amounts of raw umber and black paint to white paint). With a contrast as bold as this, use the darker colour for quite small areas.*

Dusty blue *White paint was added to blue paint to create a dusty-coloured foil to the swirling patterns of the accompanying damask. Adding black, white, or brown paint to colours that appear to clash will tone them down to produce a friendly combination.*

ROCOCO DINING ROOM

Used since Roman times, trompe l'oeil (meaning literally, "to trick the eye"), is a cheap and effective decorative device. It is the perfect instrument for bringing a sophisticated theatrical air to a room, with designs that will delight and surprise your guests. For a light-hearted atmosphere choose a Rococo scheme of decoration. This eighteenth-century European style, typified by gracefully curved shapes and pale, clear colours has been encapsulated here on a wall, using a range of trompe l'oeil effects made with inexpensive materials.

TROMPE L'OEIL reached great heights of popularity and sophistication in eighteenth-century Europe. For this scheme I combined features of period architecture (including arches, trelliswork and a dado) that were a popular subject of *trompe l'oeil* both in the home and the theatre. All these features were made using a simple, logical system of painted shadows and highlights (see pp.320–22).

Two-dimensional features

Once the main areas of the design were drawn out they were colourwashed with thinned emulsion paint. Then I marbled the dado panels with water-based washes. All the lines of the *trompe l'oeil* mouldings, skirting board, arches and trelliswork were painted with emulsion paint.

The swirling Rococo images between the marbled panels and on the arched frames are photocopies. I coloured them with emulsion paint so they blend with the rest of the decoration. The selection of colours – lilac, lavender and cold peach – are all typically Rococo. The finishing touch was to give all the colours a soft, dusty quality, by painting the whole wall with a coat of diluted white emulsion paint.

Room for illusion

The joy of *trompe l'oeil* is that large, dramatic architectural features, which in reality would take up a lot of space, can be created with paint on walls in the smallest of rooms. A bold *trompe l'oeil* design, like the one here, will look effective even if there is a considerable quantity of furniture in front of it, but for greater elegance use a small amount of furniture, which has a delicate design, preferably, and is made of wood or contemporary steel, like the wine rack, shown here.

Rococo fabrics Choose fabrics authentic to the period, like damask in soft, dusty colours, for billowing curtains and drapes.

ANALYSIS

GILDED RIBBONS

Gold was a popular Rococo colour. The bows were cut from a lincrusta frieze and gilded. They conceal the picture hooks from which the plaster panels are hung.

"ANTIQUE" PANELS

I antiqued these new plaster panels. Their musical and naturalistic motifs and light, elegant design are typical of Rococo decoration.

PLASTER MOULDINGS

Gild plaster or wood mouldings and incorporate them in your Rococo wall decoration; look for swirling, asymmetrical designs like this.

PHOTOCOPIES

The details on the arches and between the marbled panels are black and white photocopies, which I painted.

DADO DECORATION

To create an overall sense of space and lightness all the heavier trompe l'oeil *paintwork (a moulded dado rail, a skirting board and marbled panels) is positioned low on the wall.*

Techniques

Three-colour colourwashing pp.250–51
Antiquing plasterwork pp.272–3
Marbling p.294
Gilding – metal leaf pp.302–3
Using photocopies pp.318–9
Trompe l'oeil pp.320–22

COLONIAL LIVING ROOM

Early settlers in North America took with them the decorative ideas of the countries they were leaving, so Colonial homes had much in common with eighteenth-century European country houses. But these Americans developed a particular taste for the simple and practical, reflecting the morality of the Founding Fathers, with their preference for plain living and scrupulous honesty. A lack of clutter, rustic furniture, simple panelling and plain walls, with a predominance of earthy colours, are the hallmarks of Colonial style. Its spare, clean lines create a light and airy tranquillity that is very appealing.

Early Colonial houses were often modest, with low ceilings and small windows, so decoration needed to make the most of the available light and space. In your own home, this style can be helpful in rooms that are small or are lacking in light.

Paint schemes

Where light is a problem, one option is to paint a coloured dado but to highlight the ceiling, walls and cornice in white. This reflects the maximum amount of light and suggests a bright canopy over a low, coloured "wall" (see the English Baroque Parlour setting on p.67).

Here I decided instead to emphasize both the cornice and the mouldings, which combine to trace a thin boundary line, delineating rather than hiding the wall's architectural form. Against this frame of oily green the areas of white wall are not imprisoned; instead, they seem to "float" independently.

Borders and stencils

The walls here are painted on lining paper, which was popular in grander Colonial houses, though more modest homes were usually whitewashed. Coloured and patterned paper borders and garlands were sometimes pasted on: stencils developed as the poor man's imitation of these. Avoid too much decoration, though, if you want to preserve the straightforward lines of Colonial style. The white wall provides a suitable background for a few carefully chosen ornaments.

Border patterns *The complex and delicate pattern on this reproduction wallpaper shows the Colonial preference for natural motifs of fruit and flowers.*

ANALYSIS

CONTEMPORARY PAINTINGS

Both of these American oils sit perfectly with the colour scheme, hung quite high in the tradition of the late eighteenth century. You may find it easier to make a painting the starting point for choosing colours than to find a picture to match a room that is already decorated.

COLOUR SCHEME

The choice of green comes from a set of eighteenth-century colours researched by an American firm, which I matched by mixing up eggshell paint. The white paint was mixed with very small quantities of blue and brown paint to give it the cool cast of cheap distemper, used in modest Colonial homes.

WOODEN FURNITURE

The tallboy was made of mahogany in America at the end of the eighteenth century in imitation of English originals. However, much furniture continued to be imported, like this limed oak chair (liming is a simple technique you can do yourself), until American woodworking and wrought iron craftsmanship developed.

MOULDINGS

The dado rail, skirting board and door architrave are copied from originals and are composed of a number of smaller mouldings pinned and glued together (see pp.22–3). The cornice is a simple dentilled reproduction.

CARPET

Sometimes canvas floorcloths were painted and patterned in imitation of imports like this Axminster carpet. I stained the new pine floorboards a deep mahogany colour to match the tallboy.

Technique
Liming wood pp.260–61

STYLING DECISIONS

BECAUSE OF the simplicity of Colonial decorating, it is important to use paints that approximate the colour and finish of early Colonial paints. Use traditional milk paints, distemper or emulsion paints for walls and earthy coloured oil-based paints such as eggshell for woodwork.

Collector's pieces

A simple interior makes a good empty canvas in which to display collections. Settlers imported from Europe, so any eighteenth-century English and Dutch pieces will naturally sit well in a Colonial room. The restrained Classicism of the mouldings used suggests that you might add the occasional grander piece, like a gilded mirror.

Painted and stencilled American country furniture, like the chair on the right, is another option. Even modern furniture will look at home if painted in authentic colours using eggshell paints.

Collections of ceramics These were often made a feature in Colonial homes. Display them on a high shelf round the room or against a mahogany or painted surface. Choose vigorous hand-painted ware, and combine it with spongeware, like the large jug, and creamware.

Colourways

Inspiration for Colonial colour schemes can come from original fabrics or hand-painted furniture, as well as the colour chart, above right. If you ever get the opportunity, visit Sturbridge village in Massachusetts, USA, now a working museum, where many of the buildings are decorated with close approximations to the original colours. For authenticity, copy the earthy tones of background and border colours, rather than the primary hues used for painting details: being cheaper, these subdued colours were more commonly used. The cool whites and subtle blues, greens and browns of Colonial rooms can be quite tricky to reproduce accurately. However, some variation in colour is authentic: tones varied because until after World War II there was no standardized system for mixing tints. Pigments also varied from region to region.

Traditional quilting, left.
A famous trademark of early
American craftsmanship,
quilts were handmade for
beds and cushion covers.
Hang a beautiful specimen
on the wall, or use small
remnants of larger quilts for
covering cushions.

Collections with a theme,
right. Small pieces with a
common surface texture or
colour can form the starting
point for a collection. The
colour of the pewter here, en-
livens the wooden decoy duck.

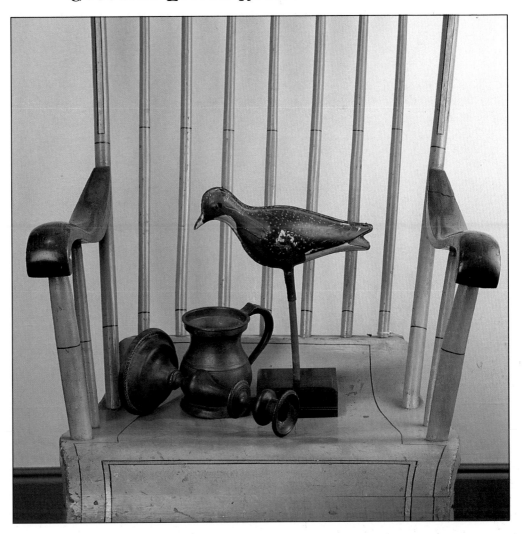

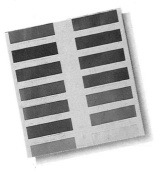

Authentic colours, above.
This swatch is representative
of the tones used in early
American homes.

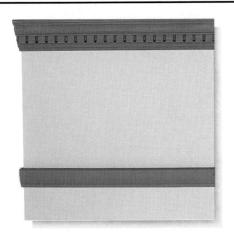

Muted green *A soft pink oil-based coat*
of red ochre and burnt sienna added to
white, was covered with a layer of the
oil-based eggshell used in the living room
scheme. When dry, it was rubbed with
methylated spirits to reveal the pink
paint beneath.

Soft brown *Popularly known as*
"pearwood", this tone is perfect for
painting doors and other woodwork.
Mix it by combining raw-umber
coloured paint with raw-sienna
coloured paint until you have the right
balance of coolness and warmth.

Earthy reds *Bright reds were rather*
rare, as the pigments had to be
imported. Earthy red pigments, such as
red ochre, were locally available and so
more common; I matched these authentic
pigments by mixing different shades of
eggshell paint.

REGENCY DRAWING ROOM

A room that soaks up the morning sunlight is the sort of bright and cheery setting that is ideally suited to the rich and confident character of early nineteenth-century Regency decoration. This English style, which embraced a mélange *of foreign influences, is typified by a taste for furnishings such as striped wallpaper and flamboyantly patterned brocades, in wild and exciting hues of magenta, emerald, and azure blue. Applied over-generously, the rich palette of Regency decoration can appear cloying, so I included just a few of the lightest and most frivolous elements, painting the wall with stripes and, as the* pièce de résistance, *picking out and gilding the ornate plaster cornice.*

DURING the rule of the Prince Regent (later George IV) in the early nineteenth century, new and pure forms of ancient Classicism (see p.59, for example) vied with the fussy exuberance of Regency style.

The Brighton Pavilion, with its exotic mixture of lavish and frivolous decoration, is testament to the style in its most extreme form.

Tamed exuberance

To adapt the sort of excessive decoration used in the Regent's Brighton Pavilion to a domestic setting on a modest scale I focused lavish decoration in one area only: on and around the cornice. Blue paint and gold metallic powder were used to decorate the cornice, and painted rope was attached to the wall in a double-wave formation. The cornice design is Gothic; this was one of the many styles that was absorbed at the time.

Simple stripes

The wall is decorated with stripes in magenta-pink emulsion over a chalk-white emulsion background. The formality of the stripes gives the scheme a measure of composure and the linear pattern lends it a slender elegance, which is counterbalanced and enlivened by the bright colours and the eyecatching decoration of the cornice.

To soften the newly painted stripes, I brushed the whole wall with a thin wash of off-white emulsion. The lightness and warmth of the walls is continued in the floorboards, which were painted with pale-pink emulsion.

Regency vase Chinese art was adapted for the decoration of English ceramics; incorporate contemporary copies or modern Oriental imports.

ANALYSIS

ENRICHED PLASTER CORNICE

The cornice is a copy of a design that probably predated the Regency era – but no matter, for Regency style absorbed a variety of different elements. I painted the cornice with powder-blue and dark-blue emulsion paint, and gilded it with metallic powder. The swagged rope was coloured with blue spray paint before being attached.

CURTAIN DETAILING

In order to place emphasis on the cornice and walls, I dressed the curtains with comparative modesty, using swagged butter muslin, and fixed chunky gilded finials (made from fibreglass) to the curtain poles.

CHANDELIER

To provide a point of focus and break up the stripiness of the wall, I hung the extraordinarily ornate chandelier low in the room.

PAINTED REGENCY STRIPES

Before painting the pink emulsion stripes, I drew vertical lines in pencil over a chalk-white emulsion basecoat. Low-tack masking tape was used to obtain a neat painted edge (the tape was removed before the paint had dried). The stripes were softened with a wash of off-white emulsion diluted 1:5 with water, which I brushed out as in step 3 of Three-colour colourwashing.

COLOURED FLOORBOARDS

The pine floorboards were sanded and then painted with pink emulsion diluted 1:4 with water (as in step 2 of Colourwashing wood). *They were protected with matt oil-based varnish.*

Techniques

Three-colour colourwashing pp.250–51
Colourwashing wood pp.252–3
Gilding – metallic powder pp.304–5

STYLING
DECISIONS

IN CELEBRATION of the florid style of Regency decoration, rooms should be painted, furnished and trimmed with a mixture of pattern, colour and texture. Just to what extent you take this depends on whether you prefer a room to have a lavish appearance, or a measure of restraint.

Selecting and mixing

At the heart of the style lie a few distinctive features, all of which will give a room a period appearance. These are: the bold Regency stripes of wallpapers and fabrics; prints of exotic birds and flowers (often inspired by Chinese art); and bamboo and wickerwork, which were often used alongside simple darkwood furniture. Select from these as you wish.

Styles from previous centuries, such as Gothic, Rococo and Rustic (see p.339), were absorbed too, and these give further flexibility to your choice of furnishing and ornament.

Colourways

Surviving Regency furniture exhibits such a sober elegance that it seems at odds with the vogue for strikingly patterned soft furnishings. But bright colours were fashionable, and those used in interior decoration simply echoed those of period clothing. As an alternative to the pink and cream stripes, left, try some bright "English" colours, such as emerald and azure, set against stripes in a subdued pastel version of the same colours, and off-white stripes. If stripes are not to your taste, paint walls in rich pastel versions of colours such as blue, red, yellow and green.

Other colours popular in Europe in the early nineteenth century were acid yellow, turquoise blue, deep ultramarine, and lilac (look at the Empire and Biedermeier colourways on pp.61 and 65, respectively).

Bright stripes In a room with plenty of light, try an English Regency striped pattern in white and acid yellow; the latter colour was popular in Empire France.

Pattern and stripes, *left. As an alternative to painting stripes, decorate with striped wallpaper and bold paper borders and furnish with robustly decorated fabrics. Add detail in the form of visual motifs, like the gilded plastic urn here, or paper rosettes, which can be repeated at frieze height.*

Chinese starting point, *above. Wallpapers, like this, which are reproduction Regency designs, capture the spirit of the age perfectly. Use them as a starting point for a Regency room – matching their colours with textiles, like the cushions and tassels here.*

Period gilt, *above left. This gilt mirror is typically Regency. Spark off formal furniture, like this table, with patterned fabric in bright colours, such as the striped material with feathery swirls, which is reflected in the glass.*

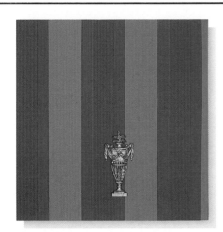

Deeper shades *I saw these intense shades of Prussian cobalt and red ochre in a print of a Regency interior and matched them with emulsion paint. Stripes in these colours would look effective in a small room.*

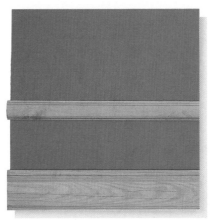

Formal green *If your preference is for unpatterned walls, try this French Empire green, which became popular in Regency England. It goes well with natural woods, such as polished pine, and would suit a formal dining room.*

COUNTRY STYLES

Age-roughened furniture and old collected objects jumble together in the timeless, relaxing setting of a country interior. Simplicity of design is the key to creating artless, rustic character in a room, while weathered finishes give history to walls, furniture and woodwork, and earthy colours and floral images are chosen to echo the rural landscape of the country.

Much of what we perceive as being a country decorating style is the creation of high street retailers, who have taken a nineteenth-century notion of country living and translated it into a popular image. What really is found in country houses may be another thing: it certainly varies the world over, which is why I have included settings from America, Sweden, England and France.

There is a timeless and pervasive quality about country interiors. In many

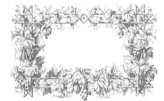

country homes, objects are collected and possessions amass in a way that seems so random it is almost organic. This is a quality to seek in any place or period setting, a feeling that all the contents have been gathered haphazardly over time and have somehow grown alike. Such homogeneity is not easy to create from scratch. It relies on a number of principles, chiefly roughness of finish, a choice of subtle and earthy colours, and simplicity of design.

Weathered wood

By roughness of finish I do not simply mean coarse: country walls and furniture are often knocked and worn, and there are associated finishes that you can exploit, such as aged and distressed paintwork, to achieve this effect. When all the woodwork in a room is painted, or weathered, in

a way that the character of the wood pokes through, the warmth and complexity of such finishes tie together apparently disparate elements (look at the Swedish Stairway on p.87). It is even easier to achieve the effect if you base your colours on local pigments, or on an artefact such as the wreath, below right.

Simple and honest

There is not much room for sophisticated finishes, such as marbling, in simple country interiors. Finishes

must respect the character of the surroundings. And, to an extent, they must be honest. Marbling is a grand deceit, whereas the rough,

pitted glaze of the terra-cotta jug, below right, clearly exposes the qualities of the raw material.

Decoration of surfaces and pattern design should follow the same principles. The rose-patterned fabric, right, represents a full-blown Victorian view of what country decorating should be. The stencilled fabric to its left has an earthier, more direct appeal. Its traditional, American, pineapple design is flat and graphic, and looks more home-made

than the carefully worked
roses and leaves. Equally,
the printed paper border,
below left, gives the idea
that it has been simply executed with a stencil.

The untrained hand
Rough-edged stencilling,
worn corners of furniture
and distressed paintwork
all contrive to suggest an
unprofessional hand. Build
the decoration of a room
with stencils, or with cheap
photocopy *découpage*.
Finally, bring the outside
in and decorate with fruit,
flowers and cane.

SWEDISH STAIRWAY

The Swedish tradition of painted woodwork, simple design and the restrained use of ornament was the inspiration for the decoration of this modest stairway. The distinctive Scandinavian blue-greens and gently faded quality of the armoire were my starting point and these qualities were extended, using a variety of paint finishes, to the stairs, dado, wall, and floor. The result is a light, airy space with an uncluttered atmosphere.

THE MOST distinctive characteristic of Swedish style is the simple and practical design of everyday objects. This stems from a tradition of craftsmanship in a remote part of the world where objects were constructed to work well and to last for generations.

This stairway is simply furnished, with a functional, discreetly decorated armoire. The richly-carved mirror, which is the only frivolous embellishment, reflects the light and makes the stairway appear larger.

Textures and colours

Follow the Swedish example, as I have done, and paint woodwork and furniture, building up thin washes of colour and creating a textured, aged finish. Link this with a wall finish with a textured appearance like the old plaster finish here and you will have a room in which all the different elements are visually unified.

My overall choice of colours was inspired by a picture of a Swedish room and the positioning of individual colours was influenced by the need to make the stairway hardwearing and to make the most of the natural light.

The dark, oily blues of the dado and the distressed paint finish serve to hide scuffmarks and the pale colour of the wall above the dado and the floorboards below it reflect the light. Grey, a colour discernable in the woodwork and the furniture, is used solo on the colourwashed floorboards to "tie" the scheme together visually.

Suitable rooms

The charming, uncomplicated look of this stairway has an authentic country feel and will suit any informal room where there is wood, or you are happy to add it in the form of mouldings (like the tongue-and-groove dado, rail and skirtings here), furniture or floorboards.

Using pale, light-reflective colours above and below the dado and including a mirror makes this scheme particularly suitable for any small room that you wish to give a more airy and spacious appearance.

Gilt enrichment To enrich a simple scheme add a little gilt in the form of a moulding, like this, or furniture decoration.

WALL TREATMENT

In imitation of warm ochre-coloured plaster I dribbled water through red- and yellow-ochre powder colour washes. A coat of mustard-tinted, diluted PVA gives the walls a light-reflective sheen that is echoed by the glaze of the peasant pottery on top of the armoire.

CARVED MIRROR

Mirrors are a practical choice for stairways as they reflect the natural light (which is often limited), creating an illusion of increased space. The style of the mirror's carving is typical of the simplified form in which eighteenth-century French ideas were adapted to suit a tradition of fine craftsmanship.

PAINTED FURNITURE

The clarity of design, simplicity of enrichment and muted colours of this small console table are typical of Swedish furniture.

BANISTERS & WOODWORK

In a balancing act of colour, the banisters, stained to a natural walnut colour, echo the warmth of the ochre walls and trace a line through a sea of moody, blue-green woodwork.

Techniques

Colourwashing wood pp.252-3
Ageing paint on wood pp.266-7

STYLING DECISIONS

IN THE LATE eighteenth century there was a resurgence of
interest in Classicism. Ancient
Greek and Roman forms of architecture, decoration and furniture
became popular and these neo-
Classical tastes spread from France
through Scandinavia.

The style that emerged in Sweden was an eclectic one in which
traditional styles of decoration sat
happily alongside Classical ones.
You can follow suit and combine
the colours and paint finishes
shown here and on the previous
page with Classical elements – but
be careful to restrain the number
you include or your room will begin
to lose its Swedish flavour.

Look out, too, for hand-crafted
country paraphernalia in the form
of basketry, weaving and leatherwork. You will find these sit just as
comfortably alongside one another
as alongside a gilded chair or an
ornate chandelier, for in Sweden
the small and the simple invariably
partner the large and the grand.

Paper detail, *above. Classical scenes,
reproduced in monochrome and on a
large scale, were a popular theme for
eighteenth-century Swedish wallpapers.
You can follow suit by adding paper
decoration in the form of a Classical
wall panel made from a large black and
white photocopy (see pp.318-9 for
decorative uses for photocopies).*

Cool light, *left. The various off-whites used in this scheme create an atmosphere of clean coolness that is typical of many Swedish interiors and suits large rooms as much as small ones.*

Classical warmth, *below left. The warmth of the ochre walls of the original scheme is strengthened by the addition of rich earth colours in the form of reproduction Classical Greek ornament.*

True rustication *In rural Sweden even the simplest of everyday objects were painted traditionally. If you can employ the friendly quality of rustic paraphernalia painted in rich autumnal colours, like this stool and foodbox, you will plant the feet of a room firmly and distinctly in Scandinavian soil.*

Colourways

The regional colours of Sweden (some of which are similar to the New England *Colourways*, see p.97) originated as subtle blends of pigments such as verdigris, carbon black, local ochres, green earths, white and a range of subtle green-blues. The right tones can be created by blending paints (if you cannot find a suitable one straight from the can) and adding a drop of raw umber or black paint now and again, to dull and antique them to an oily tone. Apply them in thin washes to create a degree of translucency.

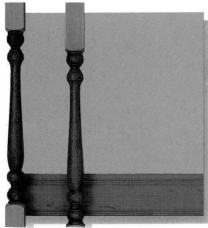

Traditional blues and greens *Combine dark green-blue woodwork with a pale grey-green background for a traditional Swedish look.*

Regal colours *Strong regal colours (like the green and red here) combined with discreet gilded carving are often found on Swedish furniture.*

Using white *This colourway contains the same dark blue as the one to its left but a whitewashed background and plaster creates a bright, airy feel.*

FRENCH KITCHEN

Country kitchens are relaxed, even ramshackle rooms – the focus of a home, where food is prepared, pickled and preserved and people congregate. They are also the meeting point between outside and inside, into which loamy vegetables, fresh eggs and muddy boots are brought and where, more than anywhere else in a home, the roughening effects of the elements can be expressed through faded stencils on old-looking walls, aged furniture and the coarseness of a tiled floor.

THE MOST sought-after quality in a country scheme like this, is a sense that everything has always been there – that all the furniture and bits and pieces have been gathered over the years and have grown to resemble each other, like a dog and its owner.

Age – real or apparent?

The quality that visually unifies all the objects and furnishings is their age, or apparent age. The stencils were painted on a wall that has a distressed plaster finish and lightly sanded to give them a faded appearance in keeping with the rest of the decoration and furnishing.

The birdcages, chair and floor are genuinely old; the screen and armoire are not, but a distressed paint finish successfully camouflages their newness, so that they seem the perfect companions to this well-worn environment.

The informality of this sort of setting lends itself to old, rustic artefacts. To avoid a relaxed, rambling style descending into chaos it is important to find some sort of unifying theme for them.

Visual links

I chose some light, wiry objects and furnishings (a collection of battered old birdcages and a rusted wine rack) to contrast with the crude nature of the wall and flooring.

These spidery forms make a visual link with the chicken wire of the armoire doors, which leads in turn to the simple farmyard image of the chicken, which is repeated in the carved decoration of the screen and a basket of eggs.

This rustic imagery is reinforced by the earthy textures of the salt-glaze pottery jars displayed on top of the painted armoire, the straw-strewn terracotta flooring and the dusty-looking wall.

Stencil design I chose two unusual variations of the ancient fleur-de-lys *(lily flower) motif.*

ANALYSIS

COLLECTIONS

A collection of battered old birdcages and salt-glaze pottery form part of the wall decoration. Connecting themes create a sense of unity – the wire of the birdcages has the same quality as the rusted wine rack and the earthiness of the pottery echoes the texture of the old terracotta flooring.

PAINTED PLASTER

The wall is newly plastered using a technique that makes the plaster look authentically old and crumbly. It was painted with emulsion paint that was thinned with water so that the flaky quality of the plaster is not lost. Truly old plaster that is in danger of becoming damp should be painted with distemper, a water-based paint (see p.328), which will allow it to breathe.

"OLD" FURNITURE

The new screen and cupboard were painted in faded colours and distressed so they look as old and well-worn as the rest of the decoration.

STENCILLED DECORATION

I found the fleurs-de-lys *designs in a book about French medieval ornament. I used emulsion paint both for the main body of the stencils and the freehand detailing, before lightly sanding the images to make them look as faded as the walls and furniture.*

EARTHY FLOOR

Country kitchens are closely linked to life on the land – you might reinforce this link with an "earthy" floor, like the terracotta (baked earth) tiles here.

Techniques
Ageing paint on wood pp.266–7
Ageing plaster walls pp.274–5
Stencilling pp.312–7

STYLING DECISIONS

FRENCH country style need not be as earthy and ramshackle as my scheme for a kitchen. The style can be "cleaned up" and refined to suit other rooms. In a sitting room, for example, tame the roughness of old walls and aged and distressed furniture with damasks and tapestries or, for an atmosphere of grandeur, brocade.

For a delicate touch include furniture painted with simple designs inspired by nature (look for cheap pieces of pine furniture to paint yourself) or include a little gold in the form of stencilled wall decoration, or furniture with a little gilded decoration (see pp.302–5 for gilding techniques).

Farmhouse naive, right. Suggest a sense of the country by introducing simple themes from nature in the form of printed fabric and painted wood.

Mediterranean colour Choose contemporary fabrics dyed with the colours of the Mediterranean and patterned pottery for a hot and summery atmosphere.

Colourways

For country settings look to local and regional colours for inspiration – local earth colours, for example, or the colour of vegetable dyes. Other sources of colour reference are those of wine, traditional fabrics, local pottery, and paintings that capture the essence of the country, particularly those of Cézanne and other post-impressionists. Look at historical sources, too. The apple green and russet red of the kitchen scheme are typically medieval and blend in well with the country setting. These colourways show the effect of a thin wash of paint over a rough plaster surface, painted white, but this creates a pleasing effect on flat surfaces too. Suitable types of paint are emulsion, powder colour (see pp.328–9), and, for really old plaster walls that are in danger of becoming damp, distemper. The latter is a water-based paint that you can buy ready-made.

Starting point, *above. The gilded decoration on the chair offers inspiration for a stencil design for walls and other furniture.*

Tailored scheme, *right. Crisp cotton fabrics contrast with faded furniture and offer just the right level of formality for a country dining room.*

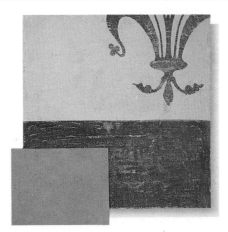

Gentle pink *To make the softest of pinks, dilute red ochre and burnt sienna powder colours in water, and paint over a white basecoat. Alternatively, if plastering a wall, use the powder colours to tint the dry plaster.*

Fresco effect *For a distressed, frescoed effect paint a thin wash of ultramarine paint over a white background (either rough, like this, or smooth) and then sand the surface. This fresh colour scheme is perfect for a sunny room.*

Historical mood *For a distinctly period country mood select unusual shades of tan and mustard for walls and floors. Stencil walls in imitation of patterned wallpaper and include pale cream fabrics to lighten the effect.*

NEW ENGLAND LIVING ROOM

The unpretentious, earthy atmosphere of eighteenth- and nineteenth-century American country interiors is the perfect antidote to the stressful pace of twentieth-century life. So why not capture the spiritual calm of the country by creating a comfortable sanctuary of wood walls, floors and furniture that look battered and worn by the passing of time? This informal American style makes the perfect choice for a living room in which to relax. I combined traditional old furniture with new wood made to look old, capturing the seaside ambience of New England homes on the bright Atlantic coast.

WOOD HAS a warmer, homelier character than any other material, especially when its paintwork is faded by years of use. Following East Coast tradition, I used wood throughout, and gave the new wood (floorboards and walls) the same quality as the old furniture using treatments such as colourwashing, stencilling, liming and sanding.

The effect of techniques, like these, which bring interest to wood without disguising its character, is visually to unify different surfaces, so giving a room homogeneity.

Simple charm

The immense appeal of this style comes from its simplicity. Apart from a traditional candle sconce, the wall is devoid of raised ornament, or relief structures, such as a cornice or a skirting board.

The wall is decorated with simple stencils, an authentic feature because in modest homes in eighteenth-century America, stencils were used as a cheap alternative to patterned wallpapers. A single leaf (a traditional American motif) is repeated at ceiling height. Framing the window there is a fish and wave stencil which, along with the model boat, is a reminder of New England's seaside location.

Colour inspiration

The soft pink and warm brown of the paintwork match colours used in an eighteenth-century Texan farmhouse. Though Texas is far removed from the brisk climes of the Atlantic seaboard, I chose these colours because they suit the informality of this scheme.

On the walls, I colourwashed diluted paint over a coat of brown woodstain and then sanded back the paint to reveal the woodstain and the grain of the wood beneath. To tone down the pink I applied a coat of tinted transparent oil glaze. A final coat of beeswax polish gives the wall a soft sheen.

Inspiration Extend the character of old painted furniture to other surfaces, enlarging patterns for stencils and painting woodwork in faded colours.

ANALYSIS

LEAF PATTERN STENCIL

Stencils were often of natural forms. I repeated a single leaf image – a traditional East Coast motif – to make a frieze, stippling with gold paint and adding freehand detail.

"OLD" WOOD WALLS

I stained the wood, colourwashed it with diluted pink emulsion paint and then sanded it to reveal the grain. To mellow the colour I applied oil glaze tinted brown with artists' oil paints.

FISH STENCIL

I made a stencil of marine imagery to underline New England's Atlantic seaboard location.

FURNITURE

Whether painted, unpainted or patterned, all the furniture demonstrates the simplicity and solidity typical of American country furniture.

WOODGRAIN EFFECT

My aim was to keep the wall surface flat, so instead of fixing on a skirting board I woodgrained the bottom plank.

FLOOR

The new pine floorboards are limed. The wood was wire-brushed to open the grain, rubbed with a water and pigment mixture and varnished.

Techniques

Colourwashing wood pp.252–3
Liming wood pp.260–61
Ageing paint on wood pp.266–7
Graining with a rocker pp.300–301
Stencilling pp.312–7

STYLING *DECISIONS*

O LD PAINTED furniture
looks similar the world over
because, in time, the character of battered paintwork and
weathered wood becomes more no-
ticeable than that of the design itself. Consequently, just about any
old piece of wooden furniture, providing it is not grand, will look appropriate in an eighteenth-century
American setting.

If you acquire cheap and uninteresting furniture give it character
by painting and ageing it, or stencilling it with early American
designs. Simple spindle-backed
dining chairs look effective when
painted black and stencilled with a
gold pattern.

Collectables and accessories

Traditional accessories include
saltglaze pottery, decoy ducks,
patchwork quilts and checked
fabrics. Children's toys or garden
and farming implements and mari-
time artefacts make a good starting
point for a collection.

*Homely furniture For relaxing in
comfort include a sturdy rocking chair.
This one has a plain polished wood
finish, but you could paint a new pine
chair like the one on the previous page.*

Traditional combination,
left. Checked fabrics and old
quilts combine well with
roughly-textured rustic
basketware and wreaths.

Kitchen collection, below
left. Saltglaze pottery has a
metallic sheen that looks
effective alongside copper,
pewter and tin.

Stencilled pattern, right.
Look for wallpapers, fabrics
and spongeware pottery with
stencil designs and use them
alongside your own stencils
on walls, floors or furniture.

On the seashore *This early*
nineteenth-century American
stencil design of seashells
could be used for decorating
a piece of furniture, such as
the back of an old chair.

Colourways

For the main scheme I mixed up
different colours of emulsion paint to
match eighteenth-century American
paint colours. Though it is satisfying to
match authentic paint colours, you
need not let historical authenticity
restrain your own taste, particularly in
an informal living room, where you
should feel relaxed with the colours
around you. Whether you choose natural colours or authentic
period colours, always apply paint in thin washes, sanding it
back to expose the woodgrain.

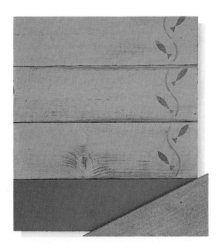

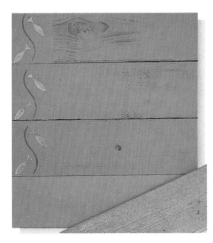

Cream combination *For a scheme*
that is restful to the eyes combine
mellow cream with green, grey and a
dash of red.

Authentic greens *These gentle*
greens were popular in eighteenth-
century Europe and introduced to
America by European settlers.

Seaside blues *Make this vivid blue*
by mixing white paint with ultra-
marine paint; the palest blue is
diluted blue emulsion.

SANTA FE DINING ROOM

The American southwest has been influenced by many different cultures and traditions over the past three centuries – Pueblo Indian, Aztec, Mayan, Navajo Indian and Hispanic – which have provided a wealth of cross-fertilized imagery. Today all these different ethnic influences are liberally mixed to create the striking Santa Fe style of decoration. With its characteristic rich colours and textures and strong sense of place, it is not a style for the faint-hearted but one to be approached boldly.

PUEBLO, Spanish New Mexican and Navajo cultures have all relied on the same climate and landscape for centuries and so, despite their differences, there is one common thread that ties them all together. This is the tradition of building thick-walled houses out of dried mud, a practice which has been adapted and maintained into the present century.

Ethnic materials

To create the sense of place that is necessary for Santa Fe style, the raw materials of the room are important. Modern equivalents of Pueblo houses tend to be painted white indoors and laid with terracotta floors, as opposed to the traditional earth floor. But most beams are still left exposed, and carved enrichment with angular patterns is reserved for doors and furniture.

The painting and decorating of a room in

Santa Fe style should serve to tie together the various images and make them seem as one. Here, I incorporated a floor of African slate, which is shot through with iron oxides, the colours of Pueblo house exteriors. For the wall, I chose a distressed white finish, imitative of old scrubbed limewash.

Navajo imagery

Although the nature of Santa Fe style seems to require a collection of ethnic objects, I wanted to experiment with transferring Navajo imagery directly on to walls, executing patterns in paint that traditionally belong on rugs and beadwork. You could copy a design directly from pottery and paint it freehand on to the wall, as I did, or use stencils (see pp.312–7). So as not to overpower the room's decor I painted a frieze and "skirting board" with simple repeat patterns, leaving the main part of the wall white.

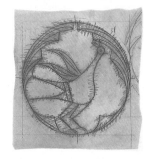

***Pueblo imagery** I drew the bird motif in pencil on tracing paper and transferred it to the wall by drawing over the reverse outline.*

ANALYSIS

WALL DECORATION

The colours and shapes of the blocks, stripes, triangles and comb patterns were taken from Navajo Indian rugs; the bird motif was copied from a piece of Pueblo pottery. All the designs were executed in emulsion paint. The leather hide hung on the wall picks up on the earth colours of the floor.

DISTRESSED PAINT FINISH

The wall was decorated to look like scrubbed limewash by dry-brushing white emulsion paint over a coat of brown eggshell paint.

SPANISH–STYLE FURNITURE

Although the furniture shows considerable Spanish influence, it is English. Hides were used again, this time as throws for the dining chairs.

ETHNIC DETAIL

The design of the papier-mâché bull-shaped pot on the floor was inspired by Aztec and Mayan imagery.

PATTERNED TILES

African slate tiles display all the earthy colours associated with Santa Fe buildings. They are an excellent alternative to terracotta, and their patterning adds drama.

Technique
Scrubbed limewash pp.254–5

STYLING DECISIONS

THE ESSENTIAL ingredient in a Santa Fe interior is the ethnic craftsmanship from which the style springs. There are all sorts of items you could collect and display: decorated leather objects, beautiful tin work, or even superstitious images. If you cannot get hold of a real Navajo rug then paint a substitute on a canvas rectangle using emulsion paints. (Protect the design with varnish.) Mexican and Spanish artefacts, too, look perfectly at home in a Santa Fe interior.

Walls and floors

Adapt imagery from Pueblo and Navajo art and even Aztec architecture into painted patterns that you can apply to walls. Or make patterns using wall tiles. Nowadays, decorated Pueblo tiles are exported worldwide. Their Indian/Mexican designs have their roots in complicated sixteenth-century Spanish and Moorish pattern.

Colourways

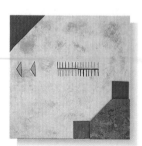

In a Santa Fe room, white walls are almost *de rigueur*, although you could veer to white tinted with an earth colour, such as raw sienna or yellow ochre, or even a bright yellow, like that on the right. Thereafter the colour scheme you choose for your room will be determined to some extent by the scale, texture, provenance and colour of the objects you want to display in it. For patterned detailing on walls, take your inspiration from the warm, earthy colours of the desert – donkey brown, yellow and stone – and combine them with the rich colours used by Indians in their weaving – rust, deep red, strong yellow and black. If you are displaying tin ware, use turquoise-blue detailing around the room. Or highlight other bright colours that appear in your collected items. Pueblo tiles offer a wide range of colours and patterns to copy.

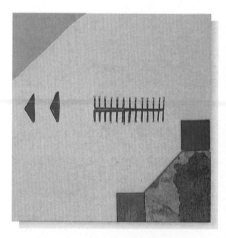

Powerful combination Canary yellow and grey-blue make a sand and sky combination that could work well in a small, uncluttered space, such as a hallway or study.

Leather decoration, *far left. An assortment of Navajo leatherwork makes an attractive display in a Santa Fe scheme. Look out for pieces with interesting beaded details.*

Superstitious images, *left. The skull, tin hand, candles and straw man decorated with a string of dried Mexican chillies, provide unusual icon-like ornamentation.*

Spanish Colonial style, *above. The beautiful turquoise-studded tin work of the mirror is offset by the simple wooden table. Both are typical of sixteenth- and seventeenth-century Spanish Colonial style furnishings, which are still being produced today.*

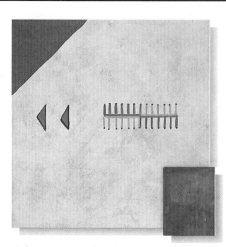

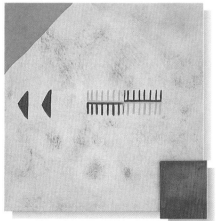

Relaxing earth colours *The pinky-brown colour of the triangle warms the otherwise cool stone-coloured background, and echoes the mellow colouring of the terracotta tile.*

Neutral tones *Walls painted in pale colours, such as donkey brown (the painted triangle) and white, allow for a contrast with a brightly painted frieze, or with other furnishings, such as a patterned rug.*

Hispanic tiles *Hand-painted ceramic wall tiles like these can be used to add colourful decoration to a Santa Fe scheme, or to provide inspiration for creating your own painted patterns for walls or floorboards.*

FARMHOUSE KITCHEN

More than any other room, the decoration of country kitchens needs to be practical and informal, for not only are they hives of domestic activity but, more often than not, they serve as cloakrooms for outdoor clothing and general repositories for the necessary clutter of country life. In this room treatment, dado, floor and furniture have been given a ready-scuffed appearance. Useful kitchen artefacts and outdoor clothing assume the role of foreground decoration, while out-and-out adornment, in the form of photocopies, is high on the wall, out of harm's way.

MUDDY, dusty colours are the most practical choice if your back door opens on to a field. I chose soft browns and greys and off-white neutrals, against which localized areas of colour (the brightly-coloured dried flowers and the blue chest of drawers) stand out. The paintwork on the chest was aged to make it appear to have yielded to the effects of time as much as the colourwashed floorboards and colourwashed wall.

Dado division

A wood dado is a wise choice for a country kitchen because it protects the lower part of the wall from wear and tear. The panelling was limed to give it a gentle white sheen.

Like the colourwashed flooring the panelling reflects the light and makes for a scrubbed, healthy atmosphere, redolent of the countryside. An equally practical alternative for a wood dado is an aged paint finish (see also the Swedish Stairway on p.87).

Confine decorative ornament to the upper part of the wall where it will survive undamaged by children, dogs and dirty feet.

Motifs and country clutter

A colour photocopy of an enormous pig (taken from a book of naive agricultural paintings) adds a humorous touch to the decoration and contrasts with the detailed rustic vignettes. I made the border by overlapping photocopies of hunting imagery.

Treat culinary and country clutter as a form of casual decoration. Old kitchen artefacts, like the bread bin, milk churns and wrought-iron utensil rack, all add character, as does the chimney-pot, which is put to good use as an umbrella stand.

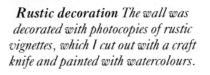

Rustic decoration *The wall was decorated with photocopies of rustic vignettes, which I cut out with a craft knife and painted with watercolours.*

ANALYSIS

PAPER DECORATION

Leave plenty of space for kitchen and country essentials by confining ornament to your wall decoration. A colour photocopy of a pig adds a humorous twist to the paper decoration of rustic vignettes and a frieze of falcons, pigeons, bows and arrows.

COLOURWASHED WALL

The dado protects the lower part of the wall from muddy scuff marks. The upper part of the wall was painted white and then colourwashed with raw umber emulsion (follow step 3 of Three-colour colourwashing).

DOMESTIC BITS & PIECES

Old kitchen artefacts add enormous character. Look for useful ones like the wrought-iron utensil rack.

STENCILLING & LIMING

The panels are stencilled with an oak leaf and acorn design. The whole area was rubbed with liming wax, which fills the wood's open pores, creating a mellow sheen.

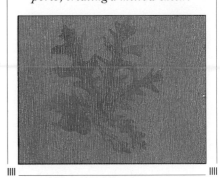

STYLING DECISIONS

BRIC-A-BRAC and muddy boots suit the rough-and-ready character of a country kitchen but for other rooms you may wish to progress to something a little more refined. For a living room or bedroom, for example, follow in the great nineteenth-century country decorating tradition and look to flowers for inspiration, using photocopies of decorative floral designs. Hand paint them and use them alongside manufactured printed borders and wallpapers, choosing designs that suit the age or location of your house.

Bolder themes

For a less delicate theme look to the orchard for ideas. Fruit and vegetables have a ripe, abundant appearance and the subject matter makes them well-suited to country dining rooms.

If photocopies are not to your taste or you want to create a grander scheme, invest in period prints and paintings. Reproductions of botanical textbook plates or designs for garden architecture, like those above right, make the perfect additions to a conservatory where – by their subject matter – they will reinforce the association with the outdoor world.

Animal motif Naïve animal paintings in the form of a wall plaque, like this, or a firescreen or coathooks have a simple, rustic charm about them.

Link with the garden, *left. To link a conservatory or kitchen with a country garden include elegant metal garden furniture and prints of garden architecture.*

Delicate flavour, *below left. To give a room an unfussy country authenticity, contrast floral wallpapers, fabrics and borders with the rough graininess of wood that has been limed and colourwashed.*

Refined air *Bring a refined, scholarly air to a country dining room by introducing botanical prints and contrast polished oak furniture with limed oak.*

Colourways

Cool and unassertive neutrals, like the off-white and pale brown of the main scheme complement soft primary colours, such as dusty blues, pinks and greens. For another gentle and unassuming colour scheme in a bedroom, for example, choose shades of cream for both walls and woodwork. To make a stronger statement, look to deeper, richer colours like those of the right-hand colourway. If you live in the country give a room a truly indigenous look by painting it with local, rural colours traditionally used on the outside of buildings.

Dark and light *For a sober, period atmosphere in a dining room include dark oak (or pale wood stained the colour of oak).*

Pale cream *Use cream-coloured emulsion paint on woodwork and walls for a homely, traditional country atmosphere.*

Deep colours *To give a room an ancient, almost magical appearance, choose red ochre for walls and black for woodwork or floors.*

SHAKER PARLOUR

The more minimal a room's decoration and furnishings the more you scrutinize the elements in it. The clean, elegant lines and unfaltering craftsmanship of American Shaker interiors and furniture have a visual confidence and honesty that will satisfy even the most demanding eye. The Shakers were a religious group; their creed of purity and simplicity extended from their forms of worship to the decoration of their homes and the design of the objects in them. This interpretation of a Shaker room, with its plain walls, bare floorboards and beautifully crafted furniture has a refreshing simplicity that will suit any modest room.

SHAKER interiors can be nothing but minimal, for the simplicity of Shaker furniture was applied to decoration. Walls were usually painted in pale, subtle colours. The wall here was colourwashed to resemble bare plaster – a finish which is in keeping with the Shaker code of unadornment. (As an alternative to colourwashing use the plaster finish on pp.284–5).

The soft colour of the wall contributes to the sense of tranquillity and complements the warm tones of the beech furniture and the muted brown paintwork of the simple wood mouldings.

Simple furnishings

The Shakers had the minimum of everyday objects in their homes but what they had was made to last. The beauty of Shaker objects is bound up with their function and their lack of ornament, which focuses the eye on their shape. The furniture, the clock and the boxes are all Shaker designs, but any well-made furniture with graceful lines would suit a room decorated in Shaker style.

To avoid clutter the Shakers hung possessions such as lamps, clocks and furniture high on the wall. Instead of traditional style Shaker pegboards I used old school coathooks, which I screwed to a plank of painted wood.

Functional fabrics

Choose modest, functional fabrics. Upholster furnishings with ticking, gingham and canvas. Use butter muslin for your curtains and fine white linens for your table. If you prefer patterned fabrics opt for checks and stripes. Simple white fabric can be used to make blinds; a suitable alternative to curtains.

Industrial fittings To meet the Shaker ethos look to factory fittings – the idea of using coathooks instead of Shaker pegs came from an old commercial catalogue.

ANALYSIS

STORAGE SPACE

To avoid clutter in a room the Shakers used built-in storage and hung objects (and furniture that was not in use) out of the way, high on the wall.

WALL FINISH

I made a bare plaster wall effect by colourwashing with three colours of emulsion paint: a biscuit colour, then pink, and finally, white.

DADO RAIL

The simple dado rail is made from standard timber mouldings (see p.22). I mixed raw umber and raw sienna emulsion paints to match an early nineteenth-century milk paint colour.

SHAKER FURNITURE

Shaker furniture was beautifully crafted. Few authentic pieces survive but well-made Shaker designs like these look just as effective.

FLOOR

I brushed the floorboards with a raw umber wash (step 1 pp.252–3). When dry, I lightly sanded them and sealed them with sanding sealer before applying several coats of varnish.

Techniques

Three-colour colourwashing pp.250–51

Colourwashing wood pp.252–3

CARIBBEAN KITCHEN

*The warm climate and colourful way of life of the West
Indies are the inspiration for this Caribbean style, which
relies on strong colours and simplicity of decor for its
appeal. Any sunny room would be suitable for this
treatment; bright light allows you to play with colour
combinations that otherwise you would never dare touch.
This is especially true in a seaside location, where a room
can bask in the bright reflected light that bounces off water.
Furnishings need not be extravagant. Simply assemble a
few brightly painted objects that share a common quality,
like the distressed painted pieces here, and then dress them
with casual simplicity.*

IT IS IMPORTANT to choose
the right materials for this
style. In this scheme I used a
large quantity of wood, both
as a decorative and as a structural
material. Because pine is warm,
yielding and wears easily, unlike
hard polished mahogany, it estab-
lishes a relaxed and friendly interior. This effective use of wood can
also be seen in the New England
scheme on page 95 and the Swedish Stairway on page 87.

Importance of colour

The use of colour is what makes
this setting stand out from any
other. The colours are used in
strong rainbow hues, as they appear
in the Caribbean. The contrast is
uncompromising; yellow is the
complementary colour of purple,
and it was a risky decision to use
both colours together in such volume. But the distressed finishes
help break up the surface and tie
the textures of the different areas
together. Most importantly, I used
a yellow cornice to frame the room
and contain the wall colour, which
effectively makes the purple
recede and play a supporting role.

Old furniture

The element that finally ties this
scheme together is the combination of furnishings. Although the
chair and table are of slightly different colour and design, they go well
together because the finish on both
is worn, revealing the natural qualities of the underlying wood.

*Natural ideas The colours of nature
provide perfect inspiration for painted
interiors. You could even carefully dry,
wire and hang fruit as decoration!*

ANALYSIS

CORNICE

*Although the cornice is a modern copy,
the pattern matches almost exactly some
of the cornices used in early Colonial
houses in the West Indies. The paint
finish was aged and distressed to reveal
some of the stained wood beneath.*

DISTRESSED WALL

*To achieve the scrubbed-look paint
finish, I painted the surface with one
coat of pinky-brown eggshell, and when
it was dry I dry-brushed emulsion on to
the wall in indigo and purple. Finally,
using a rag soaked in methylated spirits,
I rubbed away at the whole wall to
reveal the pink underpainting.*

DRESSING THE ROOM

*Seaside imagery, bright colours and
simple painted furniture establish the
setting's location. Starfish and shells
look decorative placed against strong
colours. Metal kitchenware and
colourful fabrics are also typical of
many Caribbean homes.*

DADO

*The dado was built out of old
matchboarding and then painted
bright yellow to take the colour up the
wall from the skirting board. Although a
heavily distressed finish does not look as
realistic as one more subtly executed, it
can be appreciated in its own right.*

PATTERNED FLOOR

*The floor tile pattern was based on one
seen in a Jamaican interior. Using
masking tape to make crisp edges, I
painted the design on the floor with
emulsion and then applied several coats
of protective varnish on top.*

Techniques

Scrubbed limewash pp.254–5
Ageing paint on wood pp.266–7

Styling
DECISIONS

THE CHEERFUL atmosphere evoked by a Caribbean style of decoration makes it suitable for any bright room. Although the decorative finishing might seem a little rough-and-ready, care and precision should go into the choosing and positioning of furnishings. Space is also important: clutter will ruin the effect.

Bright and natural
Simplicity is the keyword for furnishings. Choose natural fabrics, such as muslin, cheesecloth, gingham and cotton ticking for your tablecloths and cushion covers. Incorporate blinds and shutters in plain or painted wood, and furniture from virtually any period, particularly simple painted items and Victorian Colonial pieces. Finally, add colourful points of reference such as bowls of fruit, flowers and seashells, all of which provide reference to a vivid natural world outside.

Relaxed appeal, below. An informal display of a cane chair and straw hats creates a friendly atmosphere.

Colourways

Natural colour combinations are always a good starting point for a scheme, especially in a Caribbean setting where the light is bright. The watermelon, below left, is a good example. You could take the dark green and pink-tinged red as your two main complementary colours and add black details, softening the effect with the scrubbed limewash technique. For a subtler result, try tinting one of the colours with white to produce a strong pastel. Plain white walls are also very common.

Nostalgic air The use of cloudy white over blue gives a peaceful feel, which is ideal for a bedroom.

Robust blue Strong blue woodwork strikes a more formal note, which would suit a dining room.

Restrained alternative The emerald green on the cornice contrasts quietly with the dark-blue woodwork.

Exquisitely simple, top left. The soft, natural fabrics of the draped mosquito net and old-fashioned quilt serve to quieten down the colourful exuberance of the setting, so making a charming and restful bedroom.

Colourful arrangement, left. The colours of tempting tropical fruit and vegetables make a bright and inspiring starting point for a colour scheme, as well as a cheerful decoration. Arrange them informally with cheap kitchen-ware, cloths and old tin cans.

Colonial atmosphere So as to give your room a more mature Colonial feel, display a few old books, Victorian table cabinets and writing paraphernalia on a highly polished darkwood bureau or side table.

MEDIEVAL STYLES

Several periods of history have taken up medieval decorative styles. There is the domestic interior of the Middle Ages with its richly coloured tapestries; the Gothic arches of medieval churches; the eighteenth-century Gothick style, characterized by fanciful ornament; and finally there is the Victorian Gothic Revival style.

The interiors of medieval houses varied in their decoration, depending on their size. Cottage interiors tended to be undecorated, whereas in grander houses there was room and money for opulence. The two

settings on pages 115 and 123 interpret interiors that might have been found in the grander homes of the period. Such rooms were usually sparsely furnished and walls were simply painted. What gave character to these rooms were the colourful furnishings. Wall hangings, tapestries, cushions and rich damask fabrics, like the yellow and blue fabric, below right, were combined to create a colourful mixture of patterns,

suggestive of medieval pageants. To balance this profusion of colour, the wood panelling was plain and unpolished. Today you can find reclaimed panelling or buy reproduction wainscotting.

Gothick decoration
In the eighteenth century, interest was rekindled in medieval Gothic building styles, and *Gothick* decoration was born. This idiosyncratic style is typified by a

delight in the application of superficial ornament that has a wonderful light frothiness and fantastical irreverence. Because Gothick style was really skin-deep decoration for the sake of pattern, it is easy

and inexpensive to achieve, relying as it does on details, such as the decorative beading, above left, that can be applied to furniture, or paper photocopies of medieval designs, such

as the gryphon, below left. The favourite colours of Gothick style are white against pink, powder blue, sulphur yellow or soft green.

Gothic Revival style

The Victorians took the Gothick style a stage on, in reverence of the architectural massiveness of medieval cathedrals. This style became known as Gothic Revival. Medieval decoration was reproduced in glorious colours and combined with current Victorian tastes to create the style. Flowers, birds and animals all figure in the reproduction designs of fabrics and furnishings, revealing a lively medieval world. The crown wallpaper, right, is an example, and is still printed today.

EARLY ENGLISH KITCHEN

A robust environment, where the decor is earthy and hardwearing, is well-suited to the preparation of food. This unsophisticated kitchen setting has a rustic charm akin to that of medieval folk art and an accessibility derived from its humble workaday appearance. The basic components of the scheme – painted walls and stained floorboards – are unassuming. What gives this scheme its medieval appearance and theatrical quality are the beams, knights and dado panelling, and the rustic painted images of vegetables and cooking utensils.

THE OLD BEAMS that give the scheme its medieval structure are in fact resin imitations of wood. I varnished and painted them to look as worn as the wall, which I painted and rubbed to look like old-fashioned scrubbed limewash.

The resin knights, carrying heraldic devices, add a decorative touch to the corbels and take on the role of medieval grotesques. Their aged paint finish was gilded, and antiqued with wax.

Rustic wall decoration
The scrubbed-limewash-effect wall was decorated with thematic images of simple country fare,

cooking utensils and a simplified medieval coat of arms. These images, painted in red ochre, stamp their identity strongly on the wall through their rhythmical repetition. If you have a fitted kitchen, paintings like these can be interspersed between units.

Balancing colour
It was important to develop a colour scheme that did not detract from the variety of finishes and the detailed use of colour in areas such as the knights and painted chest. For this reason I kept the dado panelling and floorboards subdued in colour, simply staining them dark brown.

AGEING NEW BEAMS
Apply a coat of French enamel varnish and then white emulsion. Rub the dry paint with methylated spirits; this dissolves the varnish, which stains the paint layer.

MOTTLED WALL
Walls painted with limewash, a paint that contains lime, were often scrubbed clean. I imitated a scrubbed limewash finish by dry-brushing white emulsion paint over a pink eggshell basecoat. When dry, a rag soaked in methylated spirits was used to soften the effect and wear away the emulsion, revealing patches of the basecoat.

DADO & FLOOR
The dado panelling was stained dark to make an unobtrusive background to the furniture. The floorboards were stained the same colour, and then varnished to give them a hardwearing finish.

KITCHEN CHEST
This sturdy chest makes a useful piece of kitchen furniture. I gave it an aged paint finish in medieval colours and gilded part of the panel detail with metal leaf.

"MEDIEVAL" PAINTINGS

To recreate the style of early paintings, paint images with a red-ochre powder colour PVA wash (see p.333).

When dry, erase some of the image with a piece of damp sponge. Finally, seal the surface with matt varnish.

Techniques
Scrubbed limewash pp.254–5
Ageing paint on wood pp.266–7
Antiquing pp.270–71
Gilding – metal leaf pp.302–3

STYLING DECISIONS

WHILE MEDIEVAL imagery abounds in the kitchen setting on the preceding page it has few ostensibly Gothic features. Trefoil arches and other architectural or heraldic details like chevrons can be painted to spice up panels on uninteresting furniture and create a Gothic impression. Another option is an ecclesiastical approach. Add devotional items, such as a reclaimed carved panel, or a stone plinth as reminders of church decorations.

Medieval and modern

Contemporary wood furniture in the form of kitchen fittings, for example, will harmonize with a medieval arrangement as long as the design is appropriate and they match the colour scheme. Choose dark hardwoods, like oak or elm, if possible from sustainable sources, or stain pine dark brown. Look for inexpensive old furniture to paint with medieval shield designs.

Heraldic theme The subject of this Victorian design is medieval chivalry; look for furnishings that incorporate this theme.

Small objects in old ivory, worked brass and forged iron provide authentic medieval detail. Blacksmiths are a good source for reproducing medieval chandelier and candelabra designs.

To bring a medieval flavour to your dining room or kitchen, display plates, drinking vessels and candlesticks made from wood.

Colourways

We are fortunate to have a direct visual link with medieval colours through European churches, cathedrals and monasteries. For inspiration look at stained glass, wall paintings, altar decorations and fabrics. These reveal the remnants of the warm, earthy colours much used in the Middle Ages, such as ochres, siennas and greens. Books about heraldry are worth consulting too, because they provide a valuable source of information on the combined use of medieval colour and decoration. Instead of the earth-coloured painted images in the main scheme you could include vividly coloured paintings of heraldic devices. Victorian Gothic style is a useful point of reference for medieval colour schemes because medieval colours were reproduced and adapted for fabrics and wallpapers (see the modern reproductions on pp.119–21).

Church imagery, left. Gothic ecclesiastical objects, including a candlestick, a censer and an icon, lend the setting a religious air.

Medieval Venice, right. These cardboard models of medieval Venetian architecture echo the imagery of the period. The colour and the pattern of the table's veneer inlay could be adapted to painted wall decoration.

Sackcloth and ashes, below. Use hessian as an alternative to dark dado panelling. Rich damask emphasizes the red ochre of the wall painting.

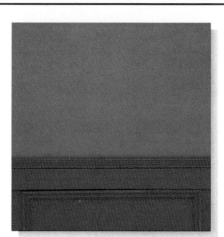

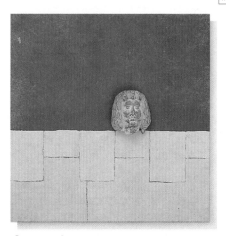

Moody scheme The matt red ochre and drab green combine to create an historical, authentic effect and would suit a dining room or hallway. To enliven these colours add painted details in medieval azure blue, scarlet, emerald and gold.

Dusty pink The colour of dark wood is controlled by this dusty pink: an asset in a room where you want plenty of dark wood or dark wood finishes for doors, beams and decorative details.

Stone colours This colourway is a tongue-in-cheek reference to the Tower of London because of its medieval quoin-stone pattern, which would look effective as a dado beneath a stone-coloured wall. For a monochrome scheme paint woodwork in white.

GOTHIC REVIVAL STUDY

This is an interpretation of the robust Gothic style that grew from the whimsical and decorative Gothick style of the early eighteenth century (see p.127). This Gothic Revival – a European phenomenon, which also spread to the United States – gave us the great Victorian public buildings of the middle 1800s, like London's Houses of Parliament, decorated with sombre authenticity and feudal pomp. This style was also adopted on a domestic scale, using less grandiose decorative treatments, and in England was incorporated into the interiors of many Victorian houses. Here is a simple Gothic Revival scheme with a medieval authenticity that is lightly borne.

I T IS NOT the structure of this arrangement that draws one's attention. Rather, the emphasis is on the overall pattern, and texture of different surfaces, such as the chessboard wall and the castellated dado (both reminiscent of medieval castles), and the bunched knot of the curtain. The wall was painted with diluted emulsion, and the checks were applied with a square sponge. The panelling of reproduction wood was grained according to my imitation *clair bois* (pale wood) technique and then antiqued with wax.

Window decoration

Within this scheme the window decoration provides a focus where different surfaces converge, and are enriched by the use of varied patterns and shapes. The blind was made from fabric with a stylized Gothic pattern, while the curtains and the swagged pelmet, which disguises the top of the blind, are a nineteenth-century fabric design.

This arrangement, based on superimposing contrasting fabrics (thick chintz, stiffened cotton and soft muslin) gives a theatrical touch to the window.

ANALYSIS

PELMET

The pelmet was constructed from a length of heavy chintz, knotted in the middle and tied back at either side to a curtain pole. Gilded plaster castings add rich detail.

GOTHIC-STYLE BLIND

The roller blind has a Gothic profiled outline. I glued fabric to a stiff paper backing and then cut around the pattern. Two thin metal rods were sewn across the backing so the blind keeps its shape.

CASTELLATED PANELLING

A moulding was attached to the linenfold panelling, arranged in a medieval castellated pattern. The background was painted red and the "teeth" gilded with metal leaf.

AUTHENTIC DETAIL

The plaster cast on the table is a model of a Victorian Gothic tower; it lends a scholarly atmosphere.

PATTERNED FABRICS

Nineteenth-century designers reproduced medieval tapestry and damask patterns with extraordinary enthusiasm, and many of their "archive" designs are still in production today in the form of weaves, like the wool carpet, and cotton prints, which can be used for making curtains and blinds.

Techniques

Antiquing pp.270–71
Clair bois pp.296–7
Gilding – metal leaf pp.302–3

CHEQUERED WALL TECHNIQUE

Print checks with emulsion paint, using synthetic sponge glued to a piece of plywood.

When dry, paint the wall with emulsion (diluted 1:2 with water) to soften the contrast between the colours.

STYLING DECISIONS

THE OPPRESSIVENESS of Victorian Gothic architecture, typified by dark wood and black stone, has not been popular since the advent of Modernism. But now that so many Gothic buildings are being cleaned, these architectural styles have revealed a freshness of colour and a richness of form that appeal more to contemporary tastes.

Fabrics and wallpapers

The dominant theme among nineteenth-century Gothic fabrics, papers and furnishings was not so much medievalism of the Middle Ages as a form of Gothic decoration that appealed to Victorian taste. Many nineteenth-century designs continue to be produced today and will instantly give any room a Gothic appearance.

Furniture

Carved Victorian furniture – until recently unfashionable – is widely available second-hand.

Some furniture makers are now adopting Gothic imagery in a simplified form for furniture with clean, modern lines. In moderation, such pieces can be introduced effectively into a Gothic Revival room.

Wall sconce Accessories that have an ancient patina, like this wall sconce, sit well in a Gothic Revival room.

Colourways

Glorious colours decorated the walls, wooden screens and carvings of medieval churches. Rich reds and maroons, *terra verde* and yellow ochre were used in abundance. Ultramarine and various shades of verdigris were also popular. It was with these medieval colours that the nineteenth-century Gothic Revivalists constructed a system of colours to decorate churches and public buildings. Because they documented their architectural heritage, their system was an accurate reflection of the medieval palette. But inevitably, contemporary taste influenced the tone of the colours, and where a gap in the range of authentic colours existed new ones were added. The result is a wide-ranging collection of colours that are still available today in the form of reproduction wallpapers, fabrics and textiles, and that can be matched with modern paint.

Rich setting, *left*. *Mix colours and pattern for a sumptuous nineteenth-century Gothic effect that works particularly well in hallways. All the fabrics are new; the antique chairs have marbled backs.*

Period colours, *above. Authentic medieval colours, like red ochre and this un-usual soft green, can be found in Victorian wall-paper and fabric designs.*

Stick-on Gothic, *right. Look out for running mould-ings that can be glued to shelves and existing features.*

Modern interpretation, *above. The modern Gothic chair looks at home alongside the reproduction eighteenth-century screened cupboard and linenfold panelling.*

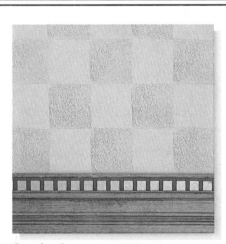

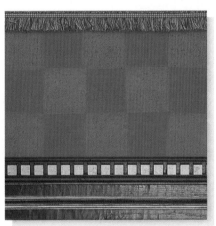

Gentle alternative *This colourway has the same background colour as the curtains in the main scheme on page 119 and a similar heraldic green: a gentle and accessible option.*

Medieval mixture *This powerful combination of red ochre sponge-printed with raw umber, and glossy black and gold woodwork would be most suited to a dining room, illuminated at night by candles.*

Strong and neutral *The colours of medieval pageantry, much loved by the Gothic Revivalists, include those shown here. Used sparingly, but together, they are best seen against a neutral background like pale pink, with just a little gold.*

MEDIEVAL BEDROOM

The romantic, chivalric associations of the medieval period were visually transcribed into this moody, almost magical decor using paint, gold leaf and eyecatching furnishings. The inspiration for the wall decoration came from a magazine photograph of a vaulted ceiling in a monastery, frescoed in blue and studded with gilt stars. Even without the "props" – the crown chandelier, the sun-and-star fabric and the opulent bed – the decoration of the walls and floor would convey a strong image of a medieval interior, such as a castle bedroom.

THE TEXTURES and colours of plaster, metals, stone and wood were the main features of even the grandest medieval rooms. These earthy materials are represented here, in the gilt of the stars, the old metal chandelier, the aged plaster dado (colourwashed with diluted raw sienna, red ochre and cream emulsion) and the floor of slate, shot with iron oxide patterns. Even the blue pigment in the paint used on the wall is suggestive of the ultramarine used by medieval craftsmen. These natural materials, together with the romantic images redolent of the period, are the force of the scheme's impact.

Canopied bed
Some rooms do well without a focus of any kind, relying for their appeal on a rhythm of decoration and a balance of colour and light (see p.67, for example). Others revolve around a centrepiece: a fireplace or a special item of furniture. Here, the centre of attention is a sculptural combination of fabrics, which unites the chandelier and opulently furnished bed into a single feature. Any simple modern bed can be transformed with cushions and tapestry throws.

Balance and colour
The fabric overhanging the bed is patterned with stars on a deep blue background. By extending this theme to the wall I suggested a canopy of stars in the night sky.

To continue the rich blue as far as the floor, however, would have been too overpowering. So a "wall", in the form of a pale dado (capped by a rust-effect moulding) was included. The dado is high so that it does not appear "squashed" under the weight of the dark blue. To compare this with other dado effects see pages 20–21.

Candle lamp *This is a modern design in blackened and polished steel. A special type of lens concentrates the light into a brilliant flare.*

(see p.67, for example); see pages 20–21.

STEEL CHANDELIER
The theatrical shape and size of this chandelier brings to mind a medieval corona (a chandelier that was suspended from the roof of a church).

BLUE WALLS
The intense blue of the aged plaster wall was created with two coats of dark-blue eggshell and a softened coat of transparent oil glaze tinted with ultramarine artists' oil paint.

FABRICS
The hanging printed chintz and butter muslin are new, while the cushion fabrics and the tapestry throws on the bed are antiques.

GOLD LEAF & RUST
Refined metal in the form of a gilt star and corroded metal in the form of a rust-effect dado rail and genuinely rusty candlestick make a magical combination.

Techniques

Three-colour colourwashing pp.250–51	
Softened glazework pp.256–7	
Ageing plaster walls pp.274–5	
Rust pp.288–9	
Gilding – metal leaf pp.302–3	

STYLING DECISIONS

ARCHITECTURAL focal points, such as window casements, beams, doorways and fireplaces dominated medieval rooms. However, unless your home is many centuries old, you will have to introduce "medieval" materials, such as stone tiles for flooring, and roughly plastered walls, in the same way as I did in the main scheme on the previous page.

Monastic simplicity

An atmosphere of contemplative calm can be produced by leaving all natural materials unadorned. Choose a minimum of simple furniture: chests, trestle tables and bench seats have a period feel. Unstained woods look best and simply constructed modern pieces in wood or metal harmonize well with a medieval arrangement.

Decorative abundance

For a richer, warmer look, dress up the sort of background shown in the main scheme with colour and pattern using paint or textiles. Take your key from the French medieval *châteaux*, where the walls were painted with heraldic designs in rich colours, or were hung with finely woven tapestries.

Textile warmth *The rich texture and sumptuous gold and deep purple of this cushion convey a feeling of warmth to the comparatively austere plaster wall and stone flooring.*

Metal furniture, *left.*
Patinated metal furniture is
ideal in a medieval setting.
Another natural element, the
marble of the table top, is
introduced to expand the
theme of earthy minerals.

Monastic icons, *below*
left. The monastery that
inspired the decoration in the
main scheme was decorated
with icons hung above tiled
stone benches: use candles
and reproduction icons like
these to transport an
ecclesiastical atmosphere to a
domestic setting.

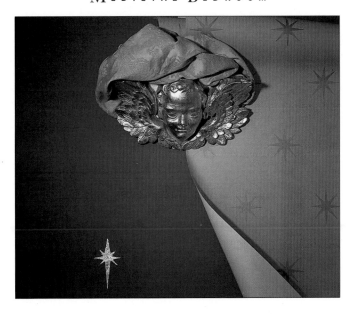

Wallpapering, *left. As an*
alternative or accomp-
animent to painted and
gilded walls use wallpaper.
Papers inspired by heraldic
or romantic themes are even
more effective when com-
bined with gilt and rich
fabrics, such as damask.

Colourways

Illuminated manuscripts convey the
love of bright colours during the
Middle Ages. For decoration with a
magical, fairy-tale quality choose
vibrant colours that are complemented
by the warm glow of gold, using them
for walls or dados, counterbalanced by
paler colours. If you cannot find paint
in the colours you require, make them
yourself by mixing universal stainers with emulsion, or artists'
oil paint or stainers with eggshell (see p.333). For a deep
finish, like the wall in the main scheme, paint transparent oil
glaze tinted with artists' oil paint over an eggshell basecoat.

Regal red *For a richly aristocratic*
look, use another time-honoured
colour: red ochre. A gilt star sets the
scheme on fire.

Vibrant blues *This blue evokes the*
sea and sky; a colourful but light
option suitable for a small room.

Gentle pink and aqua *The*
combination of pale plaster-pink and
blue-green (a shade with an ancient
history) is authentic.

GOTHICK BATHROOM

This bathroom decoration, which was quick and inexpensive to produce, incorporates a style of medieval detailing that became popular in the early eighteenth century. Known as Gothick (the old way of spelling Gothic) this usually manifested itself in fanciful, lace-like ornament (usually in the form of white mouldings) on conventional eighteenth-century buildings. The "sugar-icing" decoration on the wall and bath here, looks suitably light and frivolous against the lead-effect wall.

THE INSUBSTANTIAL quality of lace-like Gothick design would not easily withstand being liberally employed throughout a whole house because it tends to be visually indigestible in large quantities. But used sparingly, as delicate wall decoration in a small room it gives a pleasing, ethereal look.

Decorated arches
A repeated arch design, which looks rather like the frame of a trelliswork garden screen, runs across the wall, its shape echoed by the stencils on the bath. As well as being decorative in its own right this arched "screen" implies a sense of privacy.

This decoration was simple to produce. I used white emulsion paint for the arches, and enlarged photocopies taken from a pattern book for the details and finials.

I cut out the photocopies, brushed both sides with diluted PVA and stuck them to the wall. Once dry, they were painted with very dilute emulsion and sealed with waterproof acrylic varnish.

Colour contrasts
For maximum contrast I offset the arches and paper tracery against dark grey. This was not a popular Gothick colour but it makes a dramatic background and the overall appearance of the detailing is very much in keeping with the flimsy style of eighteenth-century Gothick ornament.

The surface of the painted wall has a silvery patina like that of lead – the material of old-fashioned plumbing. The tracery is painted the colour of white porcelain, another material that is frequently found in bathrooms.

In order to make a feature of the bath and link it with the rest of the decoration I painted it with grey eggshell paint, and ornamented it with Gothick stencils.

Gothick detail *This intricate twisting design is a medieval leaf pattern. Stick photocopies together to make a Gothick border.*

ANALYSIS

PAINTED ARCHES
The characteristic Gothick arch is the ogive. I painted this shape as a framework in which to concentrate the photocopied finials and other Gothick decorative details.

LEAD-EFFECT WALL
For a paint finish that has the same soft, dusty patina as lead, dribble and sponge light-grey emulsion over a basecoat of dark-grey emulsion.

STENCILLED BATHTUB
Without guiding marks it is difficult to line up a stencil on a curved surface. Before stencilling, measure out and mark the intended position of the stencil with chalk. Use a flexible measuring tape, not a ruler. This design was stippled in white eggshell paint, and scarlet artists' acrylic paint was used to add freehand detail. To protect the bath's paintwork from water splashes, I varnished it.

GARDEN GREENERY
An urn and cachepot containing greenery make a handsome addition and extend the garden theme of the arched "screen". The colour of foliage complements the dark lead-effect wall.

LIMED FLOOR
The new wooden floorboards were colourwashed with grey-brown emulsion paint, wire-brushed to open the grain and then limed (with a water and pigment mixture). They were protected from water with matt varnish.

Techniques

Colourwashing wood pp.252–3	
Liming wood pp.260–61	
Lead pp.284–5	
Stencilling pp.312–7	
Using photocopies pp.318–9	

STYLING DECISIONS

I N THE early eighteenth century many different decorative
styles were being explored and
interpreted by English designers
and architects. Medieval detailing
was just one of these and the sort of
delicate decoration used in the
bathroom scheme can be combined
with furnishings typical of other
popular eighteenth-century styles.

Eighteenth-century variations

Rococo and Chinoiserie furnishings, fabrics and objects all have a
strong eighteenth-century feel; see
pages 74–5 and pages 82–3, respectively. Look too, for reproductions of eighteenth-century fabrics
or wallpapers that are not specifically medieval, Rococo or Chinoiserie in style.

Whatever eighteenth-century
elements you do choose to include,
it is important not to be tempted to
intermix elements of the more
"muscular" Gothic style that flo-
wered in the nineteenth century
(see pp.118–21). These would destroy the whimsical atmosphere of
the eighteenth century by imposing a heavy, Victorian feel.

*Materials and papers The paper
border fits in well with the eighteenth-
century reproduction wallpaper and
fabrics; a rich alternative to light
Gothick decoration.*

Colourways

The main characteristic central to
fashionable eighteenth-century
interior decor was a taste for white
decorative plaster, placed against a
plain, often stridently coloured
background. Though the dark grey
used in the main scheme is not a
colour typical of the period it takes this
taste for contrast to its ultimate
conclusion. But such strong combinations are not to
everybody's taste or suitable for every room and there are
plenty of other eighteenth-century colours to choose from
that are suitable for walls and flatter white decorative detail.
Favourite hues included powder blues and pinks, and soft
greens, all carefully balanced against white woodwork and
mouldings. The colourways shown on the page opposite
provide gentler options to the "sterner" combination of
colours in the bathroom setting.

Eighteenth-century look, *above. Printed fabrics and papers – whether inspired by medieval imagery or not – have a place in a Gothick setting.*

Period prints, *left. I chose this Batty Langley reproduction print in an ebonized frame because it fits into the monochrome setting, and adds import to the bath. Other images that recall the period are horticultural prints.*

Glassware, *right. Use glass in a bathroom to suggest water and transparency. The carved bracket is pickled pine (see p.338).*

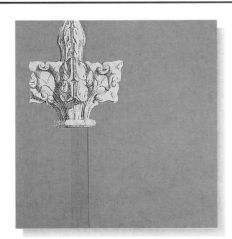

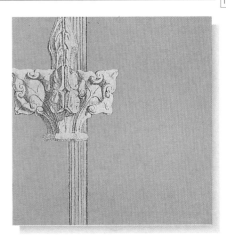

Powder pink *This is an authentic eighteenth-century colour scheme. Pleasantly warm, this pink was also popular in Rococo interiors. The arch is painted a delicate violet that sits comfortably against the pink.*

Modern alternative *An off-white background sets off an imposing blue; a distinctly modern yet formal option for a colour scheme.*

Gentle green *This calm green complements the golden-yellow, painted paper vertical. This colour combination makes a less dramatic alternative to the colours used in the main scheme.*

RENAISSANCE STYLES

Marble, polished oak and silk are the sumptuous materials of a Renaissance room, where objects are finely crafted and floors richly patterned. Settings from this period express a wealth of influences – Classical to medieval – and decoration is varied with wild, fantastic images featuring alongside geometric forms.

At the heart of the Renaissance in Europe lies the Italian city of Florence. It was here, between the years 1300 and 1500, that a bold, new generation of ideas sprang up, and forged new ways of looking at the world. Classical forms of architecture vied with the medieval; and in art, scientific observation of nature went hand in hand with traditional influences. From this boiling pot of ideas and impulses evolved a rich, many-faceted visual style.

Variations
As the Renaissance spread through Europe, both art and ideas changed, weakened or revitalized by the cultures they met. In Northern Europe they adopted heavy forms. In England they became whimsical and fantastical and mixed with the national building style in stone, plaster and polished oak. My interpretation can be seen on page 133. In the Low Countries, interiors were typified by monochrome patterned floors, deeply coloured wall decor and screened windows.

Using patterns
One universal characteristic of Renaissance decoration was a taste for geometry, not just in the formal, symmetrical layout of buildings, but using geometrical images as playful devices. Obelisks, spheres and astrological patterns such as the marbled floor shown in the magazine cutting on the right, all figure in Renaissance decoration, along with knot patterns and the idea of division and sub-division of shapes, as in the wall decoration shown on page 133. Although wall decoration was rare on the Continent, floor patterns were often complex and ranged from the startling monochrome layouts of Dutch interiors to the marble inlaid designs of many Italian church and palazzo floors.

If you are putting together a room or house in Renaissance style, consider the essential components – first, a mixture of visual imagery: wild and fantastical, referring back to the ancient world; geometrical; and quasi-mythological. The sun engraving, shown above right, which was taken from an English bookplate, is an ideal candidate for a stencil, or a freehand decorative detail. Second, look for fabrics

and materials, antique or reproduction, that reflect the exquisite craftsmanship of the time: fine damasks, worked leather, silks, thick tapestries, polished oak and marble, real or *faux*. And third, choose objects that enhance the sense of period such as carved furniture, stone ornaments and urns, old pewter and glass, hidebound books and maps. Finally, use colours that echo contemporary materials, such as the deep hues of Italian marble, and the earth colours of leather and old wood.

TUDOR RECEPTION ROOM

A reception room is the perfect place for decoration that has a theatrical flavour – especially when, like this, the effect is both flamboyant and invitingly warm. A room in a grand, sixteenth-century English house (built during the reign of Elizabeth Tudor) was the inspiration for this scheme. My interpretation is in a scale to suit a contemporary interior. It is panelled with English Renaissance shapes and painted and textured with scenic bravado – fit for a small gathering or a full-blown party.

IN ENGLAND in the sixteenth-century, the buildings of the rich were carved, painted and plastered in a witty native style that combined traditional, medieval forms of decoration with the shapes and patterns of Renaissance ornament.

Panelled walls

Traditionally, walls were panelled. The panelling here was made from shapes cut from hardboard, which I arranged to make a formal geometric pattern, of the sort popular in Renaissance Italy. I textured the shapes with dusty shades of emulsion. All the shapes were then painted with raw umber artists' oil paint in imitation of old, crumpled leather; the small squares were painted to look three-dimensional using *trompe l'oeil*. The idea for the shapes and colours of the panels came from a photograph of some marble panels in a large Tudor house.

The panel decoration and the raised rectangles (made up from timber moulding) contrast with the flamboyant curved shapes and obelisks. The latter were made by stippling paint around masks (shapes cut from oiled manila card) held over the cream wall.

Cornice

The cornice was attached at a height of only 2m (7ft) in order to reduce the proportions of the wall to the sort of scale you will most likely have in your home. It creates a wrapround band of "sugar-icing" decoration and divides the sombre brown of the upper wall from the coloured panels below and along with the rest of the off-white paintwork lightens the overall effect.

The solidity and strength of the reproduction stone plinth and urn give the room a sense of decorum that throws the flighty theatricality of the main wall decoration into high relief. This kind of lively decoration creates an atmosphere that would suit any room in which you might receive friends.

Strapwork panel *The pattern on this typically Renaissance strapwork design from Northern Europe could be adapted for use as a stencil.*

ANALYSIS

FRIEZES & CORNICE

The spheres, obelisks and swirling designs of the friezes, made by painting around card masks, are typical of Renaissance architecture. The choice of a Classical cornice reflects the revived fashion for ancient Classical designs.

"LEATHER" PANELLING

The panels were made from lightweight hardboard and were stuck to the wall with a strong adhesive. They were painted with emulsion and then raw umber artists' oil paint.

OFF-WHITE WALL

The main body of the wall was colourwashed with off-white emulsion paint. The lower part of the wall is less heavily decorated than the higher part to create a visual pause and to allow the stone ornaments to take their place without the overall effect becoming confusing to the eye.

STONE ORNAMENT

The stone plinth and urn lend an air of seriousness to the arrangement. They are also historically in context and add to the theatricality of the setting.

Techniques
Colourwashing pp.248–9	
Leather pp.282–3	
Trompe l'oeil p.322	

STYLING DECISIONS

OR A historically authentic treatment incorporate furniture and fabrics that are sixteenth-century in style.

Furniture was carved, solid in shape and often made from polished oak. Ornamental stonework looks fitting in this setting too, along with thick, heavy tapestries and drapes. There are plenty of reproductions on the market as well as contemporary interpretations of sixteenth-century designs.

Smaller artefacts that suit the style are pewter mugs and candlesticks, wooden bowls and plates and – to reflect the European exploration of the world and the air of discovery – leather-bound books and old maps.

Contemporary mood

The whimsical character of English Renaissance decoration makes it suited to a modern interpretation. For a light, contemporary mood, include simply-designed furniture and fresh-looking natural fabrics like calico and muslin.

Using masks To decorate your wall with Renaissance designs, cut shapes from oiled manila card and use them to shield the wall while you stipple paint around them.

Modern mood, *left. Use pale, natural fabrics and paper friezes to introduce a soft, modern feel. Here, calico uphol-stery updates a dark wood Renaissance-style chair.*

Outside in, *below left. Topiary was fashionable in the sixteenth century and is typical of the Renaissance interest in geometrical shapes. It looks effective against a pale, panelled background.*

Spirit of adventure
Expansion and conquest overseas were motivating forces in sixteenth-century Europe – this collection of unframed maps and antique globes conjure up this spirit of adventure and enterprise.

Colourways

The whites, creams and pastels of the original scheme have a degree of authenticity because they were inspired by marble panelling in a sixteenth-century English house but the beauty of an offbeat decorative style like this, is that it suits some unusual colour schemes and paint finishes. To create a bright mood use a vibrant yellow as your main wall colour; for a moodier, authentic sixteenth-century look, introduce the darker earth colours. If you imitate leather on panels, use colours that will blend in with the top layer of brown artists' oil paint.

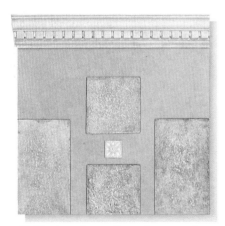

Delicate scheme *Raw sienna and raw umber over white create a warm parchment colour that pairs elegantly with a dusty pink.*

Darker colours *Create a mysterious mood by using darker colours, such as the slate grey, deep blue, and burnt sienna colours here.*

Vibrant yellow *White and canary yellow make for a vibrant, sunny combination; the off-white leather-effect panels make a soothing contrast.*

Florentine Hallway

Postcards, holiday photographs and guide books are all a rich source of inspiration, so why not reproduce the styles, materials and colour schemes that you most like, in your own home. Here, elements of Florentine Renaissance architecture – a corbelled stone window, marble floor, and intricate marquetry inlay – have been reproduced using paint and other cheap materials. To solve the problem of decorating a small space, like a narrow hallway, emphasize just one or two elements of decoration and keep the rest simple.

T**HE ART** and architecture of sixteenth-century Renaissance Florence was eclectic. Ideas absorbed from Ancient Rome were combined with medieval and Byzantine styles. You should feel just as free to incorporate the elements of decoration you most admire.

Key elements
Start by analyzing the key elements that give a place its identity, such as the architecture and local colours, patterns and materials.

If you are decorating a limited space try to emphasize one, or at the most, two main elements, like the floor or a doorway. This way you will develop a simple interior reminiscent of old Italian buildings. Then add a few smaller details, like a light fitting or picture. If you also restrict the number of colours, and reproduce natural materials you will give a room, however small, a fresh, elegant and uncluttered

Classical capital Renaissance designers were influenced by Classical architecture; this capital is a good example of their work.

appearance. The simple timber mouldings and resin corbels that I used to construct the "blind" window are painted to look like *pietra serena*, a stone used in Florentine Renaissance architecture. Strong architectural features, like these, give a room a powerful sense of time and place.

Another material much used in Italy is marble. I painted a wood floor in imitation of different marbles; coats of polyurethene varnish make it hardwearing.

Imitation details
Finer details can also be convincingly imitated. The "inlays" on the wall are photocopy enlargements of prints of Renaissance wood marquetry in Florence's Santa Croce church. They make effective, historically accurate decorations. The shape of the reproduction scrollwork lamp echoes the patterns of the photocopy "inlays". The colourwashed wall shows off these details to their best advantage.

ARCHITECTURAL FEATURES
The mouldings and corbel of the "blind" window are painted to look like pietra serena (*a type of stone*).

FINE DETAILS
Photocopies of wood marquetry were coloured with thinned, raw umber artists' oil paint. Pasted on the wall and protected with varnish, they serve as instant "inlays".

COLOURWASHED WALL
To convey the idea of sun-bleached ochre walls I colourwashed with three layers of emulsion paint (raw sienna, yellow ochre and cream) to build up a veiled effect. I chose a cool colour as a contrast to the rich "stonework".

MARBLED FLOOR
The floor is painted in imitation of four different types of Italian marble: white Carrara marble, green serpentine marble, yellow Siena marble and pink Brescia marble.

SKIRTING BOARD
To continue the theme of stone, the skirting board was also painted to resemble pietra serena.

Techniques
Three-colour colourwashing pp.250–51
Pietra serena pp.278–9
Marbling pp.290–93
Using photocopies pp.318–9

STYLING DECISIONS

ALTHOUGH a small hallway or lobby looks best with the absolute minimum of furniture and clutter, in other larger rooms you can be more expansive. In a sitting room, for example, you might decide on a heavier, more theatrical Renaissance look and include ornate furniture and weighty stone ornament, with rich fabrics for drapes and curtains.

For a lighter treatment with a slightly Rococo air (see pp.74–5) include painted details like swags, urns and flowers and soften the appearance of real or *faux* marble with rich fabrics and textiles.

Alternatively, emphasize the Classical, and include contemporary furnishings, like those on the right: paper borders with a Classical motif, fabric printed with Classical designs and a black glass urn.

Less is more

The key to styling a room like this is to exclude the irrelevant and the mediocre. If you do this you will find that each element in your room, whether it be a marbled skirting board or stone urn, will demand more attention and the contrast between the colour, texture and solidity of each element will be enhanced. By adhering to the maxim "less is more" you will not loose the qualities of lightness and space that are characteristic of so many Italian interiors.

Florentine design This sixteenth-century wood inlay has a light and capricious design typical of Italian Renaissance features.

Colourways

For centuries, Italian decorators relied on the basic earth colours to tint their limewash and distemper. The names of the pigments indicate their origins: burnt sienna, for example, which comes from Siena and the umber colours which originated in the region, Umbria. When mixed with, or brushed over, white paint, these colours radiate an immediacy and strength. Mix the earth colours together for softer effects and use neutral colours such as cream, or bright secondaries, like the green of Italian shutters, to counterbalance the stronger tints. If you use the earth colours judiciously, you can be more daring with vibrant colours. The bright, yellow ochre on the walls of the hallway treatment on page 137 has been offset by the colour of the *pietra serena*, which was made with two earth colour paints: a dark grey-brown and pale grey.

Contemporary Classicism, *left.* Complement Renaissance Classicism with modern monochrome furnishings such as these.

Theatrical air, *right*. For a rich slightly theatrical mood, include prints of Renaissance art, antique textiles and marble (either real or painted).

Marbled paper, *below*. The inlay on the wall was made from marbled wrapping paper (a speedy alternative to imitating marble with paint).

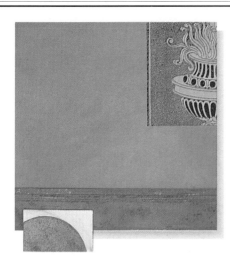

Raw sienna A strong wash of raw sienna will heat a room to a Mediterranean sultriness. Balance its strong influence by including rich colours and textures elsewhere.

Red ochre This ancient-looking colour is particularly dramatic with black and white, steely-grey and rust.

Soft brown Mix raw umber, burnt umber and white to make a soft brown, which can be enlivened with a Florentine pattern and gold.

DELFT DINING ROOM

Seventeenth-century Dutch interiors – so beautifully portrayed in paintings of the period – provide the perfect inspiration for creating a light, cool room scheme. Their graphic simplicity and the shifting emphases of light and shade derive from the use of broad shapes, contrasting textures and deep, moody colours. Follow this decorating tradition, using simple techniques such as stencilling and colourwashing, and furnish your room with a few artefacts that capture the mood of the period.

DARK colours are often avoided when decorating a room because of the fear that they will create a cramped and gloomy atmosphere. But dark colours can be used successfully to create all sorts of different moods (see pp.58–61 and pp.126–9) and if, as here, furniture and ornament are kept to a minimum, to create a surprisingly light, spacious atmosphere.

Pattern and texture

The boldest, richest elements of this scheme (the stencilled patterns, the carved reproduction panelling and the heavy tapestry hanging) are on the wall. Grouped together like this, rather than scattered randomly, they form a strong retaining band of colour and pattern that frames and unifies.

Black and white marble flooring (I used plastic tiles) is typical of the interiors depicted in Dutch paintings. The calm and rhythmic geometry of the tiles serves to steady the curves and complex patterning of the wall decoration. The white tiles have the advantage of reflecting the natural light. Keep the floor clear of rugs in a scheme like this, to create an air of emptiness in contrast to the busy wall decoration. Instead, hang rugs on walls or use them to drape over your not-so-favourite pieces of furniture.

Minimal furnishings

The risk that accompanies so much colour and pattern is that a room might begin to look cluttered. The secret is to stick to essentials only. Whenever possible, place furniture against walls and confine any ornaments to high shelves so that they form part of the wall decoration, leaving the floor area empty.

This kind of decorating requires a certain ruthlessness, but offers an unmatched level of sophistication when it comes to evoking mood and manipulating the quality of light in a room.

Delft plates In place of genuine Delft plates you can photocopy pictures of plates, colour them and stick them to the wall (see pp.318–9).

ANALYSIS

UPPER WALL

The upper wall, colourwashed in brown-grey, makes a cool, reflective background for a row of contemporary plates that follow the Delft tradition in their use of pattern and colour. The impressive "carved oak" frieze and rack are reproduction mouldings.

TAPESTRY

Look for affordable reproductions that have the colour and texture of an old tapestry. Alternatively, copy a tapestry design using acrylic paints on canvas; spatter lightly to give a flecked, woven appearance.

FLAMBOYANT STENCILLING

Many Dutch interiors had stamped and gilded leather wall panelling in large-scale intricate patterns, or printed wallpapers in imitation. I stencilled the wall to look like boldly-patterned wallpaper, using grey-blue paint. To soften the effect slightly, I spattered the wall with dark blue and then white emulsion and gave it a thin coat of white emulsion diluted 1:6 with water.

PERSIAN & TURKISH RUGS

These were essential decorating accessories, but used on furniture rather than flooring (which was left bare to create a sense of space). Use rugs to cover cheap and uninteresting tables, and complement them with rush-seated or simple leather-covered chairs.

TILED FLOOR

Traditionally, floors were tiled with black and white marble squares. These are much cheaper – and more practical – plastic alternatives.

Techniques

Colourwashing pp.248–9
Spattering pp.262–3
Stencilling pp.312–7

STYLING DECISIONS

P IECES from other periods, reproductions and even modern designs will sit quite happily together in a Dutch seventeenth-century setting as long as they complement the colours and textures of the rest of the room. The pictures on the right are reproductions of nineteenth-century paintings but were chosen because they are reminiscent of seventeenth-century still-life paintings and the colours of the frames blend in with the antique tapestry.

Choosing materials

Include furniture made from light-coloured wood, wrought steel or any other materials that would have been familiar to a seventeenth-century Dutchman, such as rush-work and leather. Choose hard flooring, in the form of tiles or floorboards, as a contrast to textiles.

Marbling (see pp.290–95) and woodgraining (see pp.296–300) were popular in the early seventeenth century, so consider these as an alternative to stencilled pattern.

The right spirit You can recreate the spirit of a period without the genuine article. These pictures are large, framed postcards of nineteenth-century prints but they are reminiscent of Dutch still-life painting and the colours of the frames and mounts blend in with the antique tapestry.

Delft wallpaper As an alternative to stencilling, use contemporary wallpapers with complex interlocking patterns like those popular in seventeenth-century Netherlands; this wallpaper is in Delft colours.

Archetypal artefacts The gilt fish-eye mirror and reproduction brass chandelier convey the period of the setting at a glance. Offset gilt and brass with green damask, which is a cheap alternative to tapestry.

Inspiration from tiles
Reproduction tiles – like the ones here – come in a vast range of designs and, as well as for flooring, they can be used for hearths and walls, or to tile a table or worktop. Use the colours of glazed tiles as inspiration for colour schemes – cobalt blue and grey, for example, or the more unusual mossy green and aubergine colours.

Colourways

For the main scheme I used a combination of colours authentic to the period – moody blue as the background wall colour, offset by grey-blue, shades of white and brown. Another authentic but richer colour scheme consists of washes of earth colours on the wall, marbled woodwork (with gold detailing) painted partly in dark grey-green, partly in orange scarlet. If you favour a less rich effect, use monochromes: black stained wood, black and white stencilling, and a black and white floor; for a calm scheme choose natural shades.

Natural shades *For a calm look, use natural shades like pale leather (spattered to give it a gritty texture), terracotta and pale wood.*

Terracotta *The colour of terracotta, a material often associated with the Mediterranean, makes a warm background to Dutch furnishings.*

Blue and grey *For a starker, more graphic impact place Delft blue, pewter grey and grey-black against a pale, colourwashed background.*

VENETIAN STUDIO

If you like unassuming, yet atmospheric decoration, and have a collector's instinct, then follow the precedent for display set by the merchants of Venice, for they knew the effectiveness of placing the detailed against the plain, and the richly-formed against the simple. The modesty of raw materials, like the ancient-looking plaster wall here, makes an effective canvas against which to display furniture and any group of randomly-assembled objects, whether in a garret studio or imposing reception room.

IN sixteenth-century Venice, merchants imported various goods from all over the Mediterranean and beyond, and of course kept some of the finest merchandise, such as rugs, silks and carvings, which they proudly displayed in their simply-decorated homes.

Today's collectables and clutter, like the artist's trappings here, benefit from having a simple environment where, instead of battling for attention against a heavily ornamented background, they can stand out as a group.

Natural themes

Abandon any manufactured and "fussy" finishes like wallpaper and dainty paint effects and go back to basics in favour of simple surfaces that are elemental in appearance. Suitable colours for walls and furnishings are those of the earth, which include ochres and umbers (see the *Colourways* on p.147).

The ancient-looking plaster wall opposite has a simple elegance and creates a spacious atmosphere by reflecting the light. It was colourwashed with diluted emulsion in the colours of natural materials: grey, unpolished marble for the upper wall and terracotta for the dado. To imitate ancient plaster walls, follow the technique on pages 274–5.

As an alternative to textured plaster walls, leave untextured plaster walls unpainted or, if replastering, tint raw plaster with powder colour (see p.333).

The theme of natural colours and materials is continued in the wooden skirting board, which is painted to imitate terracotta, and the (plastic) terracotta flooring. The only concession to ornamental detail is the paper *trompe l'oeil* pasted on the wall.

Which room?

Although the simple elegance of plaster walls and the paring back of wall decoration create a spacious atmosphere, this approach is best for medium-sized or large rooms.

Rope pattern *The rope course is the only ornament used on the wall. The heavier rope, positioned near the ceiling, facilitates a lighter and more complex repetition of the theme below it.*

ANALYSIS

PAPER ROPE

Use PVA or spray glue to stick printed paper designs to walls. Blend them with the wall decoration by painting the paper with a dilute wash of your wall colour.

"ANCIENT" WALLS

The ancient-looking plaster wall, in fact newly plastered using a special technique, was colourwashed with diluted emulsion paint to give it the appearance of unpolished marble.

FURNITURE & COLLECTABLES

A simple, textured wall makes an atmospheric backdrop for the artist's clutter and collection of masks, bottles and brushes. For an "earthy" look, choose robust furniture made from natural materials, like the wood and leather chair here.

RED OCHRE DADO

Reserve the strongest colours in a natural colour scheme for the dado and by so doing follow an ancient Mediterranean tradition. For true simplicity I decided against having a painted line or dado rail and took the wash of red ochre down over the skirting boards to meet the terracotta flooring.

Techniques

Colourwashing pp.248–9
Ageing plaster walls pp.274–5
Terracotta pp.284–5
Using photocopies pp.318–9
Trompe l'oeil p.322

STYLING DECISIONS

FOR FLOORS, consider polished floorboards, terracotta tiles or terracotta-coloured flooring, which complement the natural look of the plaster walls and enhance their status. Carpeting, on the other hand, will deaden the effect. Paint skirting boards an earth colour or stain them brown.

Wholeheartedly natural

To continue the natural theme choose natural fabrics and materials, such as calico and muslin, wood and leather. Any collection of artefacts made from natural materials, such as a collection of terracotta bowls, or earthenware jars will look at home in a room itself apparently constructed in substances that come straight from the ground.

Rich additions

Rich fabrics and artefacts look effective too – especially against a clear background. The natural, robust appearance of walls and floors will sing a solid bass to the descant of the rarefied, more refined textures and colours of gilt, silver, carving, and rich textiles. Look for furnishing fabrics with deep colours, perhaps with gold.

Marble inlay Designs like this one for an Italian marble inlay make a good starting point for designs for home-made stencils.

Venetian drama, above. To emphasize the theatrical flavour of Renaissance Venice, choose and use images from the theatre and the opera, like the mask, the printed silk hanging and the paper swag here, and select dramatic materials like marble or stone.

Clearly collectable The Venetians are renowned for their glass – for a delicate, magical and light look, display glass in all its forms and contrast delicate fabrics with robust ones.

Rich mixtures *Treat your windows and furniture like works of art by choosing rich fabrics.*

More minimal, *left. For a sterner look, eschew the comfort of padded furniture and rich hangings and opt for furniture like this chair, which has the harder, earthier qualities of wood and hide. Using the painted leather technique on pages 282–3, transfer a leather-like finish on to other surfaces, like skirtings.*

Colourways

For a Venetian setting choose the warm, earth-pigment colours of Italy — umbers, ochres and siennas. To cool down the effect of your scheme put these colours alongside marble-grey and soft cream; to heat them up, deep reds and gold. For a dramatic effect on walls use the earth pigment colours all over or follow in the ancient Mediterranean tradition by using them to paint a dado, or, for a less dominant effect, in the form of fabric and accessories. Paint plaster walls with diluted emulsion paint, to retain the plaster's dusty appearance.

Strong reds *To create a dramatic effect in a small room, why not grab the bull by the horns and use a tomato-coloured wash and deep red detail?*

Terracotta and cream *Soften a bright terracotta dado with a cream wall, restating both colours in the form of a frieze.*

Yellow ochre and cream *A strong yellow ochre is calmed by cream and a paper* trompe l'oeil *in white-cream and marble-grey.*

147

VICTORIAN STYLES

The reign of Queen Victoria saw a wide variety of architectural and decorative styles, ranging from the formal, austere and patterned interiors of the 1830s to the simpler Arts and Crafts rooms seen at the turn of the century. The schemes illustrated in this section represent slices of Victorian styles, interpreted to fit contemporary tastes.

The Victorians had a great love of pastiche and pattern and crammed together details and designs from lots of different periods and countries. Today this might seem rather claustrophobic, but the style can be successfully adapted so as to flatter a variety of settings. Victorian wallpapers and

fabrics, like those shown right, were highly patterned and richly coloured. Medieval motifs and floral patterns were popular. Often several patterns of wallpaper were used within the same decorating scheme. For example, a richly embossed wallpaper might be used for the dado, and then a flowery design used for the rest of the wall. Boldly patterned carpets and drapes added further colour.

Using fabrics

Drapes were used in abundance, sometimes even to excess. In addition to the heavy curtains with their tassels and decorative pelmets, there would be lace or net curtains covering the windows. Tables were covered with lace cloths, and mantelpieces were decorated with runners and borders. As a result, many Victorian interiors tended to be quite gloomy during the day, although at night, with the addition of gas lights, the atmosphere became quite cosy.

If you are not keen on dark colours and heavy patterning, you can still create a Victorian interior using the lighter and simpler Victorian decorating style that was more fashionable towards the end of the period. This style used paler colours and softer fabrics, such as muslin and printed fabrics with simple patterning.

Victorians were obsessed with details and collecting

all sorts of knick-knacks helped to fuel this. If you do not like too much clutter, however, you can still create an authentic feel by devoting an occasional table or corner of a room to a collection of objects.

If Victoriana is an interest, you may be familiar

with the kind of kitsch pieces available, like the sugary *découpage* prints, above, and the floral picture and tray, right. So much mass-produced material of the 1800s can be found in markets, and, although it can look pretty in the right setting if used with discretion, it does give the period a bad name.

However, there are many worthwhile Victorian pieces you can collect, such as carved mouldings (reproduction plastic ones are available), shell boxes, silverware, and porcelain.

Victorians were also great travellers and liked to display souvenirs of their adventures. These were often from Africa and the East, such as lacquered boxes and gilded Indian ornaments.

Victorian furnishings

Much Victorian furniture is of mahogany, and chosen for its ornamental quality rather than its shape. *Papier-mâché* was another fashionable material of the time. It was used to make small tables, chairs and even bedheads. It was often lacquered and decorated with mother of pearl or a painted design.

Wicker and rattan furniture was also popular, especially for use in conservatories. This furniture was often painted green, white or vibrant chalky colours.

Marble and tiles were popular surfaces, especially in bathrooms. These finishes can easily be imitated with paint.

Intricate scrolled or chunky cast metalwork was also prevalent. This was used outside as iron railings, and inside for decorative structures.

COLLECTOR'S HALLWAY

A Victorian house naturally responds well to a period scheme, though a Victorian ambience can be created in a house of any period by using the rich, dark colours and highly patterned papers and fabrics fashionable in the late nineteenth century. These make for a strong period atmosphere when dressed with collections of accessories inspired by the period, like the assembly of architectural remnants here. There is no better place to display a collection than in a hallway or stairway, where visitors can stop to admire it, and where pieces can be amassed and added to, studied and compared.

THIS VICTORIAN treatment was inspired by the Classical collection of the great British architect of the early nineteenth century, Sir John Soane. He spent time in Italy studying all things Classical and acquired details of ancient buildings to hang in his stairway, thereby popularizing new and original forms of neo-Classicism.

Combining styles

In true Victorian collector's style, this scheme brings together elements from different periods and countries in a harmonious whole. Classical ornamentation, an Eastern runner carpet and dado wallpaper by the Victorian designer, William Morris, blend pleasingly.

What gives this scheme sparkle is the collection itself. After filling the area above the stairway with an abundance of interest, it begins to peter out beneath the painted frieze in order to give the eye a rest and prevent the narrow hallway area becoming in any way claustrophobically cluttered.

The informal arrangement of objects of different shapes and sizes contrasts with the rigid structure of the hallway, which is divided into distinct horizontal bands by the dark skirting board, dado rail and maroon frieze, all of which make a striking contrast with the yellow wallpaper and paintwork.

Styling a hallway

The kind of formal simplicity shown here, and of the neo-Classical treatment on page 55, is appropriate for a hallway, a place of adjustment and preparation, both for the rigours and realities about to be confronted in the world outside and, conversely, for the civilizing effects of the world indoors.

Classical design *This type of design was popularized in early nineteenth-century England by the eminent architect, Sir John Soane.*

The neo-Classical treatment on page 55

ANALYSIS

CORBEL & FRIEZE

These are both reproductions of popular Victorian originals. I brushed French enamel varnish on to the plaster corbel to make it look like dark wood. The assertive tones I used to paint the frieze were adapted from the colours of London's Royal Albert Hall.

CLASSICAL COLLECTION

None of the pieces here are priceless works of antiquity of the sort collected by the Victorians: they are reproductions, some of which I painted, gilded and antiqued. I combined all these pieces with an authentic Victorian carved and gilded panel on the top left of the wall.

GLAZED WALLPAPER

The Victorians were fond of glazed wallpapers. After sealing this William Morris design wallpaper with PVA and shellac sanding sealer, I applied transparent oil glaze tinted with artists' oil paint.

WOOD FINISHES

The fashion was for dark wood and ebonized finishes. I used eggshell paint on the dado rail and skirting board, and painted the floorboards and stairway with dark woodstain.

Techniques
Softened glazework pp.256–7
Antiquing plasterwork pp.272–3
Gilding – metal leaf pp.302–3

STYLING
DECISIONS

THE DIVERSIFIED taste of the Victorians means that when it comes to accessorizing your room, you have a wide choice. A blend of historical styles is quite in keeping, though a strong Classical streak was often in evidence in family homes.

The tobacco and black colours of the main scheme are so strongly rooted in the period that almost any collection would complement the Victorian theme. So long as the finished effect in your own home is richly ornamented and patterned, it will be certain to have an authentic atmosphere.

Paintings and fabrics

One option for decorating a hallway is a collection of the dark paintings and prints of the period, perhaps of landscapes or portraits of pets.

Another choice could be soft pieces: samplers by genteel ladies mixed with tapestry remnants, rugs, bell pulls and tassels.

Colourways

The dark, moody colours of mid-Victorian decoration are used less in decoration now than the pastel tones that were also popular in the eighteenth century. If a dark, deep colour scheme does not appeal to you, choose from the range of colours that became popular in the late nineteenth century when bright textiles and wallpapers were mass-produced following the introduction of new technology and cheap dyestuffs. Gold-printed wallpapers and delicate combinations of colours like jade green and oily blue were often used to brighten rooms with dark wooden panelling. Alternatively, use yellows, which, being light-reflective, are a practical choice if you want to brighten a dark room or make a small room appear larger. Combine painted surfaces with areas of pattern in the form of wallpapers, friezes or plasterwork.

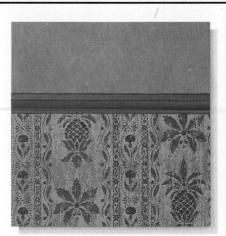

Country colours A complex stencil-patterned wallpaper can be used with strong tones for a characterful, but soft-edged scheme, which would be ideal for a country house.

Opulent effects, *left. A collection of gilded objects, combined with rich textiles from the East, makes for an exuberant style of decoration, which is suited to a room where a rich, opulent atmosphere is preferred.*

Kitsch Victoriana, *right. Markets are the places to find the sort of small items that will add Victorian character to a room, though you may be lucky enough to unearth some in family attics: the romantic print here belonged to my grandmother. Look for Victorian toys, silver and clocks as well as soft furnishings and lace.*

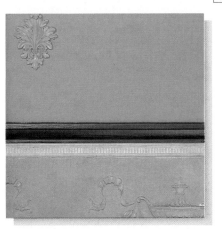

Warm combination *By changing the black edgings to russet brown, the colour scheme is warmed and softened a little, and a woody, less severe tone introduced. The wallpaper is glazed to match.*

Cool stone *A sophisticated and cool alternative results from combining this soft, beige pink with stone colours. A dado of relief lincrusta adds a degree of textural interest.*

Textile designs *The Victorians were fond of patterned fabrics and lace. Designs were often adapted from historical sources, so modern interpretations of century-old designs like these, will fit in well with a Victorian scheme.*

SCOTTISH SITTING ROOM

For centuries, interior decoration has made use of faux *(literally, false) effects. By enabling you to imitate a whole range of different materials they make it possible to create the illusion of an entirely different environment from the one in which you live. Here, for example, I used paint to imitate a stone wall, like that common in many Scottish castles and houses. Add tartan trimmings, ancestral crests and Victorian furnishings and you have an illusion of Scottish baronial grandeur that is in fact only as deep as a layer of paint and a few plastic mouldings.*

ALL THINGS Scottish became increasingly popular in England after Queen Victoria and Prince Albert bought Balmoral Castle in the Scottish Highlands, resulting in the development of a Scottish baronial style.

In the time-honoured tradition of eighteenth- and nineteenth-century decorators I used a range of *faux* effects to conjure up the image of a Victorian Scottish setting.

Sandstone and wood

I deliberately chose the warm colours of sandstone for the wall, so as to avoid too sharp a contrast with the dark wood.

The brand-new door was woodgrained to make it appear old and as if panelled in different woods. I chose a combination of paler browns than the dado panelling to give the lower half of the room a lift of lighter colour. The colours of the door, which include black outlines, link visually with the colours of the dado and the parquet-effect floor. Dark wood was much used in Victorian interiors. Using French enamel varnish (see pp.224–5) I stained the dado panelling, the plastic heraldic devices and the scrolled decoration above the doorway to match the original cupboard made of dark oak.

Many grand Scottish houses have extremely ornamental friezes. The frieze here, which came on a roll, is a typical design. The crisp white makes a refreshing contrast to the browns used elsewhere.

Scottish motifs

The heraldic devices attached to the cornice and the thistles stencilled on the door, along with an ancestral portrait, root the setting firmly in the Highlands. The tartan drops and lace frills add a humorous, frivolous touch to the scheme.

Scottish emblem The thistle is the national emblem of Scotland. It was a much-used motif in Victorian Scottish interior decoration.

ANALYSIS

ORNATE FRIEZE

A *lincrusta* frieze with ornate, swirling Victorian decoration was edged with a cast moulding. Many Scottish baronial houses have ornamental low-relief friezes, like this.

SHIELDS & MOULDINGS

The shields are plastic; I painted them with French enamel varnish and decorated them with heraldic devices. I added frills and tartan drops as a final touch. The door frame is made from a wooden moulding, which I also painted with French enamel varnish and then waxed. The "carved oak" scrolls above are made of rigid foam, stained to match the dado panelling.

DECORATED DOOR

The door is woodgrained using the same colour of transparent oil glaze on both light- and dark-coloured backgrounds. The thistle stencils and thick black lines were then added.

"SANDSTONE" WALL

To suggest the walls of an old Scottish house I painted the wall in imitation of sandstone. A thick layer of emulsion was stippled on to give a textured effect. The mortar lines were painted with grey-coloured emulsion.

CARVED CUPBOARD

The low cupboard is not Scottish but Afghan – this is in perfect keeping with the traditions of the Victorians who collected pieces from around the world.

FLOORING

High quality plastic tiles, in imitation of wooden parquet, lighten the tone of the floor. The tartan rug continues the Scottish theme.

Techniques

Sandstone pp.280–81

Graining with a brush pp.298–9

Stencilling pp.312–7

STYLING *DECISIONS*

A COMBINATION of dark woods and woody textures can do much to alter the character of a room, particularly when contrasted with natural finishes like stone (real or imitated) and plaster. The look is rich and warm, with an element of theatricality that can be exaggerated with massive and heavy wooden furniture, an approach that particularly suits sitting rooms and dining rooms.

Lighter touches

Such a dark setting is not always desirable and you can lighten the effect by incorporating other Victorian themes in your room. For example, rattan furniture, sisal flooring, wicker or furnishings in British Colonial style could all be included. These were popular in morning rooms and conservatories from the Victorian era through to the 1920s when much furniture was painted in green, white and vibrant chalky colours.

Huntin', shootin' n' fishin' The paraphernalia of sporting life can be decoration in itself, even if you are not keen on stuffed animals. Fishing flies, for instance, are miniature works of art. Paintings or prints, from steeplechases to grouse, add to the theme of Highland sporting activities.

Either side of an era Twentieth-century Lloyd Loom furniture, made from paper wound on wire, developed from Victorian wicker designs. The painting pre-dates the Victorian era, yet both are in perfect keeping with the eclectic tastes of the period.

Colourways

Tartans and heraldic emblems are important sources of colour for rooms of wood and stone (whether real or imitated). The Victorians documented and embellished existing clan tartans and heraldry, as Scotland had a sporting and romantic appeal that made it popular with many of the English, including Queen Victoria.

Books on tartans and heraldry provide a wealth of source material for adding colour in paintwork to a traditionally dark Victorian scheme. Another way of introducing colour is with paintings. The huge Victorian studies of glens and lochs by artists such as Landseer, for example, dominated the rooms in which they hung. Any original landscapes or portraits of the nineteenth century will serve, as will prints or reproductions, but surround them in carved, gilded frames to catch the light and warm the room.

Thistle stencil *Make stencils, like this, from stencil card (see pp.312–3). I cut out this stylized thistle shape for stencilling the panels of the door shown on page 155.*

Finishing touches, *right. Look for small items to reinforce your room's decorative theme. Trinkets and accessories are still made for the tourist market, so include these, or display original Victorian pieces, like the ones here.*

Soft peach *Warm, creamy tones on the wall help to soften the contrast between light and dark and lend a room warmth, even if the band of colour is quite narrow.*

Terracotta tones *A richer, bolder effect than the original scheme can be made by using terracotta-coloured emulsion paint instead of cream, bringing out the colour of the wood.*

Tartan inspiration *Simple plaids in warm colours can be reproduced in paint on walls to add a jolly, theatrical touch. Limit the area of pattern to prevent the effect becoming overwhelming.*

TILED BATHROOM

The Victorians were the first great bathroom-builders. They invented beautifully engineered sanitary ware and decorated their newly created bathrooms with polychrome ceramic tiles. In celebration of this spirit of domestic enterprise, I placed a Victorian washstand centre stage and, with period authenticity, tiled the dado and glazed the woodwork. Two ornate metalwork pilasters evoke the noble aspect of Victorian industrial achievement and their verdigris paint finish suggests a hundred years of corrosion by steam and water – an apt allusion since water is the essential ingredient of bathrooms.

THE TEMPTATION to decorate a bathroom with aquatic imagery is almost irresistible. But try to avoid the hackneyed images of Neptunes, dolphins and nymphs. Introducing colours and finishes associated with water will give you much more flexibility in your decoration and original results.

Special effects

In the bathroom scheme on page 41 I used my imitation verdigris technique to suggest the effect of water and salts on an ancient bronze bath. The same finish also seemed ideally suited to this nineteenth-century bathroom scheme – but this time to suggest the effect of water and steam on ornate Victorian metalwork.

The other main decorative component is tiling. The mass production of ceramic tiles during the late nineteenth century brought pattern into millions of Victorian homes and tiles still make a practical and decorative choice.

Dado rails, skirting boards and architraves were often heavily glazed with rich, translucent colours to harmonize with the colour and finish of tiles. I brushed transparent oil glaze on to the skirting board and dado rail and, because oil glaze does not dry hard, applied oil-based varnish over the top. A similar effect can be achieved in one step, using oil-based varnish tinted with artists' oil paints, but glaze is far easier to brush to a flawlessly smooth finish.

Green and cream

The green of the verdigris finish was the starting point for the colour scheme. I chose shades of green for the tiles, the woodwork and stencilled frieze, and cream as a neutral wall colour (green and cream was a Victorian favourite).

Bathroom frieze To make a frieze, colour in photocopies of Victorian designs, like this. Paste them in a chain and protect with a coat of varnish.

STENCILLED FRIEZE

After adding freehand detail to the stencilled leaves I drew a trompe l'oeil *frame in pencil, using my fingers to smudge the impression.*

WALL & PILASTERS

The wall, painted with emulsion, makes a flattering background to the green tracery of the ironwork and ivy-leaf frieze. The "cast iron" pilasters, which are in fact lightweight aluminium, have a verdigris paint finish.

GLAZED WOODWORK

I painted the dado rail and skirting board with green eggshell paint and then glazed them with dark-green transparent oil glaze, in imitation of the deeply glazed finish of the typically Victorian tiles on the dado.

VICTORIAN WASHSTAND

Original Victorian furniture can often be bought cheaply. This dresser (which had a broken marble top) was converted to a washstand and plumbed in.

FLOOR TILES

Marble was a popular material in Victorian bathrooms; it was even used to construct baths. These "marble" floor tiles are, in fact, very serviceable plastic.

Techniques

Softened glazework pp.256–7
Verdigris pp.286–7
Stencilling pp.312–7
Trompe l'oeil p.322

STYLING DECISIONS

FOR AUTHENTICITY, opt for the hard finishes used in Victorian bathrooms: tiles, mahogany and marble. You can imitate these finishes with paint: glazing for a tile-like finish (see pp. 256–7); woodgraining (see pp. 296–301); and marbling (see pp. 290–95).

Once the character of the room is established, develop the effect – lightening it with drapes, enriching it with brass or nickel fittings and including accessories suggestive of the rituals of ablution, such as glass scent bottles and pot pourri.

Bathroom furniture

An original roll-top, footed bath or marble-topped washstand provides an ideal centrepiece. Reproduction bathroom furniture and fittings are widely available.

Many Victorian families who lived in houses of an earlier period converted a bedroom into a bathroom, where they often retained bedroom-style decoration. To follow suit, decorate the exterior of your bath with painted designs, adapted from floral wallpaper, and floral *découpage* (protect from water with a coat of varnish).

Verdigrised metalwork A verdigris paint finish looks just as effective on functional bathroom pipes as decorative metalwork.

Bathroom drama, *left.*
Add a theatrical flourish to a bathroom wall with a Victorian border (which could also be used in an adjoining bedroom). Hang tassels at repeated intervals for a heavy rhythmic effect.

Shiny finishes, *below left.*
Restate the glazed finish of ceramic tiles and introduce a Victorian wealth of colour with other ceramics, like this vivid yellow bowl – the colour of which is echoed by a glass scent bottle and brass candlesticks.

Delicate addition, *left.*
Shades of pink (which often appear cloying and sugary in other rooms) make a wonderfully delicate contrast to the hard surfaces of tiles and bathroom furniture. Add warmth with the colour of terracotta, shown here in the form of towels and a frame with a terracotta paint finish (see pp.284–5).

Colourways

The colours of ceramic tiles formed the basis of popular schemes for Victorian bathrooms. As well as green with cream, which was a late Victorian combination that remained popular well into this century, other ceramic colours, such as rich ruby red, dark Prussian blue, or tan and brown were also used with cream, and sometimes in combination with each other. If you have authentic Victorian tiles, match their colours with your painted decoration. Fabrics and paper borders make an excellent starting point for a more varied colour palette; several companies produce mid-nineteenth-century designs.

Moody colour *Dark-red transparent oil glaze over green eggshell paint gives woodwork a subtle sheen.*

Period water colours *For an aquatic effect, paint surfaces in greens and greeny-blues.*

Pink and green *Pink colourwashing (see pp.248–9), copper and verdigris complement each other.*

ADVENTURER'S STUDY

For the Victorians, collecting from around the world became a passion and they mixed exotic goods from India and other parts of the British Empire with heavy Victorian furnishings and period finery. The spirit of the East and of Victorian enterprise is captured in this setting, reminiscent of an adventurer's private haunt. Indian stencils in gold and rich Moroccan reds convey the heat of the tropics, the colours of spices and porphyry and the richness of Eastern carpets, while the studded wall decoration and frieze suggest the riveted metalwork of Victorian buildings.

OBJECTS THAT have a common theme, like the richly patterned kelim, inlaid table and boxes here, have greatest impact when gathered in one room specially decorated to complement them. Rather than place these pieces against a museum-like background of white walls I created a sympathetic atmosphere by capturing the spirit of the part of the world they came from – the East.

Industrial inspiration

The decoration was also inspired by Victorian industrial details. I arranged circular pieces of plastic in a geometric pattern above the picture rail, in imitation of the rivet heads of an immense girder. The gilded studs below, suggest the gold-painted decorative bolt-heads of iron beams and columns.

This sense of nineteenth-century enterprise, combined with the suggestion of Eastern textures and colours, provide a strong and unusual background for the collected furnishings. Although the basic scheme is atmospheric, it is also simple enough to allow all the elements a measure of prominence.

The advantage of using small repeated details such as stencils and stick-on studs, is that you can build up a pattern slowly, judging the overall effect as you go.

In order to make Eastern furnishings look at home in a Western setting, I used a rich profusion of pattern – an essential element of both Victorian and Eastern decoration. The colours that I used are akin to the strong baked earth colours of Northern Africa, which were adopted by the Victorian Eclectics and Orientalists.

Indian woodblock Look for pictures with woodblocked designs like this, or woodblocks with which to print your walls.

INDIAN STENCIL

The motif was inspired by a detail on an Indian carpet. I used spray paint for the main body of the design before adding freehand detail in emulsion paint.

SPATTERED WALL

The tomato-red wall conjures up the heat of the East. It was painted with red eggshell and spattered with black glaze and gold paint. The gilded studs are reminiscent of the gold-painted bolt-heads of Victorian ironwork.

FURNISHINGS

The pictures and furniture were taken from a variety of sources, in authentic Victorian style. For a sense of the arcane, I used only dark woods, introducing a sinister memento mori in the form of the skull.

SKIRTING BOARD & FLOORING

When a powerful colour is used in any quantity it can be balanced by a neutral tone. I painted the skirting board and picture rail a neutral, muddy plum colour to counterpoise the red wall. The stained floorboards and dark furniture "control" and subdue the bright colours and busy patterns.

Techniques

| Spattering pp.262–3 |
| Gilding – metal leaf pp.302–3 |
| Stencilling pp.312–7 |

STYLING DECISIONS

IT IS popularly accepted that the Victorians had an insatiable greed for cultural knowledge. They flaunted their interests, mixing artefacts from all over the world with period decoration and furnishings. Adopting this approach enables you to be eclectic, whilst retaining a period atmosphere.

Collections

The strong colours and general Eastern atmosphere of the main scheme's decoration will flatter just about any collection of objects from Africa, India or the Far East and, if you mix these with dark wood furniture, your room will take on a nineteenth-century feel.

If you have a collection from one country, perhaps Mexico or Egypt, focus on the style of that particular country, choosing a traditional national motif as a stencil design and matching the colours of your spattered wall decoration to those of a rug, perhaps, or ceramic bowl.

Out of the nomad's tent Textiles from Afghanistan, Mexico and South America, European cushions and lengths of modern fringing, integrate well with the background of red wall and dark floorboards.

Eclectic mix A typically Victorian mixture of objects: two kitsch dog portraits sit comfortably alongside a faux-bronze Art Nouveau planter filled with greenery.

Colourways

The colours of the East and Africa can inject life into the sometimes murky tones of Victorian soft furnishings, while complementing their richness of texture and pattern. Jewel colours (ruby reds, emeralds and sapphires) can be used to dazzling effect, especially if combined with golds or silvers in textiles, brass or inlaid work.

Reference books reproducing gouaches and watercolours of Victorian interiors are especially useful, showing how liberating the comprehensive taste of the period can be when looking for colour schemes to harmonize with a particular collection. Reprints of nineteenth-century books on ornament are also available, often including Eastern patterns and decoration. Although the colours in these editions are not always as brilliant and crisp as in the original versions, they offer a wide range of colour reference and inspiration.

Indian collection, right. Pieces that all come from one country strongly evoke the spirit of the place. For richness of effect, display objects with different surfaces and textures together.

Colonial backdrop, above. Cane or wicker furniture and slatted blinds and louvred doors evoke the tropical atmosphere of a Colonial home during the days of the British Empire.

Dark blues *These blues are more representative of eighteenth-century than Victorian taste, but they are especially effective as a background for Chinese lacquer and ceramics. Use dashes of silver as a visual catalyst to enliven the scheme.*

Silvery greys *This less dominant colourway is particularly suitable for a small room. Dark wood furniture, Chinese ceramics, and black and white engravings are all eyecatching against pale grey. Colourwashing (see p.248) provides textural interest.*

Minty green *Taken from the Indian tea-room at Blenheim Palace in Oxfordshire, this colourway is a fresh alternative. The Eastern colours of jade, onyx and some blue or green ceramics will blend in well.*

AUSTRALIAN BALCONY

Early Victorian architecture made great use of decorative ironwork, and many Australian houses (especially in the Paddington area of Sydney), still proudly display complex railings, pillars, porches and balconies. The characteristics of ornate and intricate metalwork can be combined with the pale earth colours, typical of exterior walls, to form the basis of a restful decorating scheme. I interpreted this style in a balcony setting to create a warm, elegant decor with a feeling of settled age; but it could be adapted successfully for a conservatory or interior rooms.

As with most decorating themes, it is the details that serve to link the different elements of the scheme together. I linked the intricate balcony ironwork with the rest of the scheme by hanging a new iron casting on the wall.

Continuing the theme

To carry the theme of ornate decoration further and to give weight and grandeur to the modest doorway I constructed a portico from timber mouldings and added a lincrusta frieze and a cast corbel.

Heavily scrolled corbels with male and female heads are typically Victorian. They are available in cast plaster (which can be used outside if sheltered), resin and reconstituted stone (both suitable for indoor and outdoor use). For best results any new pieces that are introduced should be given paint finishes that tie them in with existing surfaces, so that they look well established. In order to create a sense of belonging, I antiqued the new items with finishes that were sympathetic to the materials. I gave the decoration surrounding the door a dusty-looking antique patina and the shiny new casting on the wall a verdigris finish.

Even though both these finishes are intended for indoor use, when protected from the weather by some kind of shelter, and varnished, they can be used outside.

Colour schemes

To establish a feeling of age and restfulness that this type of decoration calls for, colours are very important. The mellow colours of cream, stone, and a pink made from red ochre and white are characteristic of the exteriors of many nineteenth-century Australian houses. The metalwork of the balcony was painted chalky white, which complemented the cream of the wall behind.

Curving shapes This example of ornate metalwork shows a scrolling design of unfurling leaves, which was typical of Victorian decoration.

ANALYSIS

DOORWAY DECORATION

To highlight the door, I made a timber portico, and added corbels and a lincrusta frieze.

WALL COLOUR

The cream of the wall is typical of Australian Victorian houses. To achieve a textured wall like this indoors, see pages 274–5.

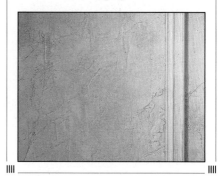

METALWORK CASTING

This new iron casting was given a verdigris paint finish. This treatment can be given to any odd pieces of reclaimed or reproduction metalwork.

PAINTED DOORS

The dark muddy-green emulsion used on the doors serves as a continuation of the green of the metalwork wall decoration.

SOFT FURNISHINGS

Dress your scheme with soft furnishings of the period. Here a Victorian lace tablecloth and fine chintz cushion cover soften the effect of the metalwork.

PAINTED METALWORK

The filigree metalwork of the balcony and pillar was painted a simple chalky white, using an exterior grade, matt oil-based paint.

Techniques

Antique patina p.257

Verdigris pp.286–7

STYLING
DECISIONS

THE TRANSPLANTING of the decorative taste of nineteenth-century Europe into the "no-nonsense" country life-style of Australia germinated a rich interior-decorating tradition, in which both foreign and unique indigenous elements were and still are combined.

To reflect the decorating ethic of nineteenth-century Australia, give walls a textured plaster finish (see pp.274–5), or treat them to

Ethnic influence *Aboriginal art can be adapted easily to an interior by painting large murals in emulsion paint. Use restraint with abstract patterns.*

resemble scrubbed limewash (see the middle colourway, opposite, and pp.254–5); then incorporate Victorian furnishings.

If you like a sober interior, choose plain dark furniture and hang monochrome prints on the wall for decoration. For a prettier look, surround yourself with Victorian fabrics, such as lace table-cloths and curtains, and chintz cushions and covers, and decorate your room with collections of Victorian ornaments.

For a truly Australian feeling, search out Aboriginal pictures and artefacts. You could even paint murals on this theme.

Scholarly air, *left. To create a room with a studious, somewhat austere air, furnish it sparsely with ebony and gilt furniture and hang Classical black and white prints on the wall. The understated sepia colour scheme is timeless. Architectural details and old books complete the effect.*

Floral furnishings, *below left. Flowery chintz, fine linen and fragile lace, all have their own place in the domestic Victorian scheme. Even this old-fashioned travelling trunk is worth including in order to show off its prettily decorated drawer fronts.*

Unusual ornamentation
In the same way that you can use Victorian metalwork to serve a decorative purpose in interiors, so this armillary sphere (see p.336), no longer needed out in the garden, can be viewed as an indoor ornament with a difference.

Colourways

The idea of bringing exterior decoration indoors to ornament walls begs the parallel introduction of outside colours in your room scheme. For example, you could use the colours of worn and corroded finishes such as rust, verdigris or crumbly plaster. Or you could adopt the colours used in traditional garden architecture, like the apple green and lavender blue of trelliswork. Look at Aboriginal art for some understanding of Australia's natural colour palette. Alternatively, follow the examples below for authentic Victorian cast iron colours.

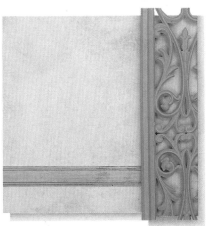

Authentic colours *Muddy green metalwork and brown woodwork make a studious combination, in keeping with a Victorian decor.*

Crisp freshness *Lavender blue set against natural wood and distressed white walls gives a clean look that has a modern feel.*

Black chic *For a stunningly modern combination of colours, paint walls peach, and woodwork and metalwork semi-matt black.*

TURN-OF-THE-CENTURY STYLES

The fluid, flowing lines of Art Nouveau ornament, flat-patterned William Morris wallpapers and fabrics, and the stylized motifs of C. R. Mackintosh are all elements of the styles of interiors formed during the end of the nineteenth century and early part of the twentieth century.

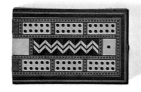

The call of the Arts and Crafts movement for a return to simplicity and honesty of design is as attractive to us today as it was approximately a hundred years ago. It restated a belief in hand crafts and the importance of individual creativity as opposed to the alienating forces of industrialization.

Roots of a style
These sentiments, which were all expressed in the decorative arts and in interior decoration, took root in England during the 1850s.

They influenced American designers, and went on to provide inspiration for Art Nouveau all over Europe.

Inspired by nature
The belief in the intrinsic beauty of natural materials, meant that Arts and Crafts furniture and domestic

objects were pleasing and simple (see the setting on p.177). Ornamentation was inspired by birds and animals, flowers and leaves. Plain oak was the staple wood but the soft sheen of limed wood, which can be seen on the carved panel, above right, is a finish that would fit in well. Walls were decorated simply, in pale, muted paint colours or with high panelling.

William Morris, founder of the firm of Morris, Marshall, Faulkner and Co.

was the most influential Arts and Crafts designer and much of his work is still produced today. His wallpaper and fabric designs were based on medieval pastoral imagery of plants and birds and took the form of abstract patterns.

In America, similar principles were incorporated into the work of the young architect Frank Lloyd Wright, while in England Charles Voysey established his own code of "simplicity and repose". Voysey produced fabric designs, below left, and furniture; the leaf from a table, above right, with its copper inlay, is typical of his work.

Scottish offshoot
Charles Rennie Mackintosh (a remarkably innovative Scottish architect and designer) used fluid motifs, such as the abstract plant form on the tracing paper, below right, to decorate his geometrical buildings and interiors. He also produced vivid and delicate designs

for stained glass, fabrics, and furniture characterized by strong geometric lines.

Linking styles

Mackintosh also drew his inspiration from the sinuous style of Art Nouveau. The graphics and accessories of Art Nouveau show an exceptional organic fluidity in their stretched and bent shapes (as can be seen in the two silver vases, right and below) but the decoration of interiors was comparatively formal. For the scheme on page 173 I used paint and gold powder to give the Art Nouveau frieze, below left, a finish that would never have been found on walls but echoes the colours and textures of period accessories.

Loose interpretation

As well as three settings inspired by specific styles, I incorporated a loosely derivative Italian one (on pp. 182–5) for a conservatory. Soft colouring, flowing forms and curvy furnishings, create an atmosphere redolent of leisurely afternoons in a turn-of-the-century home.

ART NOUVEAU DINING ROOM

The dining room is the place where gatherings and celebrations occur, and for this reason its decoration can afford to be just that little bit more showy than other rooms, with dark, rich colours that respond to soft lighting by day and candlelight by night. In this setting I used a lincrusta dado with a flowing design, and paint, powders and varnish to create a variety of extravagant effects that echo the verdigris and bronze finishes of Art Nouveau fittings and accessories.

I N THE 1880s and 1890s the sinuous lines of Art Nouveau design were applied to all sorts of decorative accessories found in the home. The style spread from England to Europe and America, but it was in France that it reached its most exuberant and then florid form. I adapted an English lincrusta dado (cutting out and then repositioning parts of the design) to create a pattern that looks convincingly French.

The paint finish

Despite the fluidity and abstract quality of the verdigris finish on the wall, neither are typical of Art Nouveau decor, which was surprisingly restrained when compared with the extravagant graphics of the period.

First I applied bronze-coloured metallic paint and then, when dry, dark-green emulsion paint diluted 1:7 with water. When this was dry, I dribbled some water-based washes (see p.333) in colours ranging from white to deep mint green down the wall. To create rivulets and crystalline pockets of colour I dribbled clean water through the wet paint. When dry, the wall was wiped with a damp sponge to blend the colours.

The effect on the dado (which was not sponged) is much more intense. Both wall and dado were protected with varnish. (See pp.286–7 for a verdigris finish that suits metalwork and a similar wall finish using emulsion paint.)

Art Nouveau originals

The furnishings, which are Art Nouveau originals, reflect the taste for dark polished wood and metalwork of all kinds. The stained beech chair is typical of the English vogue for the curving, stylized furniture that was promoted by Liberty and Co. Because of a vogue for Art Nouveau in the 1970s, copies of chandeliers are available.

Celtic flower *The fluid and organic forms that are associated with Art Nouveau were drawn from many sources, including Celtic art.*

ANALYSIS

LIGHTING

Curvilinear designs based on natural forms were adapted to accessories, like this Art Nouveau chandelier. Flower-drop shades and copies of Art Nouveau lights are available today.

UPPER WALL

On a basecoat of bronze-coloured metallic paint, powder colours and water were dribbled in layers and then sponged, to give the verdigris finish.

DADO & SKIRTING BOARD

I used the same technique on the dado and skirting board as on the upper wall, but dribbled washes of more intense powder colours in greater quantity on the band between the gilded strips, to produce a richer effect.

GOLD & BRONZE DETAILING

The lincrusta loops and ribbon were gilded with metallic powders. French enamel varnish over gold paint gave a deep bronze finish to the tapering verticals and parts of the loop design.

CHAIR & TABLE

The Art Nouveau chair illustrates the taste for dark polished woods in flowing designs. An inexpensive modern table was covered with bronze crushed velvet, which picks up the light and emphasizes the bronze of the wall and the gleam of the chandelier.

MOTTLED FLOOR

The wooden floor was given a subtle mottled appearance with the technique for fossilstone marble, using light- and dark-brown washes over a beige eggshell basecoat. It was protected with several coats of varnish.

Techniques
Sponging p.248
Fossilstone marbling pp.294–5
Gilding – metallic powder pp.304–5

STYLING DECISIONS

THOUGH antiques will add a connoisseur's fine touch to a room, there are plenty of other furnishings that you can easily obtain without burning a hole in your pocket. And where the decoration of a room relates so obviously to a particular style, you can afford to be a little relaxed about what elements to include.

Furnishing options

In the Europe of the 1880s there was a vogue for imported Japanese objects. To give a Japanese slant to a room, incorporate lacquer-work, ceramics, fans and prints.

There is little reproduction furniture available but some wrought-iron garden furniture (like that shown, right) has a suitably fluid and complex design. Edwardian furniture (much of it unfashionable and available at a reasonable price) will also blend in well.

Material themes

If you prefer, you can liberate yourself from historical restrictions and build on the theme of popular Art Nouveau materials, incorporating a variety of artefacts made from (or with a finish like) bronze, verdigris, mother of pearl or shagreen.

Original patterns, *above. Many opulent Art Nouveau fabric designs are still being produced today.*

Ornate metalwork, *left.*
The designs of this wrought-
iron garden furniture are
tamed adaptations of Art
Nouveau imagery, but the
overall impression is right
for the period.

Period pieces, below left.
Just one or two pieces, like
these round bronze castings,
are enough to add period
authenticity to a scheme.
They are decorated with the
flowing forms and stylized
human profiles that are
characteristic of Art
Nouveau imagery.

Oriental influence A
European taste for things
Japanese bubbled to the
surface in the 1880s and
artefacts were incorporated
in Art Nouveau interiors.
Oriental additions, in the
form of parasols and fans,
for example, are an inexpen-
sive and effective way of add-
ing character to an Art
Nouveau interior.

Colourways

Many European interiors of the 1880s
and 1890s were painted in muted mid-
greens, which are rather disappointing
compared to the rich colours of Art
Nouveau posters, bookplates and
graphic work. These are a rich source
of ideas for wall colours and stencils
with flowing designs. Look too, at the
colour combinations of period fabrics,
for example the mauve, and muddy greens and browns of the
fabric on the opposite page. The main scheme used verdigris
and bronze, two popular period finishes. Other fashionable
finishes were silver and gilt; decorate walls with motifs
in gold or silver leaf using the technique on pages 302–3.

Restrained combination Ochre
cream occurs in many Art Nouveau
posters and fabrics, like the richly-
coloured Liberty print here.

Exotic effect Lustrous gold leaf
when used in combination with bronze
is powerfully evocative of the most
extravagant form of Art Nouveau.

Muted option A gentle bluey-grey
paint finish makes a more subdued
alternative to the complex finish of the
wall of the main scheme.

ARTS & CRAFTS PARLOUR

Craftsmanship has had a rough time of it ever since the Industrial Revolution sparked off mass-production. But there has never been a shortage of eloquent defenders of the values of craftsmanship, among them the Victorian, William Morris. He craved the return to a pre-industrial way of life and attracted many followers. Collectively they formed the Arts and Crafts movement and caused a stylistic revolution in the 1860s by advocating a rejection of the cluttered, eclectic style of many interiors and calling for a return to something "more English", simple and traditional. The result was a set of ideas for decorating (best suited to modestly sized rooms) that create a quiet, contemplative atmosphere.

THIS ARTS and Crafts wall is lined with both matchboarding (thin tongue-and-groove boards) and plain planks of timber. In England, wainscotting, as this form of cladding is known, declined in popularity after the seventeenth century until its use was revived by the Arts and Crafts movement in the late nineteenth century.

A high shelf was often incorporated to house a display of handcrafted objects.

Natural finishes

The Arts and Crafts movement respected the honest character of natural materials. Their furniture was made from hardwoods, such as oak, which were often left plain and unpolished, with the grain clear for all to see; the chair and table here are archetypal. In accordance with the Arts and Crafts aesthetic I colourwashed the panelling with thin paint, which I sanded back so that the grain of the wood shows through. I colourwashed the floorboards too, but in different colours. To enhance, rather than disguise the plaster of the cornice, I used wax to give it a subtle finish.

Printed pattern

An exuberantly patterned William Morris wallpaper was pasted between the top of the panelling and the cornice. C. F. Voysey, who formed the more austere second generation of Arts and Crafts designers, favoured using brown paper rather than patterned wallpaper, a less expensive option then and now.

Fluid design The flowing lines of this Pre-Raphaelite design are akin to the decoration of Arts and Crafts work in silver and beaten metal.

ANALYSIS

PLASTER CORNICE

Using a simple technique I antiqued the new cornice to blend it in with the mellowed woodwork and furniture.

WILLIAM MORRIS DESIGNS

These patterned wallpapers are typical of William Morris's designs. The lower design was used as a frieze above the panelling and offset by an antique fabric wallhanging.

WOOD-PANELLED WALLS

Wood-clad walls and high shelves were popular at the turn of the century. I colourwashed the pine panelling with raw umber and then salmon-pink emulsion and sanded back the paint to expose the grain.

OAK FURNITURE

The coppery colour and grainy texture of the wall relates directly to the Voysey card table and chair. Note their simple, elegant design and the playing-card-motif inlays and cutouts.

FLOORBOARDS

To continue the soothing colour scheme to floor level, I colourwashed the floorboards with raw umber and then blue-grey emulsion.

Techniques

Colourwashing wood pp.252–3
Antiquing plasterwork pp.272–3

STYLING DECISIONS

INSTEAD OF WOOD, which I used on the bottom two-thirds of the wall in the parlour setting, you may prefer to use wallpaper. Many wallpapers and fabrics are still being produced from designs by William Morris, Walter Crane, Voysey and William de Morgan. Victorian and Edwardian furniture will fit in well, as long as it is on the light side and rooms are not cluttered with ornaments.

Rural theme

The Arts and Crafts movement placed great value on the countryside, so you can adopt a rural theme and incorporate objects made from country materials, such as clay, wicker and terracotta. The favourite chair covering of Voysey was rush, a material that has always been popular in the country.

The "new" craftsmanship

The reaction against mass-production and the renewed interest in craftsmanship towards the end of the nineteenth century is paralleled by a similar movement today. So there is no reason why an Arts and Crafts interior should not be furnished with modern hand-turned woodwork, or pale oak furniture.

Medieval overtones Nature and the beautiful tapestries of the Middle Ages inspired the intricate weaving patterns of Arts and Crafts fabrics.

Colourways

The fabrics of Morris and Co. (founded in 1861) were the first Arts and Crafts designs to be widely available and they were characterized by their carefully balanced floral and foliage patterns in predominantly muted colours: various shades of green, muddy earth colours, natural wood colours and greyish blues. Bright primary shades were reduced to pastel shades or tinted with brown, and the whole effect was sombre and rather medieval. Later, Voysey used similar colours but on strong peach and apricot backgrounds, or sometimes used a limited palette of several shades of one colour. Pale colours were used too, and walls were often painted all over in white or pale blue. To obtain the soft, non-reflective finish that suits this style, paint walls and woodwork with emulsion; colourwash wood (see pp.252–3) for the grainy finish of the blue and brown colourways, right.

Rural credence, left. This mixture of countryware reflects the Arts and Crafts movement's respect for the rural way of life and set of values.

Period designs, right. Several companies still manufacture papers and fabrics in Arts and Crafts designs; their price varies according to whether the materials they produce are hand-blocked or machine-printed.

Contemporary furniture, below. Well-made modern furniture in natural materials and patterned fabrics both fit comfortably within a traditional Arts and Crafts setting.

Pale blue *Light colours will make even the smallest of rooms appear more spacious. In order to create an effect like this on panelling or floorboards, colourwash with white, followed by dark-blue emulsion.*

Natural colour *New pine does not have the sympathetic appeal of well-seasoned wood, so colourwash it with brown emulsion to give it a more mellow, welcoming appearance.*

Muted green *This colour, which crops up in period fabrics and on wallpapers, has a soothing quality. Use emulsion paint to obtain a flat finish, like this.*

MACKINTOSH HALLWAY

This setting is based on the ideas of Charles Rennie Mackintosh, who enjoyed international success from 1896 (at the tail end of the Arts and Crafts movement) to 1906. During this time he designed everything from teapots to cathedrals. In his elegant interiors he used soft colour and a mixture of straight lines and fluid natural forms to create a sense of repose and balance. Only the minimum of furniture and freestanding ornament is required for this style, so it is particularly well suited to hallways and landings, which are best kept uncluttered, but benefit greatly from a few carefully chosen points of focus.

MACKINTOSH tended to put to use gentle colours more than any others. Lavender, which dominates this scheme, is a particularly magical colour: blue but not cold, rich but not cloying, and fresh, yet complex. It works well in bright and dark rooms as it is deep but also reflects light.

Divisions and patterns

In his interior designs, Mackintosh divided walls up with furniture, panelling or mouldings, creating linear divisions of colour in order to control the wall space and establish points of focus. To this end I introduced a chair, a white skirting board, and painted window frame and cornice.

Intertwined through all of Mackintosh's geometrical designs were the spindly and elegant forms of plants, adapted into both abstract and graphic images. I followed this idea here with the lily-leaf stencilling on the lower wall, the double-petalled tulip image on the upper wall and the abstract rose-motif stained glass window.

Archetypal shapes

The rigidly geometrical chair is a famous Mackintosh design (now reproduced by modern furniture-makers). It features the ladder and the grid, both of which are typical of his work, and occur frequently in inlay patterns, carving, low-relief patterns on walls, stencilled patterns and thin wooden mouldings, often painted black or white. I adopted this theme for the white painted frame around the window; for other ideas look at books about Mackintosh's work and adapt some of the motifs he used on furniture for example, to stencil on walls.

Contemporary design This plain blue vase, though modern, conforms to the simple elegance and organic feel of Mackintosh's work.

ANALYSIS

PAINTED CORNICE

Mackintosh believed that most ornament should be an integral part of walls, in the form of sunken panelled lights, for example, or painted pattern, rather than pictures or other hung ornament. All the wall painting here, including the white-rimmed cornice, was executed in matt emulsion paints used straight out of the tin, or diluted with water to make detail painting easier.

STAINED GLASS WINDOW

The window, which is the focus of the setting, is emphasized with a grid border in white, which echoes the pattern of the chair. Mackintosh designed much stained glass; a furniture detail was the inspiration for the design I painted on the window here.

FURNISHINGS

Look for reproduction or modern furniture, and fabrics that have the strong upright lines and/or stylized flower forms that characterize Mackintosh's designs.

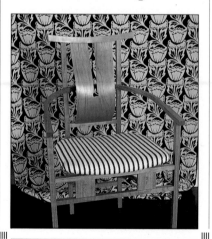

Techniques
Stained glass pp.308–9
Stencilling pp.312–7

ITALIAN CONSERVATORY

This conservatory setting combines reproduction patinated steel furnishings with paint effects to convey the atmosphere of an early 1900s Italian conservatory of the type found in fashionable seaside resorts. The use of a plaster-like wall finish is the basis of this scheme. It immediately suggests the Mediterranean with its heat, its earthy raw materials and its dustiness. Nowhere is bare plaster more effective than in rooms where natural sunlight pours in. The inclusion of mosaic patterning, which brings to mind a Classical Roman interior, completes the scheme.

THE HARD surfaces of marble, plaster and glazed mosaic were all components of the Classical Roman interior and mosaic in particular is our one archaeological link with the great Roman baths. The link between these materials and moisture is reinforced by the lush greenery trailing from the terracotta urn and the rusty-looking wall-mounted planters. If you do not have a conservatory space, you could adapt the Italian qualities of this scheme to any bright room.

Using plaster
Bare plaster, whether real or imitated is visually a fairly dense and unyielding surface, and so needs room to "breathe". For this reason it is well suited to spaces that are sizeable, such as a large dining room or airy living room. In most cases it will make a small room feel more cramped. The exception is if a room has a glass roof, because this gives the eye a vertical escape route to infinite space, which prevents a closed-in feeling.

Interestingly enough, this principle does not always apply to rooms with large windows instead of a glass roof, because the view outside may be limited or cluttered and may not give the impression of leading to infinity.

Metalwork furniture
The Italian atmosphere of this room stems not just from the use of materials and pattern on the walls and floor. It is also inherent in the metalwork table support, which is gilded and rusted to an aged patina. The florid exuberance and delicately worked forms of this type of furniture are still popular in Italy today, whether found in authentic reproductions like the table shown opposite, or hidden in the scrolling shapes of contemporary furniture.

Mosaic inspiration Look at mosaics from all periods and cultures for inspiration for the patterning in your real or imitated conservatory setting.

ANALYSIS

FLORAL DETAILING
I glued plastic castings (the type sold for adorning fitted furniture) along the top of the wall and painted them to match the wall. They set up a delicate rhythm around the room in symmetry with the planters below.

PLASTER WALL
This plaster effect (also used on the skirting board) is a fairly simple faux technique. The colours can be made slightly more pink or cream to suit your room. As a guide, choose earth colours mixed with white.

TABLE & PLANTERS
These metalwork furnishings were reproduced from original Italian designs of the eighteenth and nineteenth centuries and then gilded and rusted to an aged patina. Rusty-looking materials reinforce the idea of a humid conservatory, where metal might indeed rust.

MOSAIC PATTERNING
This was printed with ordinary washing-up sponges, chopped into 2-cm (1-in) squares and stuck on a board. For the leaf patterns, I used pieces of sponge on a board cut to a three-leaf shape. The block was then coloured ready for printing by pressing it into a tray of emulsion paint, or, as with the leaves, by quickly painting each sponge square a different colour with a small brush. I finished by outlining the leaves by hand, and lightly sanding all the printed pattern so it has a similar finish to the dusty-looking wall.

PRINTED FLOORING
This effect was achieved using the same method as that for the wall above, but masking tape was used to mark off the floor into squares for straight edges. The mosaic paint finish was then varnished.

Technique
Plaster pp.284–5

STYLING DECISIONS

THE ATTRACTION in dressing a conservatory space is that the more plants you introduce, the less furniture you need, and the better it looks.

If you want something less wild and fancy than curly, patinated furniture, choose darkwood furniture of the early 1900s. Or collect cane or wicker tables and chairs, particularly painted ones. For a seaside atmosphere choose striped deckchairs and for a more severe look modern black steel furniture.

Wall decoration and ceramics

Look round architectural salvage yards for bits of old buildings, such as stone capitals, decorative tiles or broken carvings, that you can actually plaster into your wall so they look as though they are exposed features. Or hang coloured majolica plates and reproductions of Della Robbia ceramic ware. (The Della Robbias were Italian Renaissance ceramicists.)

Colourways

Inspiration for mosaic colour schemes abounds in the many archaeological remains situated around Europe and the Middle East, and there are also several books on the subject. Mosaic colours have very often been dirtied by time, so if you match them carefully you will achieve an aged version of the colours. Brighten the colours slightly for something nearer the mosaic colours when new. The natural colours of plaster are also a starting point for colour. Consider tinting white plaster powder with powder colours or colourwash walls with diluted water-based paint; alternatively use a plaster-like paint finish, like that on the left. Use earth colours to emphasize plaster's mineral qualities. To remind yourself of the relaxed atmosphere of a room like this in a seaside setting, choose seaside stripes in bright colours and white to decorate your dado.

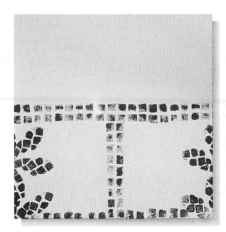

Contemporary style In a minimal setting that relies on very few plants, use an abstract mosaic pattern in black and white for a stark effect.

Relaxed living space, *far left. Collect an informal mixture of painted wicker and Lloyd Loom chairs together with coffee and card tables for a restful conservatory atmosphere.*

Establishing character, *left. A display of reproduction artefacts in granite, terracotta, marble and resin emphasize the archaeological character of the wall decoration.*

Colourful ceramics, *below. These bright and cheerful modern majolica plates with painted flowers, birds, butterflies and foliage are entirely in keeping with the green and leafy nature of an Italian conservatory setting.*

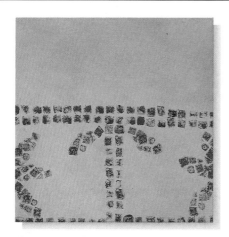

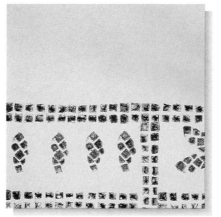

Antique feel *For a truly Roman feel, I used the earth colours of burnt umber and red oxide on a background of yellow ochre (mixed with raw sienna to cool it down).*

Seaside combination *This dark-blue and white combination is a gentler alternative to the first colourway. With its suggestion of the aquatic, it makes a peaceful, restrained pattern, an ideal background for the relaxed and soothing atmosphere of a conservatory.*

Conservatory lighting *This is a typical, if somewhat crudely cast, turn-of-the-century lamp. Alternatives to globe lighting like this are Italian metal chandeliers and candlelight for evenings.*

TWENTIES ONWARDS

Abstract painting, Bauhaus design and Hollywood Art Deco were all new twentieth-century forces that helped to purge the ideas of the previous century and to shape the style of interior decor from the Twenties onwards. Because they all exerted their influence at the same time there are stylistic similarities between them.

One of the powerful moulders of twentieth-century taste was the Bauhaus, the German design college founded in 1919. This was linked in the beginning to the turn-of-the-century Arts and Crafts movement, in that it taught crafts like bookbinding and stained glass and created a vogue for things unadorned and functional (see p.177). But what made the Bauhaus different was that from the 1920s onwards it took a more industrial direction, combining art together with technology.

The results of this combination were functional and timeless designs such as the teapot, above right, and the coffee pot on the opposite page. Designs like

this found favour with manufacturers and similar pieces are being made today.

To create a suitable period interior for such objects the decoration of the walls and floor needs to be uncluttered (see the Bauhaus Study on p.201). Metals such as chrome and steel are appropriate, and furnishings should be streamlined. Functional objects with "clean" lines, whether made in the early twentieth century or not, are the ones to seek out. The fan shown opposite is a typical example of the

sort of objects that can be found in second-hand shops and markets.

Hollywood's influence
Though Bauhaus gave design a new and pure direction

in the Twenties and Thirties (the age of Art Deco), its idealization of industrialism found little popular support. During this time, the minimal approach of Bauhaus contradicted the twentieth-century image that was being promoted by early Hollywood. This was a glamorous celluloid world that mirrored the opulent interiors of 1930s cinemas.

This style (which I captured in the Savoy setting on p.189) was luxurious, with pale woods, glass, leather, ivory and lacquer predominating.

Domestic Deco
This style also produced abstract geometrical designs, mass-produced in

the form of fabrics like the ones below, mixed with Aztec and Mayan pattern, Classical elements and

Egyptian imagery like the flower on the yellow-patterned fabric, right.

Furniture was made with rounded outlines and often decorated with exotic materials. The cocktail cabinet (and its accessories) and coffee table became

popular in the domestic interior at this time.

This approach to interior decorating spread rapidly through many homes, and

inevitably became cheapened on the way, which is one reason why there are so many Art Deco accessories available nowadays. For example, although a little kitsch, the teapot, left, and the plates, far left, reflect a taste for semi-abstracted decoration, and are now considered as succinct and rare interpretations of popular 1930s taste. Many Art Deco fabrics and wallcoverings are produced today. Much-used Art Deco motifs include stylized trees, shells, fans and sunrises (see the fabric below). Bright colours were popular, as the sample papers above, show.

Linking cultures

The decorative arts of the East have influenced Western interiors at different times and to varying extents since the seventeenth century. The Oriental setting on page 193 reflects this continuing tradition. Also, it draws its strength from an abstract and minimal approach that is reflected in much modern design: Bauhaus fabric and furniture bear a strong resemblance to some Japanese fabrics and black lacquerwork.

The setting also mirrors the way Art Deco style took ideas from so many different cultural sources, by incorporating elements from different Eastern countries (Thailand, Japan and China). Typical Eastern furnishings, including bamboo, cane, and Chinese pottery, are widely available today.

SAVOY BEDROOM

The most private of rooms, the bedroom, offers a unique opportunity to live out a little fantasy and indulge in the luxurious. Grand hotels, like the Savoy in London, have traditionally been synonymous with opulence, but nowhere has this theme been more thoroughly explored than in the films of 1930s Hollywood, such as Plaza Suite. *By combining reflective materials like chromium, ebony and alabaster, and adapting the sleek, geometrical imagery of the 1930s, you can convert the simplest room into an authentic interpretation of an Art Deco hotel suite.*

THIS BEDROOM arrangement is a more authentic representation of Art Deco style than the more widely interpretative Deco living room scheme on pages 196–9. It relies more obviously on the polished surfaces, slick finishes and geometrical patterns typical of Art Deco interiors, which I have combined to make a distinctly luxurious setting. Simple interiors, without ornate cornicing or mouldings, lend themselves most readily to this transformation.

Surface play

The wall opposite contains several contrasting elements: behind the slick, black dado blocks, the wall is colourwashed a salmon-pink colour for a matt, broken texture.

The warm terracotta and red ochre of the painted mural complement the patinated frieze and skirting board, which have depth and a metallic brashness.

Atmospheric lighting

To break up the flat wall surface and highlight the metallics, some thoughtful lighting and a few three-dimensional objects were needed. The answer lay in the use of Art Deco lamps, which fulfil both functions. Uplighters cast a soft, general glow towards the ceiling, emphasizing the patterns and reflections of the frieze. The warm texture of the alabaster pendant lamp (you could use a marbled glass version) gives a diffused luminescence, resulting in a satisfying orchestration of lighting.

Adapted stencil *This Egyptian flower was used for stencilling the dado panels. The floral head was taped over, so that only the leaves were printed.*

STYLING DECISIONS

T HIRTIES STYLE is characterized by a combination of finishes, including spray work, metallics, flat paint and broken colour. Three-dimensional objects should be used sparingly to emphasize these combinations. Examples of the period range from exquisite inlay work, sculpture by Bourraine and glass by Lalique, right down to geometrical "Depression glass", which was mass-produced in the early Thirties by various American companies.

Inspiring influences

Geometric designs from Romanesque or Aztec art, as well as motifs from Greek, Roman or Egyptian sources are all appropriate. Art Nouveau is another important influence, while the choice of metallics reflects the machine age's increasing obsession with industrial finishes. For furniture, the dominant aesthetic is the 1930s American streamlined style.

Reproduction fabrics These sugar-candy Art Deco colours make superb upholstery for old 1930s style sofas that need new covers.

Colourways

There are many choices of colour available for a Thirties scheme, as these colourways and the other illustrations on these pages show. Cream or beige tones were popular as backgrounds, wall and floor colours, and black featured in most rooms: to this basic palette you can add a variety of colours. The vivid tints of the Clarice Cliff pottery shown on the opposite page provide one starting point; the muddy mustards and browns of the poster above, another; a third option are the bright pastels, like mint green, blue and candy pink, which were fashionable at the time. Intense hues, such as the lemon yellow in the Egyptian fabric, above right, can be used sparingly, but they should not overpower the more characteristic pastel tones. The sheen of patinated metals, glass, varnished paint and polished wood will intensify any colour scheme.

Posters and lamps, *left. Prints convey the optimism and naivety of the period. Their colours and flat textures are very evocative and provide an excellent starting point for a room. Shell lamps from an earlier period make superb picture lamps here, but can also be bent on their flexible armatures and used to wash walls with light or uplight ceilings.*

Egyptian direction, *above. In 1922 the tomb of Tutankhamun was opened: an event that greatly influenced Art Deco style. Here a sphinx and fabric develop the Egyptian theme.*

Period ceramics *This set, in a traditional shape but with vividly painted surface decoration in popular period colours, was made by the British designer, Clarice Cliff, whose work was* sold widely through department stores in the Thirties. Another influential potter of the period was Susie Cooper, who also produced tableware and vases, which are now collector's pieces.

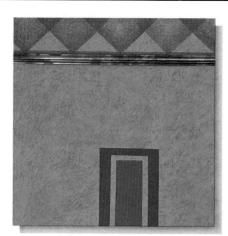

Red and green *Softly-stippled transparent oil glaze suggests the pale polished woods that were popular in the Thirties. The primitive red and green painted over the glaze are enhanced by the bronze detailing.*

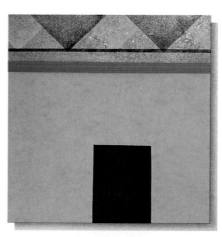

Silver and pink *Silver spray paint was worked into wet pink paint to make a metallic background for the frieze. The magenta pink is very cool; the solid green and black reinforce the formality of the scheme.*

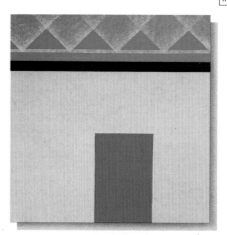

Lemon and turquoise *Sulphurous lemon with oily blue-green make an exciting basis for an Art Deco room with Egyptian hues. French-polished furniture sits well against this yellow. You could substitute red ochre for the blue to complement the dark wood.*

ORIENTAL LIVING ROOM

Eastern culture has always provided the West with a rich vein of visual inspiration and, at times, radically altered the path of design. Rather than interpret one decorative style of interior, I drew ideas from all over the East, placing emphasis on the characteristics of Oriental interiors that contribute to a spiritual quality of life, and that can be adapted to modern interiors: simplicity, elegance and the importance attached to surfaces. Here, paint finishes suggest Oriental lacquerwork and crackleglaze, while panelling, low furniture and a paper screen control space and light, making for a calm, carefully organized and minimal-looking living area.

THE LOCAL traditional houses of Thailand have always been built from painted wooden frames and panels, which give interior walls a pattern of blocks and strips. I interpreted this effect with hardboard and painted the wall saffron red, a regional earth colour.

Dividing up areas of wall in this way will help you to manipulate the space in a room and give it a rhythmic and controlled appearance.

I also experimented with the quality of natural light. Muslin hung across a window will serve to diffuse the natural light, but here I wanted to imitate the quality of filtered light common to many Eastern interiors, so I made a screen by fixing thick tissue paper (oiled with linseed oil) to a wooden frame.

Paint finishes

Lacquer and crackleglaze (a decorative cracked effect) are both Oriental in origin. I gave the side of the low wooden bench a cracked lacquer effect using the technique shown below and glazed the red wall to give a subtle depth to the finish. The theme is continued in the saffron-red lacquered trunk and two small pots on the low table.

ANALYSIS

SCULPTURE & WALL FINISH

A modern, ethnic-looking sculpture adorns the wall, which has a soft, aged finish. After painting the wall red (with eggshell) I brushed on transparent oil glaze tinted with a little raw umber artists' oil paint and softened it out.

EXOTIC WINDOW FRAME

The wood frame was given a patchy finish (using my scrubbed limewash technique) and stencilled with spray paint. To create an irregular pattern I used the stencil at a variety of angles.

LOW BENCH

The built-in bench, which is typical of Thai interiors, is in scale with the other low-level furniture. It has a cracked lacquer finish, in the tradition of Chinese lacquerwork, and Raku pottery.

CHINESE POTTERY

Blue Chinese pottery, which stands out brightly and crisply against the glossy red wall, looks perfectly at home amongst the decoration and artefacts of other Eastern cultures.

CRACKED LACQUER EFFECT

Use a decorating brush to apply liquid gum arabic (see p.332) over a dry emulsion basecoat. Leave to dry.

Apply a second coat of emulsion in a contrasting colour. The cracked effect will occur almost as you apply the paint.

Techniques

Scrubbed limewash pp.254–5
Softened glazework pp.256–7
Stencilling pp.312–7

STYLING DECISIONS

THE KEY choice is whether simply to integrate a few Eastern artefacts and forms of decoration into a room decorated in a Western style or whether to become immersed in the principles of Oriental decoration.

If you decide on the former you will be following in a long European tradition. In the eighteenth century, for example, Chinese motifs and designs were incorporated into European Rococo forms of decoration, in a style known as Chinoiserie. To evoke a period European atmosphere, decorate a room with some Chinoiserie-style

Wood carving *The modern sculpture on the previous page follows in the tradition of these old, low-relief Indonesian designs.*

furnishings, like the wallpaper, above right, or base a room's decoration on a colour evocative of the East, like jade or Chinese blue.

For the purist approach, try to absorb some of the essential philosophical principles, of say, Japanese design (principles such as minimalism, light, space and order) and decorate and furnish a room with these qualities in mind. Put modern Western furniture that has been inspired by Eastern design philosophy, into a more traditional Oriental setting, like that on the preceding page.

Linking East and West *The abstract patterns of these modern Western fabrics echo the split and threaded patterns of the Eastern bamboo and woven cane.*

Eastern colours, *left*. Western taste demands plenty in the way of soft furnishings. The colour of jade, a material much used in Oriental art, is the unifying characteristic of the furnishings and artefacts here.

Paper effects, *right*. The screen is covered with calligraphic paper, which can be bought in rolls and used to screen windows. Decorate walls with Chinese scrolls and furniture with wrapping paper, crackleglazed (see pp.268–9).

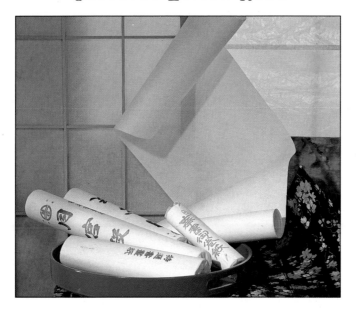

Historical accuracy, *above*. This Regency wallpaper shows the eighteenth-century vogue for Chinoiserie. The pot is similar to the imported Chinese artefacts popular at the time.

Colourways

European cultures of the seventeenth and eighteenth centuries absorbed Oriental culture, adopting background colours like acid yellow and jade green to flatter their collections of imported Eastern goods. For a period atmosphere follow suit, using these colours as a background for traditional Oriental ware or, in a more contemporary vein, against which to display modern artefacts and furniture of Eastern origin. The cracked lacquer finish shown here (and which features in the main scheme) can be applied to woodwork, using the fresh colours of Chinese ceramics.

Yellow *For a warm scheme use diluted saffron-yellow paint over a raw umber basecoat, with raw umber and scarlet for skirtings.*

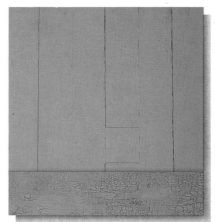

Chinese blues *The colours of Chinese ceramics are subtly combined in the cracked lacquer finish.*

Ancient browns *A mixture of raw umber and white emulsion (diluted with water) is used over red.*

MIAMI DECO LIVING ROOM

To evoke a 1930s mood, where better to turn for ideas than the sultry interiors of Miami, a city full of Art Deco architecture. Art Deco style is typified by geometric and streamlined shapes, smooth materials, like chrome and marble, and stylized motifs. This room treatment includes all these elements, but the aura of showy Hollywood glitz typical of many American Art Deco interiors has been toned down to make a setting with a friendlier, more understated character, in which an old 1930s sofa or Bakelite radio will look as appropriate as the bar and cocktail accessories here.

THIS SCHEME has a visual strength that comes from the geometric division of the wall by a dado, and a natural quality derived from the raw materials: plaster and (paint-simulated) marble. By making the floor and dado one colour, and the upper wall another, I divided the space horizontally into two distinct bands: the lower contains furniture and possessions, while the other remains refreshingly empty. Even the flamingo painting is an integral part of the wall by way of its plaster frame.

Tropical versus cool

The tug of war between the hot Miami climate and the coolness of the interiors designed to combat the heat is echoed in my choice of colour, pattern and imagery. The flamingo painting is splashed with hot colours, the armchair is covered with a tropical pattern fabric and the upper wall of aged plaster is painted in warm creams.

To counter these "hot" elements the lower half of the room is painted in imitation of a physically cold and visually cooling material, fossilstone marble, popular in many 1930s Miami interiors.

As it is not possible to use the fossilstone method on vertical surfaces (the materials used will run off), the skirting board was marbled before it was fixed to the wall, as were the hardboard tiles used as a dado. Similarly the wooden floor was marbled using the same technique and subsequently protected from wear and tear with a few coats of hard wearing, gloss varnish; see the table shown on pages 328–31.

Art to industry This stylized pattern is typical of designs produced by leading 1920s artists and adopted by manufacturers of wallpaper.

ANALYSIS

PLASTER WALLS

The texture of the aged plaster wall breaks up the light coming through the Venetian blind and contrasts with the smoothness of the other surfaces.

FLAMINGO MURAL

This stylized mural was painted with emulsion paints. The irregular frame, with its 1930s reeded outline, was made by building up layers of plaster and hemp scrim over rolled-up newspaper.

ART DECO BAR

Cocktails were all the rage in the Twenties and Thirties. The fabric covering the bar and stool is a reproduction showing stylized Egyptian flowers; Art Deco drew much of its imagery from Egyptian sources.

FOSSILSTONE MARBLE

The dado, skirting board and floor are painted to look like fossilstone marble, a material that was common in many of Miami's buildings.

DECO SKIRTING BOARD

The skirting board's rounded edges and streamlined shape give it a suitably Art Deco appearance. I combined a torus skirting board and some panel moulding.

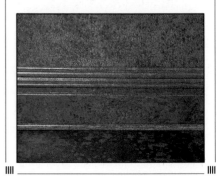

Techniques
Ageing plaster walls pp.274–5
Fossilstone marbling pp.294–5

STYLING DECISIONS

T HE FUN of Art Deco is its great flexibility. Because it is such an eclectic style, based on sources ranging from Classical Greek architecture and Egyptian pattern to South American art, Expressionism and Art Nouveau, you can include artefacts from various periods, styles and cultures.

As it is a twentieth-century style, mass-produced furniture, ornaments and memorabilia, can be included, too.

Scope for style

Within the parameters of Art Deco style you can aim for a utilitarian look by industrializing your setting with objects like old factory lamps and electric fans. Alternatively, hark back to the days of the British Empire and create a nineteenth-century feel with wicker furniture and ethnic carvings.

Standard Art Deco accessories like a Bakelite radio or Odeon wall lamp (these are glass, shell-shaped uplighters) will naturally look at home in an Art Deco setting, but so too will 1950s chrome junk-shop finds and art, both figurative and abstract, of many twentieth-century styles. Black ash or chrome furniture also fits in well.

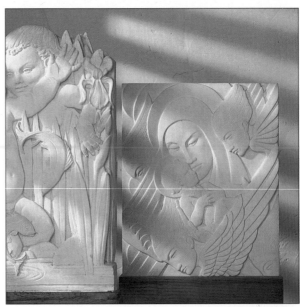

Sculpted focus Much twentieth-century sculpture and bas-relief carving, like that of Eric Gill and the modern movement, has the stylized forms and poise characteristic of Art Deco designs.

Wallpapers A few companies still manufacture authentic Art Deco wallpapers, like this one, which dates from 1925.

Ethnic deco, left. The geometric pattern and bright colours of Santa Fe style accessories and furniture make them perfect adjuncts to an Art Deco room. The ziggurat shape, loosely interpreted on the Santa Fe cupboard, was also a popular Art Deco motif.

Memphis furniture Fluidly rounded, brightly coloured, and large-scale, this modern furniture is evocative of the style of some Art Deco furniture.

Colourways

Although many modest domestic interiors were decorated in shades of beige, brown and cream, like I used in the living room scheme, public buildings were often decorated in exuberant colours. In Miami, the outsides of buildings were finished in cream or white stucco with abstract detailing in sugary colours like salmon pink, mint blue and buttery orange, or with bright greens and soft lemon-yellows. The pastel shades are effective for walls and floors; use the brighter colours sparingly, for painting doors, window frames, mouldings or for furnishings.

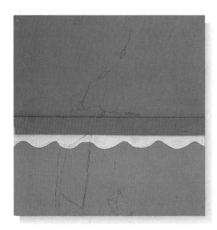

Colours of the sea Two blues are sparked into life by the pink rail – a lively colourway especially suitable for a bathroom.

Bright green This bright apple green was used in stripes on the exterior of Miami buildings. In a scaled-down form it is effective for a dado.

Soft shades Matched to the cool paint colours used in a 1930s Miami apartment, these caramel shades make for a light and breezy scheme.

BAUHAUS STUDY

Modern furnishings and decoration have been profoundly influenced by Walter Gropius's Bauhaus, a school of design in Germany during the 1920s. Forged from a new integration of art and technology, Bauhaus style created a purist vogue for things unornamented and functional that still resounds today. Look to Bauhaus ideas for some powerful inspiration to create an ordered, contemplative and beautiful setting – perfect for a room like a study. Here, simply painted walls, combined with the use of metals and a few streamlined items, establish a functional but elegant setting that has a decidedly modern atmosphere.

IN TERMS of design, Bauhaus is all too often dismissed as a monochrome world of ugly functionalism dominated by black and chrome – perhaps the profusion of black and white photographs from the period is to blame. But colour and pattern were, in fact, widely employed, and it is important to realize that functionalism can also have great aesthetic appeal.

Historical roots

Though Bauhaus style was a radical departure from tradition, it incorporated many historical precedents. My green stripe pattern, for example, which is taken from a Bauhaus design for a gym wall, echoes a tradition of using horizontal bands of colour that stretches back to Egypt via the eighteenth-century vogue for walls decorated with painted strips of imitation marble.

The technological roots of Bauhaus style are evident in the machine-age functionalism of the furniture and decor here. This approach is effective in any room in which you want to create an orderly or studious atmosphere, such as a quiet sitting room or study.

As you can see in the elegant structure of the table opposite, a lack of ornament does not imply any lack of beauty. The design is not entirely functional: the whim of the designer has dictated its unusual rounded base.

Domestic objects of Bauhaus design harmonize well with many twentieth-century homes, whose plain lines suit a minimalist approach. But Bauhaus does not have to be restricted to modern interiors. Such furnishings can be shown off to advantage in a home of any period as long as the decoration of the floors and walls is left uncluttered.

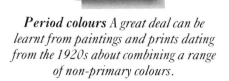

Period colours *A great deal can be learnt from paintings and prints dating from the 1920s about combining a range of non-primary colours.*

ANALYSIS

CEILING LAMP

This modern Italian lamp is designed to refract the light. It embodies the Bauhaus concept of domestic functionalism.

WALL SCULPTURE

This abstract wall decoration was cut from a sheet of hardboard and covered with hammer-finish enamel paint (see p.223). Its inspiration was a curious machine designed by Moholy-Nagy of the New Bauhaus (see p.338).

STRIPED WALL

The wall was first painted in pale sage-green emulsion paint. Then lines were drawn and bordered with masking tape before painting in darker green stripes.

SIMPLE FURNITURE

This chair, with its elegant design and fine craftsmanship, is in the style of the 1920s French cabinet-maker, Jacques-Emile Ruhlmann.

FLOORING

Sheet steel, for use on fire escapes, was cleaned and then varnished with a metal lacquer. Similar designs can be bought in aluminium.

STYLING DECISIONS

THE JUDICIOUS use of raw materials is an effective way of bringing Bauhaus style to a room. Metals such as chromium and steel are appropriate, as is glass, while polished wood adds warmth. Instead of sheet steel flooring like that used in the main scheme, you could cover your floor with plain linoleum or paint floorboards black or steely grey. Allow functional items a prominent position in a room; small objects should be tidied away, for a minimal setting demands an absence of superfluous bits and pieces.

Softer lines

For a more luxurious look, turn to French furniture of the 1920s which, inspired by Art Nouveau (see pp.172–5), was more fluid. Art Deco accessories (see pp.196–9) make another alternative. Different twentieth-century styles can be gathered together successfully in a Bauhaus style interior, providing it is not crammed with pieces.

Functional decor, top right. Fans, light fittings, clocks, radiators and heaters should be prominent, in celebration of their functional worth.

Collections, below. Simple displays, such as this assortment of industrial glassware, Lalique sculpture and moulded ware, blend well with the clean lines of a modern interior.

Colourways

Black and chrome are such dominant colours in the range of reproduction Twenties furniture that it is often thought, mistakenly, that a decorative scheme in colour would be inappropriate for a Bauhaus interior. And yet much original Twenties furniture was upholstered in coloured leathers and fabrics. There are also period paintings that make useful reference for schemes in colour (Klee's and Kandinsky's work, for example).

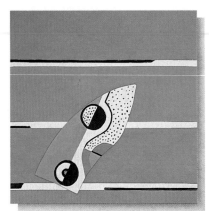

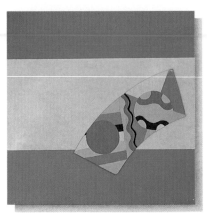

Subtle pinks *Muddied violet and pink are kept in check by black and white. The brown tone of the colours evokes a strong sense of the period.*

Violet and brown *Lemon yellow adds a flash of light to this more sombre juxtaposition of brown and violet.*

TOOLS
MATERIALS
& TECHNIQUES

INTRODUCTION

*To master the techniques in this section, first practise them.
Wall finishes can be tried out on the wall you are going to
decorate and painted over in white. You can also practise
techniques that use transparent oil glaze on the surface to be
decorated as long as you wipe it off before it dries.
Experiment with waxes and pastes on scrap wood. To get
an impression of different colours, prepare large sample
boards and hold them up in different parts of the room.
The effect of any colour is intensified when all four walls
are painted the same; to judge the impact of this, paint the
inside of an old paint can (see opposite). I never apply
paint with a roller because the texture spoils subsequent
paint layers. Quantities for mixing materials are given as
proportions (to dilute eggshell paint 1:4 with white spirit,
for example, use four times the volume of white spirit as
paint). Information on making paints, tinting emulsion
and eggshell, estimating quantities and special tips on
glazework and finishing are included on pages 332–5.*

**Home-made tool for
painting straight edges**

Colour sample boards

**Airtight container useful
for storing powders**

**Electric sander,
and paint tin in
a paint kettle**

Setting up and finishing
Always lay down plenty of dust sheets and put paint tins in paint kettles to catch drips (this also makes it easier to carry tins without a handle). Attach the paint kettle to the ladder with a snap-hook. Always work in a well-ventilated area and do not drink, eat or smoke. Certain materials should only be used with rubber gloves, goggles or a mask (dust masks prevent powder particles from being inhaled; use a special respiratory mask to avoid inhaling fumes if using solvents). Safety tips are given with each technique and on pages 324–31. If you stop for an hour or so, cover your brushes with a rag dampened with water (for water-based paints) or with turpentine (for oil-based paints). Clean your brushes and close all paint containers before finishing for the day.

On the workbench: dust mask and protective goggles

Thick rubber gloves

Long ruler and spirit level

Plastic paint kettle attached with a snap-hook

Colour test in empty paint container

DECORATING BRUSHES

ECORATING brushes are used to apply and manipulate different sorts of paint in a variety of ways, as well as to apply waxes, pastes and powders.

Styles of brush

There are many designs of decorating brush: round, domed, flat-ended, pointed and chiselled, and they range in size from one hair wide to 25cm (10in) wide.

Though the scale of the job and the medium in hand dictate the size and basic composition of the brush needed, many design variations are simply due to manufacturers' whims or a particular country's decorating traditions.

But one thing is certain: for nearly all work nothing betters pig bristle. Lily-bristle brushes, made from white hog-hair, are the best decorating brushes you can buy and are worth the investment. The bristles are soft, flexible and have flags (split ends) that disperse the paint and soften out the brush-marks. For advice on cleaning brushes see pages 218–9.

Old but serviceable
emulsion brush

Flat, oval, or round?

The flatter a brush the less paint it can hold, yet flat brushes are the most widely used in the United States and Britain; oval brushes are the most popular design in the rest of Europe. The round brush, which holds a generous amount of paint, is an old British design; the one shown below, right, is quite small by traditional standards.

Oval brush

Old medium size
flat brush

Lily-bristle
flat brush

Old-fashioned
round brush

An old friend, *above.*
This 10-year-old brush, still in use even though it has a split ferrule, has a flexibility and character all of its own.

DIFFERENT GRIPS

For brushing out or softening hold the brush, as shown, top, and for wide sweeps, as above.

Short-bristled
sash brush

Lily-bristle
sash brush

Wide sash
brush

Medium size
well-chiselled
emulsion brush

Large well-chiselled
emulsion brush

Sash brushes
These 3–5-cm (1–2-in)
brushes are known as sash
brushes because they were
traditionally used for
painting window frames –
in fact they are useful for all
sorts of small-scale work.

Short-bristled
emulsion brush

Lily-bristle
emulsion brush
(stained through use)

Emulsion brushes
The size, bristle length and flexibility of
emulsion brushes make for efficient
coverage with any type of paint. The
bristle ends of the two large brushes
above have been worn to a chisel edge: a
benefit, for this gives a smoother flow.
The thick, short-bristle brush is another
popular design of emulsion brush; it can
also be used as a cheap stippler. The
largest brush is what I call a "tosher"
and is used for covering huge areas.

FITCHES & LINING BRUSHES

FITCHES and lining brushes are used for small-scale and detailed work. Each subgroup has different characteristics and their use varies accordingly. Some of these brushes are designed specifically for decorative painting and others are artists' brushes.

Fitches are extremely useful for painting furniture and picking out mouldings. They come in a variety of shapes, with either round or square ends. Fitch is the old name of a member of the weasel family, from which hairs were plucked to make this type of brush. Today the best fitches are made from white lily bristles (and are rather similar to artists' hog-hair brushes).

Lining brushes made from hog-hair, ox-hair, polyester and sable are used for delicate freehand painting, lining furniture and marbling. Fitches and lining brushes can be used with both water- and oil-based paints.

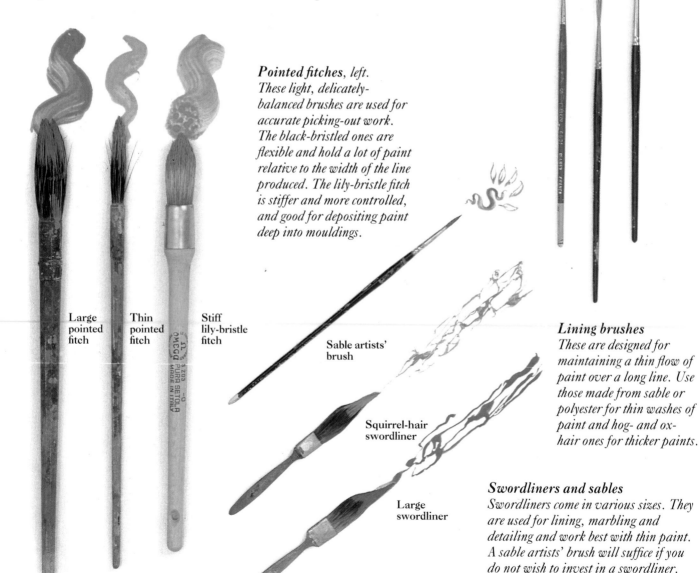

Pointed fitches, *left.*
These light, delicately-balanced brushes are used for accurate picking-out work. The black-bristled ones are flexible and hold a lot of paint relative to the width of the line produced. The lily-bristle fitch is stiffer and more controlled, and good for depositing paint deep into mouldings.

Large pointed fitch

Thin pointed fitch

Stiff lily-bristle fitch

Sable artists' brush

Squirrel-hair swordliner

Large swordliner

Lining brushes (left to right): ox-hair liner, hog-hair liner, polyester liner

Lining brushes
These are designed for maintaining a thin flow of paint over a long line. Use those made from sable or polyester for thin washes of paint and hog- and ox-hair ones for thicker paints.

Swordliners and sables
Swordliners come in various sizes. They are used for lining, marbling and detailing and work best with thin paint. A sable artists' brush will suffice if you do not wish to invest in a swordliner.

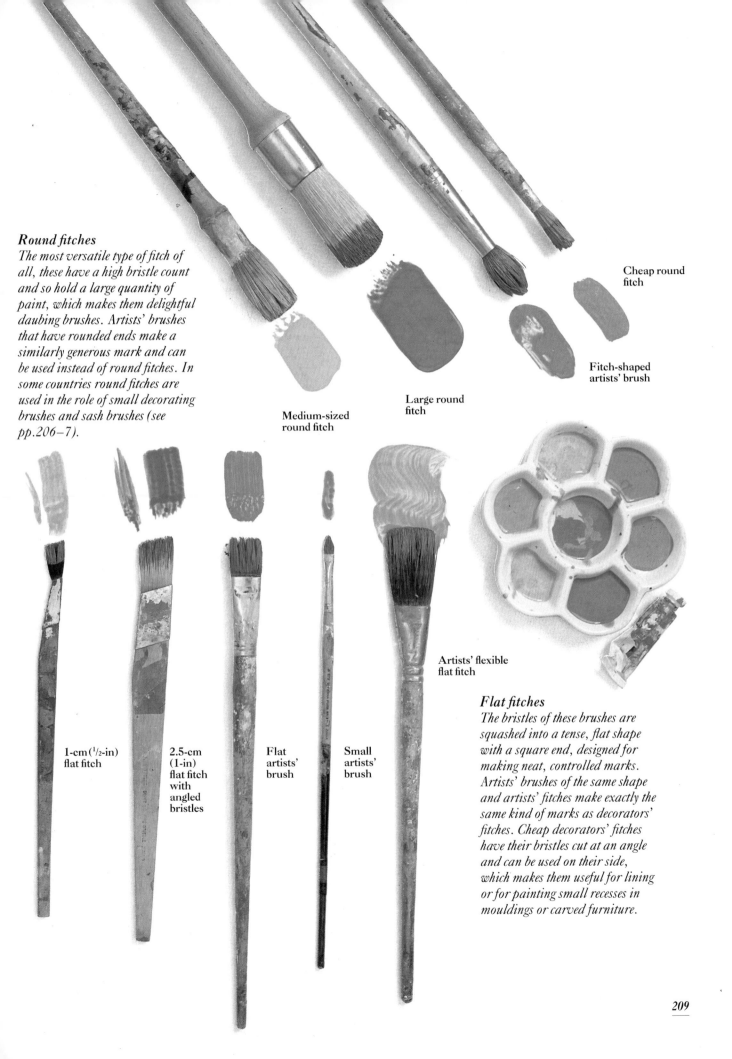

Round fitches

The most versatile type of fitch of all, these have a high bristle count and so hold a large quantity of paint, which makes them delightful daubing brushes. Artists' brushes that have rounded ends make a similarly generous mark and can be used instead of round fitches. In some countries round fitches are used in the role of small decorating brushes and sash brushes (see pp.206–7).

Medium-sized
round fitch

Large round
fitch

Fitch-shaped
artists' brush

Cheap round
fitch

1-cm (¹/₂-in)
flat fitch

2.5-cm
(1-in)
flat fitch
with
angled
bristles

Flat
artists'
brush

Small
artists'
brush

Artists' flexible
flat fitch

Flat fitches

The bristles of these brushes are squashed into a tense, flat shape with a square end, designed for making neat, controlled marks. Artists' brushes of the same shape and artists' fitches make exactly the same kind of marks as decorators' fitches. Cheap decorators' fitches have their bristles cut at an angle and can be used on their side, which makes them useful for lining or for painting small recesses in mouldings or carved furniture.

BRUSHES FOR SOFTENING & VARNISHING

SOFTENING brushes are gently pulled over wet paint or glaze to eradicate brush marks and to give a smooth finish. The badger-hair softener is the best and this is reflected in its price; the lily-bristle softener is the next best and is less expensive.

Alternative softener

The dusting brush is an excellent, cheap alternative to badger-hair or lily-bristle softeners. Made from long, soft, hog-hairs set into a resin stock and designed for smoothing wet paint, they also make effective softeners (see p.213 for the other uses of this versatile brush).

It is worth investing in high quality varnishing brushes and treating them with care because with unsuitable brushes you will achieve a disappointing result.

Choosing a varnisher

There are many different types of varnisher, including the chisel-headed brush shown below, which delivers varnish a little at a time, creating a smooth, even layer. Novices sometimes prefer a lighter brush like a long-handled lily-bristle brush or a glider.

As with all brushes, try your hand at as many as you can until you find the one that suits you.

Pointed brush for applying shellac

Brushes for varnishing
Many different types of brush can be used for varnishing, including the chisel-headed lily-bristle brush, which many people use for painting. Gliders are thin, light brushes for applying thin varnishes that need a lot of brushing out. Long-handled brushes with a generous head of bristles, like lily-bristle and hog-hair brushes, are suitable for thicker varnishes that need to flow on to the surface, rather than be brushed out. Varnish brushes should never be used with paint, for minute traces of dried paint will work their way on to your pristine varnished surface. Clean varnish brushes immediately after use and do not store next to paintbrushes.

Small glider

Large glider

Chisel-headed lily-bristle brush

Soft hog-hair brush

Brush for shellac
To apply a coat of shellac (as opposed to shellac varnishing, see p.339) use a pointed brush. Keep the brush solely for this purpose.

Stock and bristles of a decorating brush

Brushes for softening
A dusting brush (also known as a jamb duster) or the stock and bristles of a thick decorating brush can be used as effective softeners for oil glazes and emulsion washes. Make sure that you clean excess paint off the bristles as you work and that no solvent touches the resin stock – it will dissolve.

Small softeners, right. Badger brushes come in a range of shapes, their price varying according to their size. Small badger brushes are designed for softening paints and glazes on accessories and furniture. The fan badger is designed for small areas and mouldings and the pencil badger reaches into corners of frames and the panel mouldings of furniture, pulling out the frequent accumulations of colour that get left there. Other soft brushes such as delicate artists' fans, camel-hair softeners, squirrel mops and even make-up brushes can be used instead of badger-hair brushes.

Dusting brush used as a softener

Badger-hair softener
This brush, which is the crème de la crème of softening brushes, has entered the mythology of specialist decoration, partly due to its price, which is eight to ten times that of a similar-sized decorating brush. The badger-hair softener is made from the finest badger hairs set into a resin or rubber stock. Only the tips of the bristles are used, to tickle the surface of the paint to a flawless finish. I, like many others, use a dusting brush or lily-bristle softening brush instead. They are cheaper and give a good result.

Fan badger

Pencil badger

Camel-hair softener

Badger-hair softener

Small artists' fan

Make-up brush

211

SPECIALIST BRUSHES, ROCKERS & ROLLERS

THE BURGEONING interest in decorative paint techniques, fostered by the Victorians, and the previously unsurpassed displays of graining and marbling at the Great Exhibitions of Paris and London, led to the first-ever organized production of specialist tools.

Until then, the style was for more abstract finishes and artists just made do with the tools they had to hand or made their own.

Though there is now a greater range of specialist tools and brushes on the market than ever before, many just duplicate or approximate the roles of others.

The maximum number of special tools you will ever need for the effects in this book is shown here. Some of these are expensive, but wherever possible I have suggested cheaper brushes that can be used successfully to approximate the marks they make.

Checking roller and oak grain effect

Checking roller
To create an oak grain effect, paint is wiped over the steel plates of a checking roller as it is pushed along a flogged surface.

Stippler and feather
Stipplers are used to lift off flecks of glaze. The large stippler, below left, has long, finely-flagged bristles and leaves a finely freckled impression; a stronger mark can be made by increasing the pressure. If you do not want to invest in a stippler use a lily-bristle decorating brush instead. The feather was dipped in solvent and used to produce the veined lines typical of marble.

Gilding tools, *right.*
The value and fragility of gold leaf means that only the finest camel-hair brushes should be used with it. A gilders' tip is used to handle sheets of gold leaf and a mop (which must be kept grease-free) is used to dust on metallic powders.

Stencilling brushes
These have stiff, tightly-packed bristles and they are used with a brisk, dabbing action.

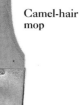

Camel-hair mop

Large stencilling brush

Stencilling brush made from a fitch

Small stencilling brush

Gilders' tip

Large stippling brush and feather

Lily-bristle
fantail
overgrainer,
right

Synthetic
fantail
overgrainer,
right

Horsehair flogging
brush dragged and
patted into glaze

Dusting brush
used here
for graining

Graining brush
and the mark
it makes

Pencil
over-
grainer

Floggers, dusters and grainers, *above*.

Each of these brushes plays a part in creating realistic woodgrain effects, while the flogger and duster have other uses too. Flogging brushes can be pushed, dragged, patted or even stippled into glaze to produce different wood effects; they also make effective draggers. The ever-useful dusting brush, which makes an excellent cheap softener, mottler and stippler, can be dragged through glaze to make a simple woodgrain impression. Graining brushes make a woodgrain texture that can be softened with an overgrainer or dusting brush. Pencil overgrainers are used to add broad bands of grain.

Rockers and combs

These are used to create authentic-looking woodgrains, fantasy woodgrains and abstract patterns. A rubber rocker will magically create the distinctive heartgrain whorls (shown right) typical of pine, which look especially convincing once the pattern has been flogged, dragged, or softened. It is easy to create fantasy grains and abstract patterns using a comb made of steel or rubber.

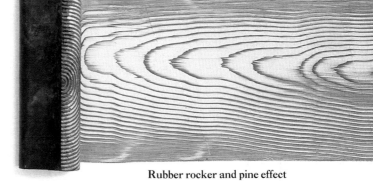

Rubber rocker and pine effect

Rubber comb and an
abstract pattern

STENCILS

THOUGH there is an abundance of ready-made stencils available, making your own allows you to be more original and to get the correct scale of design for your purposes. The *fleurs-de-lys* designs here, were inspired by illustrations in a book about medieval ornament, and they are fresh with the spontaneity that mass-produced designs often lack (see the wall in the French kitchen scheme shown on pp.90–93).

Only a few easily-obtainable tools and materials are needed to make and use stencils (the techniques are shown on pp.314–5). I nearly always use oiled manila card rather than acetate. The latter is useful for designs that need to be lined up for repeat runs but slippery to cut and altogether less "user-friendly" than manila card. I use emulsion paint (or sometimes spray paint) for most of my stencilling – they come in many colours and dry fast.

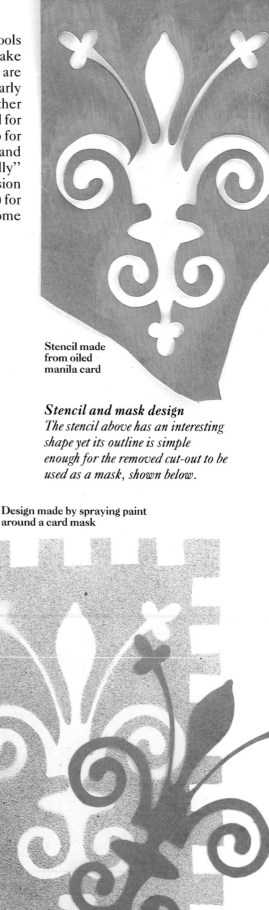

Stencil made from oiled manila card

Stencil and mask design
The stencil above has an interesting shape yet its outline is simple enough for the removed cut-out to be used as a mask, shown below.

Design made by spraying paint around a card mask

Freehand designs on tracing paper

Book of medieval ornament

AGES Nº5   MOYEN-AGE

Transferring designs
A freehand interpretation of a design from a book of medieval ornament, left, is shown on the tracing paper above (on one drawing the area to be cut out has been filled in for clarity). A photocopier with a facility for enlarging and reducing can be used to reproduce and change the scale of a design.

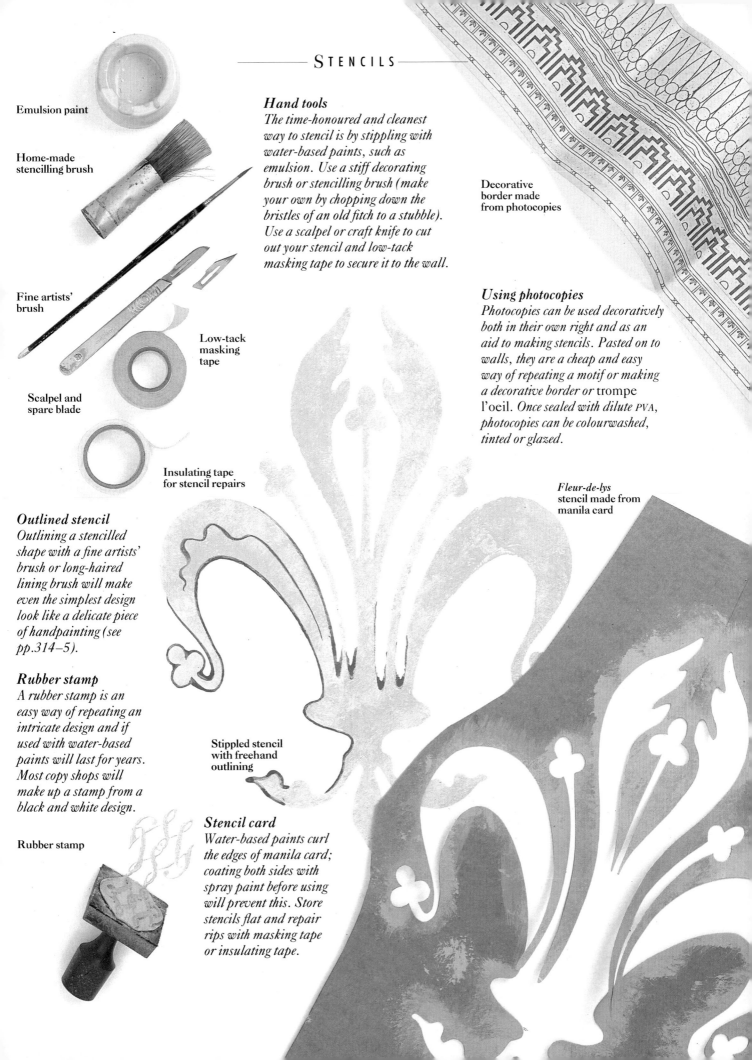

Emulsion paint

Home-made
stencilling brush

Fine artists'
brush

Scalpel and
spare blade

Low-tack
masking
tape

Insulating tape
for stencil repairs

Hand tools
The time-honoured and cleanest way to stencil is by stippling with water-based paints, such as emulsion. Use a stiff decorating brush or stencilling brush (make your own by chopping down the bristles of an old fitch to a stubble). Use a scalpel or craft knife to cut out your stencil and low-tack masking tape to secure it to the wall.

Decorative
border made
from photocopies

Using photocopies
Photocopies can be used decoratively both in their own right and as an aid to making stencils. Pasted on to walls, they are a cheap and easy way of repeating a motif or making a decorative border or trompe l'oeil. *Once sealed with dilute* PVA, *photocopies can be colourwashed, tinted or glazed.*

Fleur-de-lys
stencil made from
manila card

Outlined stencil
Outlining a stencilled shape with a fine artists' brush or long-haired lining brush will make even the simplest design look like a delicate piece of handpainting (see pp.314–5).

Rubber stamp
A rubber stamp is an easy way of repeating an intricate design and if used with water-based paints will last for years. Most copy shops will make up a stamp from a black and white design.

Rubber stamp

Stippled stencil
with freehand
outlining

Stencil card
Water-based paints curl the edges of manila card; coating both sides with spray paint before using will prevent this. Store stencils flat and repair rips with masking tape or insulating tape.

SCRAPERS, SPOONS & OTHER TOOLS

NO DECORATOR should be without a range of "sundry implements": a useful hotchpotch of tools and bits and pieces raided from toolboxes, and, more often than not, from the kitchen, the latter being the reason I so often treat paint mixing instructions as recipes.

Ingenious uses

As you try out new techniques you will discover ingenious new uses for old brushes, tools and other items. A small length of picture moulding, for example, is a useful aid to painting straight lines. The rebate of the moulding serves as a straight edge, raised just above the surface, against which to rest the ferrule of a lining brush and paint a clean, straight line, without fear of it smudging.

Window scrapers take blades and can be used to scrape paint off glass and other surfaces; they have a spacer to allow the necessary margin of paint to be left on the glass when painting window frames.

Another useful little gadget, which I discovered a use for in several techniques, is a little wire mesh basket designed for making herbal tea infusions. It has a handle and opens up so you can fill it with powders, such as powdered charcoal, whiting or fuller's earth, for dusting over surfaces.

Stiff
scrubbing brush

Wire brush

Masking tape

Household brushes and tape
Keep a scrubbing brush and a wire brush for cleaning brushes, and masking tape for painting stripes and other shapes.

Picture moulding

Wallpaper scraper

"Painters' mate"

Window
scraper

Small
scraper
for mixing
pastes

Scraper suitable
for cleaning
surfaces

Scrapers
Scrapers are invaluable for mixing filler and small quantities of plaster, making pastes, skimming the dried skin off paint, cleaning surfaces and stripping wallpaper. They range in size from the small black window scraper to the "painters' mate", which has a huge, lightweight blade that can be held as a mask when painting mouldings and straight edges.

Miscellaneous tools

All these tools get used time and time again for mixing and applying paints and solvents. The tea infuser is used for dusting on powders, the screwdriver for opening cans and old kitchen knives for mixing paints, handling small quantities of powders and for fine filling. The kitchen dropper, which has a calibrated side, useful for measuring fluids accurately, can be used for dripping solvents on to painted surfaces. The whisk is used for mixing paints and the ladle and spoon for measuring liquids and powders.

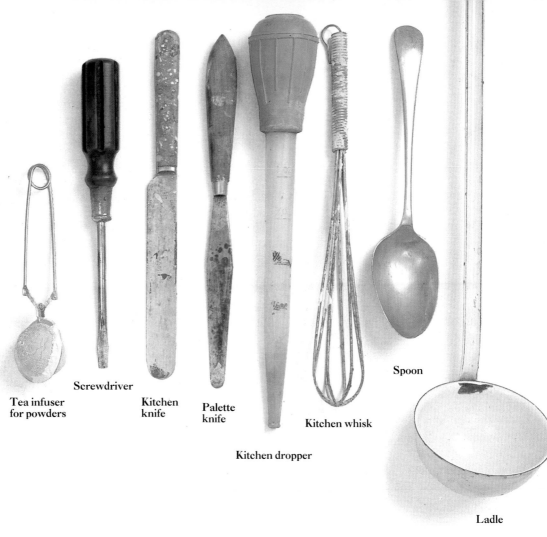

Screwdriver

Tea infuser
for powders

Kitchen
knife

Palette
knife

Kitchen whisk

Spoon

Kitchen dropper

Ladle

Other equipment

Sponges and lint-free cotton rags are used to dab, rag and mottle paint. Natural sponges have a beautiful random quality which you can go some way towards imitating by ripping up a car sponge. For cleaning up, use rags or mutton cloth (also known as stockinette) and, for preparation and finishing, a sanding block and several grades of sandpaper and wire wool, down to flour grade sandpaper and grade 0000 wire wool.

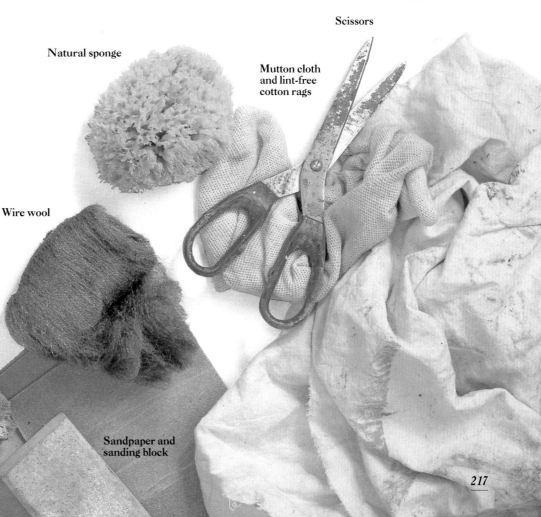

Scissors

Natural sponge

Mutton cloth
and lint-free
cotton rags

Wire wool

Ripped-up
car sponge

Sandpaper and
sanding block

CARE OF BRUSHES

IT PAYS TO take care of your brushes as, treated well, a good brush can last for as long as fifteen or twenty years.

Preparing new brushes

All new brushes, good and bad, have a few loose bristles that should be removed before you use the brush. To do this, tap the ferrule (the metal brace on the brush handle) firmly on a table edge, or spin the brush between the palms of your hands. The loose bristles will then work their way out. (This will also dislodge any dust.)

If this does not work, you can always copy the traditional decorator's trick of breaking in a new brush. This is to use the new brush for exterior painting work, for a while, only bringing it indoors when you are sure no more bristles are going to work loose. By this stage, the shape of the brush tip will have been worked to a tapered chisel head – the standard shape for fine paint-finishing.

Cleaning and storing

Ideally all brushes ought to be cleaned thoroughly on the day they are used, and then dried and stored. It is all too easy to leave a brush standing in a jar of solvent for weeks on end until you find the solvent evaporated away and the brush stiff and bent, its bristles stuck to a cake of grey residue at the bottom of the jar. Yet the point about buying expensive brushes is that you never allow yourself to treat them in such a vindictive way!

Store all brushes in a clean, dry atmosphere, preferably in a cupboard where dust cannot settle on them. And make sure the space is ventilated to stop mildew forming.

If you intend to put away your brushes for more than a few weeks, wrap the bristles in newspaper so the brushes keep their shape, and secure the paper around the brushes with a rubber band.

To store brushes in the long term, drill through the handles of large brushes and suspend them from hooks. Small brushes can be stored upside-down in a jar.

You can leave a brush with paint on for an hour or so, provided that you wrap it in a rag (dampened with water for water-based paints or turpentine for oil-based paints) or tin foil. This will keep out the air and stop the paint drying.

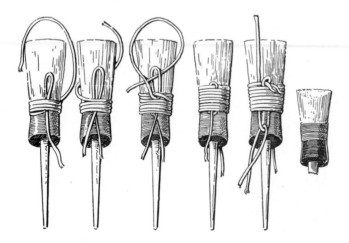

Making a chisel head Decorators used to bind new round brushes with string, carefully "working in" the bristles to create a chisel head.

CLEANING BRUSHES

Always start by leaving the brush suspended in solvent (see the table on pp.328–31 for the appropriate solvent) for a few minutes. Work the brush in the solvent until it looks clean, then wash it with warm water and soap. Do not use detergent as it can be too harsh. Rinse the brush well in clean water. It is best not to leave brushes suspended in turpentine overnight, as this tends to harden the bristles. If soaking in water, make sure the water does not cover the handle, which can swell and split. If your brushes have been left standing in solvent for weeks and seem beyond repair, try revitalizing them with a proprietary brush cleaner.

Scrubbing a paintbrush This is the ideal way of dealing with dried-on emulsion paint.

Using a wire brush For paint that has really dried hard, a wire brush is all you can use!

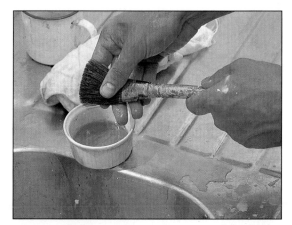

Using solvents Water-based paints such as emulsion are so quick-drying that, no matter how fast you work, they dry on to the brush. To clean, dip the brush into methylated spirits and work the solvent into the bristles with your fingers. Brushes used for oil-based paints such as eggshell should be cleaned with turpentine.

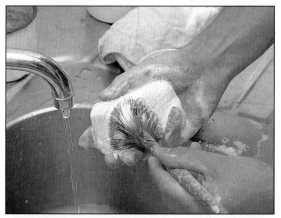

Using soap Brushes that have been cleaned with methylated spirits or turpentine should be washed using warm water and simple unperfumed soap. Work the soap well into the bristles so that you reach the ferrule and then wash the brush repeatedly until the rinsing water runs clear.

Shaping brushes Flick as much water as possible out of the brush so that it does not take too long to dry. Then comb the damp bristles out using a scrubbing brush. Finally, squeeze the brush between your fingers to shape it.

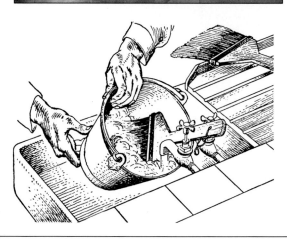

Washing large brushes Another way of cleaning large brushes is to swish them around in a bowl or bucket of water. This lets the water circulate freely between the bristles. The dirty water should be changed frequently.

BRUSH STORAGE

Decorators have used a variety of gadgets for suspending brushes in water or solvent; modern equivalents are sold today. Hanging up brushes is a traditional method of storage.

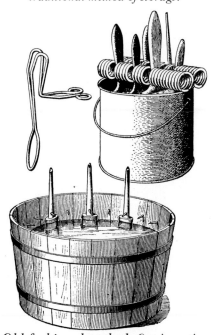

Old-fashioned methods One invention for suspending brushes was a spring system; another used special hooks. A simpler solution was to drive nails into a wooden pail.

Air ventilation The best way to store paintbrushes is to hang them up in a ventilated cupboard. This lets the air circulate between them and the brushes will keep their shape much better than if they are stored flat.

PIGMENTS & HOME-MADE PAINTS

INTERIOR decoration has ancient origins. Over six thousand years ago the citizens of Jericho painted the lower half of their walls with a red pigment, iron oxide, mixed with a binder in the form of a primitive glue. Today's paints, both manufactured and home-made, are not so very different: pigments (concentrated natural or synthetic colours) are mixed with a binder that dries on exposure to the air.

Making your own paint

Home-made paint has pleasant handling qualities and gives a unique finish. The ingredients are cheap and you can make exactly the colour you want.

Pigments are readily available as powder colour and are contained in artists' oil paints for decorating with. Powder colours can be mixed with a range of glues, including PVA and bone glue to make a paste that closely resembles the paint made over six thousand years ago. Artists' oil paints and universal stainers can be mixed with transparent oil glaze to make a translucent glaze suitable for many decorative finishes.

It is important to bear in mind that some pigments have much greater staining power (colour strength when diluted or mixed) than others and some fade in contact with materials. The table on pages 324–7 gives details of their various properties.

Kitchen knife

Palette knife

Tools for mixing
Old kitchen knives and palette knives are ideal for mixing up paints. Use a kitchen sieve to grade powder colours before mixing.

Transparent oil glaze
One of the most useful decorating media is a nineteenth-century invention called transparent oil glaze, which you can buy ready-made or make yourself (see p.332). Pigments, in the form of artists' oil paints, or universal stainers, are mixed with it to create a medium with unique qualities.

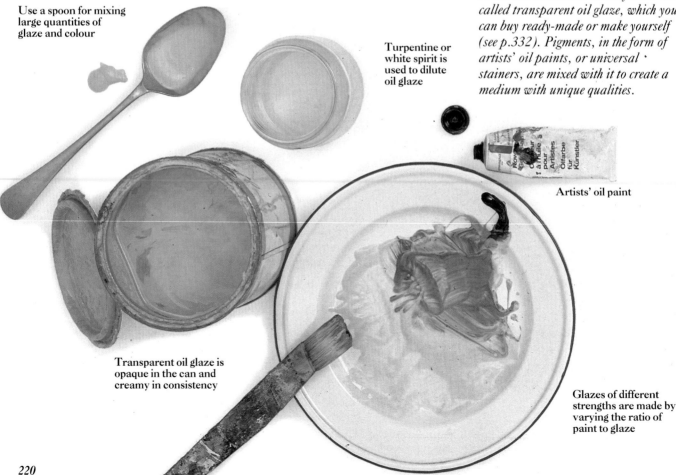

Use a spoon for mixing large quantities of glaze and colour

Turpentine or white spirit is used to dilute oil glaze

Artists' oil paint

Transparent oil glaze is opaque in the can and creamy in consistency

Glazes of different strengths are made by varying the ratio of paint to glaze

Rabbit-skin glue can be used to make paint and is an ingredient of gesso (see p.230)

Cooled bone glue is a clear jelly

Bone glue (also called pearl glue) is soaked and then heated

PVA can be mixed with powder colours to make paint

Simple water-based paints

The ingredients above are types of glue, which can be mixed with water and powder colours to make an extremely cheap paint with qualities that are ideal for colourwashing and special effects, such as grisaille *(see pp.320–21)*. To make a traditional glue-based paint, like that used in the theatre, use an animal gelatin such as bone glue or rabbit-skin glue. These are available from specialist suppliers *(see p.340)* and need to be diluted with water and heated to transparency in a double boiler *(above right)* before powder colours are added. Alternatively, you can follow the instructions on page 333 and make paint from powder colours and PVA, which is a modern, water-based glue.

Raw sienna is a tan brown

Burnt sienna, an intense terracotta red, is made from heated raw sienna

Yellow ochre, an intense mustard colour, dilutes to a bright, sunshine yellow

Red ochre is also called red oxide

Earth colours

The earth colour pigments, whether in powder form, like those shown on the left, or contained in tube colours, as artists' oil paints, have the most ancient origins. They are called earth colours because they are dug from the ground and their names often indicate their origin. The Umber colours, for example, come from the Italian region of Umbria, and terra verde *(Italian for "green earth")* is exactly that. Their natural charm as colours makes them invaluable for tinting, dulling and antiquing. The earth colour pigments, both in powder and liquid form, are cheaper than other pigments.

Raw umber is an excellent brown for antiquing (see p.270)

Burnt umber is a richer, more chocolatey colour than raw umber

PROPRIETARY PAINTS

THE ARRAY of paints on the market may at first seem bewildering, but once you know which paint dilutes in which solvent, you can begin to distinguish the main categories of paint. It is the binder in the paint – which is used to hold the paint together – that determines which solvent can be used to dilute the paint and to clean it off brushes. Some paints, such as gloss and eggshell, are oil-based and these are all soluble in white spirit, while others, like emulsion, which are water-based, are water-soluble.

As a general rule, paints that have the same binder can be mixed together. So you can mix emulsion with another water-based paint like artists' acrylic. A look at the information on the side of the paint container will tell you what kind of paint it is and you can refer to the table on pages 328–31, which gives the properties of proprietary paints.

Spray paints
These tough, quick-drying paints (often formulated for retouching car bodywork) are useful for colouring small areas and for stencilling. Different colours can be sprayed one on top of another to give delicate blendings of colour. Look for CFC-free sprays and use in a well-ventilated area.

Water-based inks are available as writing ink, artists' ink or concentrated watercolours

Shading from a spray paint

Spray paints

Gouache and acrylic paint can be mixed with water-based inks

Inks, above.
Water-based inks are a useful addition to the painter's repertoire. They can be spattered in antiquing techniques (see p.268) and can be used instead of powder colour for mixing into PVA to make a quick-drying, transparent glaze. Indian ink gives the densest black, even when diluted, and dries to give a waterproof finish.

Primers
Most bare surfaces need a coat of primer so that subsequent coats of paint will bond (see pp.232–45 for surface preparation).

Tube colours
Acrylics and gouache are water-soluble artists' paints. Gouache is denser and has less intense hues than acrylics. Both can be used for colouring water-based paints.

Tubes of water-based gouache

Zinc primer (left) for aluminium

Red oxide primer (far left) for steel

Water-based artists' acrylics

Thick and flexible acrylic primer for canvas

Specialist paints

There are a number of specialist paints on the market, like this paint which creates a broken effect like that of hammered metal.

Hammer-finish enamel paint

Gloss: an oil-based paint

Oil-based or alkyd paints

Paints like gloss and eggshell, which are usually loosely described as oil-based, are these days usually bound with a synthetic alkyd resin. They can be tinted with universal stainers or artists' oil paints.

Household enamel paint

Modellers' enamel paint

Eggshell paint

This oil-based paint gives a reasonably "flat" finish that is the ideal base for oil glazes. It is slow drying and requires even and careful application.

Green oil paint mixed into gloss

Eggshell: an oil-based paint

Paint finishes

Note the different reflective qualities of the various types of paint on the plate, above.

Artists' oil paints

The composition of artists' oil paints – pigment and linseed oil – has barely changed since the fifteenth century. Like universal stainers, they can be used to tint oil-based paints, oil glazes and varnishes.

Paint manufacturer's colour swatch cards

Poster paints

Poster paints are water-based. They are useful for freehand work and for tinting other water-based paints.

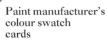

Poster paints

Emulsion: a water-soluble paint

Artists' oil paints

Universal stainer – widely available chemical dye

Emulsion paint

This tough, water-based paint can be used to paint walls, floors and furniture. It can be tinted with universal stainers.

223

VARNISHES & GLAZES

VARNISHES are categorized according to their main ingredient and the solvent with which they can be diluted. The three groups of varnish that are shown here are: oil-based (which dilute in turpentine), water-based (which dilute in water), and alcohol-based (which dilute in methylated spirits).

Each type of varnish within these groups has varying qualities and properties and, according to these, different decorative and practical uses (for a summary see the table on pp.328–31).

The conventional role of most household varnishes is to form a protective coating over a plain or painted surface but these, and other types of varnish, can be used decoratively, to create a layer of translucent colour. Some specialist varnishes, such as French enamel varnish, come ready-coloured; most household varnishes do not, but they can be coloured with tube paints or powder colours (see the table on pp.328–31).

Using oil glaze

For a really smooth layer of translucent colour it is best to use transparent oil glaze. It is less sticky than varnish and much easier to manipulate to a flawless finish. It does not dry hard but can be protected with a layer of clear varnish.

Crackle varnish:
a two-part varnish

Crackle varnish

This is sold as a pack of two varnishes that work against each other to create a decorative cracked finish on many surfaces (see pp.268–9). Crackle varnish was invented in eighteenth-century France to imitate the fine web of cracks (known as craquelure) *on Eastern lacquerwork and pottery.*

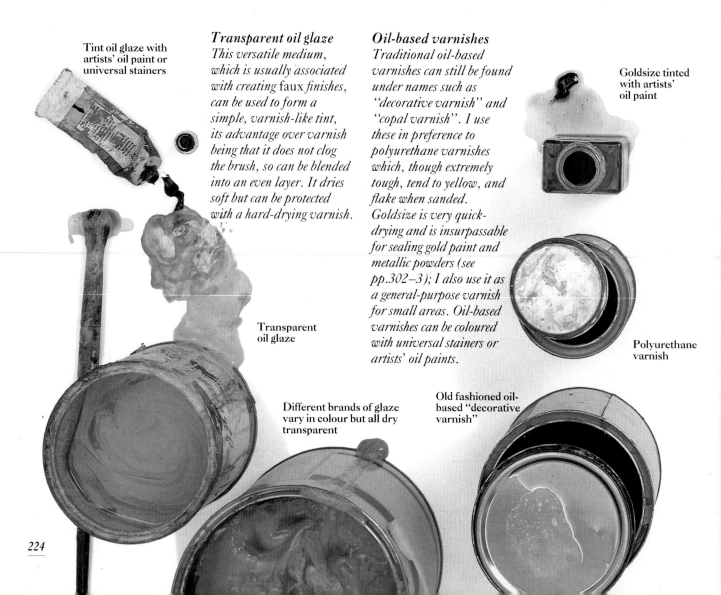

Tint oil glaze with artists' oil paint or universal stainers

Transparent oil glaze
This versatile medium, which is usually associated with creating faux *finishes, can be used to form a simple, varnish-like tint, its advantage over varnish being that it does not clog the brush, so can be blended into an even layer. It dries soft but can be protected with a hard-drying varnish.*

Transparent oil glaze

Different brands of glaze vary in colour but all dry transparent

Oil-based varnishes
Traditional oil-based varnishes can still be found under names such as "decorative varnish" and "copal varnish". I use these in preference to polyurethane varnishes which, though extremely tough, tend to yellow, and flake when sanded. Goldsize is very quick-drying and is insurpassable for sealing gold paint and metallic powders (see pp.302–3); I also use it as a general-purpose varnish for small areas. Oil-based varnishes can be coloured with universal stainers or artists' oil paints.

Old fashioned oil-based "decorative varnish"

Goldsize tinted with artists' oil paint

Polyurethane varnish

Shellac
Made from a sticky brown goo secreted by the lac insect, shellac is used neat for some techniques (like that on pp.270–71) but when diluted with methylated spirits makes a quick-drying varnish. There are several grades, ranging from standard brown shellac to fine-grade orange shellac. Bleached shellac, sold as white polish, is used for French polishing pale woods.

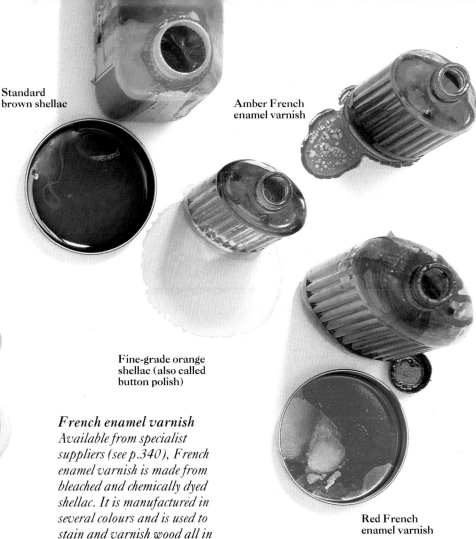

Standard brown shellac

Amber French enamel varnish

Fine-grade orange shellac (also called button polish)

Red French enamel varnish

White polish is bleached shellac

Sanding sealer

Sanding sealer *Shellac is the main ingredient of sanding sealer, which is used for sealing bare wood prior to varnishing.*

French enamel varnish
Available from specialist suppliers (see p.340), French enamel varnish is made from bleached and chemically dyed shellac. It is manufactured in several colours and is used to stain and varnish wood all in one process. Some colours are bright and coarse, but can be diluted with methylated spirits to create subtler tones. The earthier colours, such as amber and chestnut brown, are amongst the most pleasing.

Water-based varnishes, *right. The past ten years have seen the increased use of acrylic and vinyl resin varnishes that are held in suspension in water. For most general varnishing I use PVA and its waterproof sister EVA (both vinyl varnishes). PVA and EVA are cheap, widely available and can be used to seal porous surfaces such as plaster, as a protective varnish for wallpaper and photocopy découpage work (see pp.318–9) and for binding home-made paints (see p.333). For small areas I often use artists' acrylic varnish, which is waterproof and non-yellowing.*

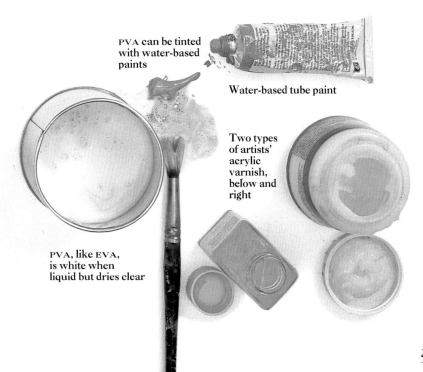

PVA can be tinted with water-based paints

Water-based tube paint

Two types of artists' acrylic varnish, below and right

PVA, like EVA, is white when liquid but dries clear

225

SOLVENTS

SOLVENTS are most commonly associated with the practical tasks of diluting paints and varnishes and cleaning brushes (see the details on pp.328–31), but they can also be spattered and sponged on to painted and glazed surfaces to make random patterns.

Effects with solvents
The solvents featured here are turpentine (white spirit can be used as an alternative), methylated spirits, water, and acetone. Some paint and solvent combinations have no effect at all, but when there is a reaction it is often dramatic. The results are ideal for marbling (see pp.294–5), scrubbed limewash (pp.254–5) and general patinated effects (pp.306–7). The thinner the layer of paint or glaze on to which the solvent is applied, the more striking the finish will be.

When spattering with solvents, remember always to protect your eyes with a pair of goggles (when spattering with acetone it is important to protect your hands too).

Acetone
Acetones are a range of complex solvents that react with oil-based paints such as gloss and eggshell. They are dangerous, so should be used with care and never in a confined space. Acetone reacts immediately when spattered or lightly sponged on to wet paint, but must be left for 30 minutes after being applied to dry paint and then rubbed with a clean cloth to reveal a pattern of spot marks and worn areas. Any remaining solvent will evaporate and any untouched areas of softened paint will re-harden.

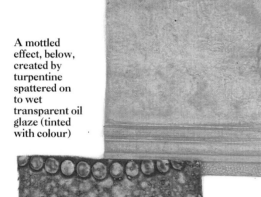

A mottled effect, below, created by turpentine spattered on to wet transparent oil glaze (tinted with colour)

Turpentine flicked on to wet oil-based paint produces soft patches, left

Acetone flicked on to dry oil-based paint and then rubbed, creates spots and worn areas

Turpentine and white spirit
Turpentine is a clear solvent that is distilled from pine tree resin. White spirit (also called turpentine substitute), which is slightly thinner and much more unpleasant smelling than turpentine, is used more widely because it is cheaper. White spirit and turpentine react identically on wet oil-based paints and oil glazes, but do not react at all on dry surfaces. When used on diluted oil-based paints, above, they produce subtle patches, while their effect on oil glaze, left, produces mottled patterns of extraordinary detail. Both are highly toxic.

Turpentine, above, has the same properties as white spirit (also called turpentine substitute)

Always protect your hands and eyes when using solvents

Methylated spirits flicked on to dry emulsion and then rubbed gives a patchy finish, right

The effect of methylated spirits on a layer of wet, diluted emulsion, below

Methylated spirit can be spattered on to wet or dry French enamel varnish, below

Methylated spirits

Methylated spirits is ethyl alcohol, "denatured" by the addition of naphtha and methyl violet to render it undrinkable. Use it principally to dilute shellac or French enamel varnish (see pp.224–5). You can also flick, sponge or dribble it on to wet or dry emulsion to create a distressed effect. When spattered on to French enamel varnish, left, it creates patterns of a marble-like depth and complexity, similar to those created by turpentine or white spirit on a wet oil glaze; the effect of methylated spirits spattered on to wet emulsion is "flatter".

Methylated spirits

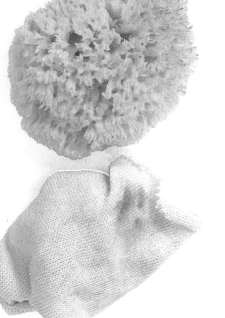

The soft effect of water spattered on to a coat of wet, diluted emulsion

Water

Water is the cheapest of solvents. It is used to dilute water-based paints such as emulsion and can be used to create patterns on surfaces painted with a coat of watered-down emulsion or a wash of PVA. The unique pattern created by water complements that produced by methylated spirits and the two look highly effective when worked together. As with any fluid that is also the diluting agent, take care not to apply too much water, or you will wash the paint away. Water is also used in a number of techniques before applying washes of paint.

Applying solvents

It is easiest to use a brush to flood a horizontal surface with solvent, but for vertical surfaces like walls it is better to use sponges or rags, making sure you wring them out first.

Water is a convenient solvent, but slow to dry

PASTES & POWDERS

YOU CAN use simple materials to make pastes and mixtures that will transform the most mundane of surfaces, imitating wood, for example, that has the patina of years of dust and polish, weather-worn sandstone, faded terracotta or ancient, encrusted verdigris. *Faux* effects like these have an ancient heritage – in the eighteenth century a mixture of lime, sand and plaster dust was used to imitate stone.

Using plaster

The potential of plaster as a decorative wall finish is often overlooked. Smooth plaster is usually painted, while textured plaster effects tend to be associated with attempts to disguise shoddy structures. Smooth, bare plaster walls have a refreshing elegance – you can colour white plaster by adding powder colours. Ancient plaster walls have a dramatic simplicity that you can imitate by applying plaster over blobs of wax (see the technique on pp.274–5).

Finding suitable materials

Some of the materials shown here, for example whiting and fuller's earth, are only found in specialist suppliers (see pp.340-41) but those like sand and plaster are available from builder's merchants or do-it-yourself shops.

Plastic shapes

Using pastes

Use pastes and powders to transform ordinary plastic shapes, like those above, into pieces of verdigrised ornament or antique wood.

Wet plaster

Textured plaster

Decorators' white plaster

Plaster

Decorators' plaster is available in standard grey or pink, as well as white, which is a useful medium for tinting with powder colours. Like plaster of Paris, decorators' plaster is a gypsum plaster, but because it has a much slower drying time it can be manipulated with a plastic bag or trowel.

Powdered rottenstone

Beeswax furniture polish

Waxed ornament

Beeswax mixed with rottenstone

Fuller's earth

Gesso

For centuries gesso has been used to prime wood to make a completely smooth finish over which to paint or gild. The basic recipe comprises whiting and rabbit-skin glue (see the instructions on p.332 for how to make this traditional version and a synthetic variation using PVA).

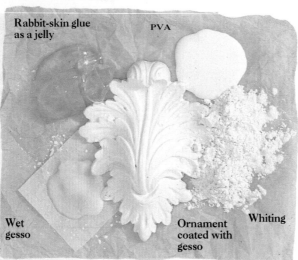

Rabbit-skin glue as a jelly

PVA

Wet gesso

Ornament coated with gesso

Whiting

Waxes, *above.*

Antiquing waxes are easy to make and can be used as a decorative finish in their own right, or in the ageing and distressing of wood, where they are used to simulate the effect of years of dust worn into furniture polish. To make an antiquing wax, mix beeswax polish and a little turpentine and then add colour in the form of fuller's earth, powdered rottenstone or powder colours. Alternatively, oil paints or even shoe polish can also be used to colour wax.

Mixing pastes

Most pastes are extremely quick-drying and mucky, so mix them in disposable containers such as jam jars and yoghurt pots. Use a knife for mixing – a brush will become hopelessly clogged. Keep lids and plastic film at hand to cover the containers and prevent the pastes drying up too quickly.

Palette knife and rottenstone

Emulsion

Whiting

Whiting can be patted on to the damp paste

Methylated spirits

Paste for imitation verdigris

Verdigris paste

Some metal effects, such as the imitation of verdigris, require a crumbling texture. Use a paste made from emulsion paint, whiting and methylated spirits. The whiting adds body to the paste and the methylated spirits curdles the paint to give it a crumbly consistency.

Beeswax furniture polish

Limed ornament

White powder colour

Liming wax

Liming wax

Wood used to be disinfected with a paste of caustic lime. Now an inert antiquing wax is used. This contains beeswax furniture polish and a harmless white pigment such as white oil paint or powder. It is simple to make but is available ready-made. Liming wax can also be used for antiquing plasterwork.

PVA

Sand

Sand and PVA paste

Sand texture

A sand texture is used for imitating rust and some types of stone, where an all-over gritty texture is needed. Cover the surface in glue (either spray glue or undiluted PVA) and pat, blow or throw dry sand at the surface. Use fine-grade sand for small objects such as lamps.

Sand

PVA

Deep sandstone texture

To imitate the highly-textured relief of some of the more distressed and eroded types of stone, apply a paste on top of the sand texture, shown left. Mix sand and undiluted PVA to make an extremely thick paste and apply this with a spatula. Paint the surface when the paste is dry.

GILDING MATERIALS

THE ART of gilding has a mystique about it – justifiably so in the case of water gilding, which is a highly specialized skill, but oil gilding (see pp.302–3) is simple and it need not be expensive.

Oil gilding involves laying transfer leaf (either real gold or its inexpensive counterpart, Dutch metal) over a layer of a tacky varnish called goldsize. For a silky smooth finish, the area to be gilded is prepared with several layers of gesso. This comes ready-made in white, red or ochre or you can make your own using the ingredients shown below (see p.332 for detailed instructions). Red gesso glows through transfer leaf and any tiny cracks in it to give a rich warmth and antique appearance; yellow ochre gesso serves to disguise cracks in the transfer leaf and intensify its colour.

Powders

Metallic powders (available in a wide range of colours, including gold) can be shaken on to tacky goldsize for a gilt finish. They can also be mixed with varnish to make gold paint and used with transfer leaf to imitate an effect called combination gilding; the real version is created by a combination of oil and water gilding. Suppliers of gilding materials are listed on page 340.

Oil-gilded emblem patinated with French enamel varnish

Self-adhesive gold tape

Sprayed surface gilded with transfer leaf

Ready-made gesso comes in red, ochre and white

Rabbit-skin glue as a powder, below, and as a jelly, after heating, below left

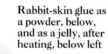

Whiting

Home-made gesso mix

Gesso

Layers of gesso are painted on and polished to make a surface smooth before gilding (see pp.302–3). Gesso is available ready-made or you can make your own from whiting (powdered chalk) and rabbit-skin glue or PVA (see p.332 for gesso recipes).

Special effects

Water gilding is often done over a layer of coloured clay (usually red), which shows through cracks in the gold leaf. You can imitate this effect with oil gilding, by applying transfer leaf over coloured gesso (buy this ready-made or colour home-made gesso with red ochre powder colour) or red spray paint. Use self-adhesive gold tape to imitate strips of gold leaf, and French enamel varnish, dilute emulsion or ink to patinate your work (see pp.306–7).

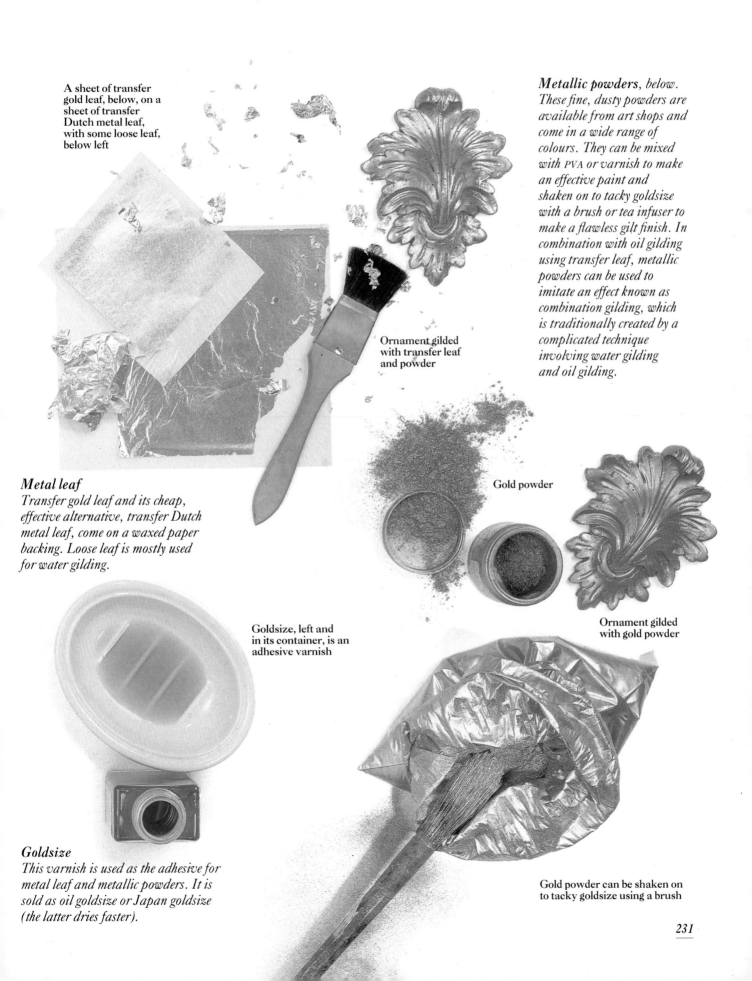

A sheet of transfer
gold leaf, below, on a
sheet of transfer
Dutch metal leaf,
with some loose leaf,
below left

Metallic powders, *below.*
These fine, dusty powders are
available from art shops and
come in a wide range of
colours. They can be mixed
with PVA or varnish to make
an effective paint and
shaken on to tacky goldsize
with a brush or tea infuser to
make a flawless gilt finish. In
combination with oil gilding
using transfer leaf, metallic
powders can be used to
imitate an effect known as
combination gilding, which
is traditionally created by a
complicated technique
involving water gilding
and oil gilding.

Ornament gilded
with transfer leaf
and powder

Metal leaf
Transfer gold leaf and its cheap,
effective alternative, transfer Dutch
metal leaf, come on a waxed paper
backing. Loose leaf is mostly used
for water gilding.

Gold powder

Ornament gilded
with gold powder

Goldsize, left and
in its container, is an
adhesive varnish

Goldsize
This varnish is used as the adhesive for
metal leaf and metallic powders. It is
sold as oil goldsize or Japan goldsize
(the latter dries faster).

Gold powder can be shaken on
to tacky goldsize using a brush

231

PLASTER & STONE

THE PRIMITIVE quality and archaeological associations of bare rough plaster, stone, marble and terracotta are most suited to rooms with a Mediterranean, country/ethnic, ancient or medieval slant. But polished marble and some glazed terracotta, particularly when they are laid in complex patterns, are also suited to rooms decorated in a grander, neo-Classical style.

Appreciating uneven plaster
Old, crumbly plaster walls make such an atmospheric alternative to flat, plainly painted walls that I devised a special technique (see pp.274–5), in which new plaster is applied and textured to resemble genuinely old walls. The plaster should be mixed in a bucket as shown below.

Flat plaster
Smooth plastering is a highly skilled operation and usually best undertaken by a professional plasterer. Small holes or unwanted cracks, however, can easily be disguised with filler (a fine plaster, available in small quantities).

Tools
To apply new plaster you need a trowel, for filling cracks, a scraper, and for scraping off loose plaster, a shavehook. Hemp scrim together with fibreglass make up the fibre in cast plasterwork, like the moulding at the top of the page.

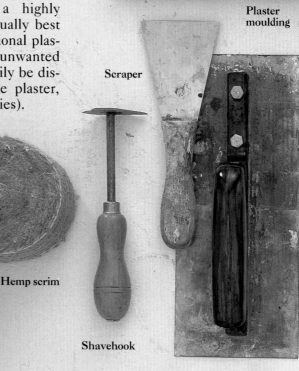

Plaster moulding

Scraper

Hemp scrim

Shavehook

Trowel

WORKING WITH PLASTER

Mixing plaster *Shake plaster into water until it peaks just above the surface. Mix and then transfer to an upturned dustbin lid for working.*

Stabilizing *Old and flaking plaster walls, distemper and old porous paint should be brushed with stabilizing solution before decorating.*

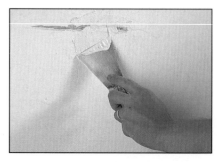

Filling *To fill small cracks, rake out any loose plaster, dampen the surface and apply new plaster or filler with a scraper. Sand flat when dry.*

Plaster mouldings

Decorative plaster is an essential element of many period styles. Standard designs, like the one above, are readily available from most DIY stores and builder's merchants; less common designs can be obtained from specialist suppliers. In the last century, mouldings were made in position (a basic frame was shaped and precast enrichments plastered in), but today they are usually precast in quick-setting gypsum plaster. They should be plastered into walls (by a professional) or, in the case of lighter mouldings, screwed in.

Black granite

Terracotta tiles

Made from fired clay, terracotta is perhaps the warmest coloured building material and suits country and Mediterranean style interiors, in particular. To appreciate its natural qualities, use it in the form of clear-glazed or unglazed wall or floor tiles (the latter should be bedded in sand and cement). Alternatively, reproduce the qualities of terracotta with paint (see pp.284–5) and varnish the finish to make it hardwearing. Or, colour concrete tiles with woodstain and coat them with matt varnish.

Terracotta tile

Serpentine marble, left

Marble and stone

Marble is the name given to any stone that can be polished to a hard, glossy finish, including granite. Scagliola (a dough of pigment, lime, marble dust and glue) is a traditional fake-marble material. Paint has long been used to imitate marble – the price of real marble makes this or the use of marble offcuts popular (some marbles scratch too easily to be used for floors). Other stones that can be used for floors include slate and sandstone.

African slate floor tiles, above

233

DECORATING PLASTER

MANY DECORATIVE paint effects, such as colour-washing and patterned glazework, are suitable for smooth (and sometimes rough) plaster walls. The preparation required for special paint effects varies; details are given with each technique.

Decorative mouldings

Plaster also comes in the form of mouldings, which have formed an integral part of many interiors since the eighteenth century. As an alternative to painting these (and possibly glazing them too, as shown on pp.256–7), I devised a simple method of antiquing (pp.272–3), which gives plasterwork a natural-looking, mellow bloom.

Types of plaster

Most modern decorators' plasters are gypsum plasters. Quick-setting plaster of Paris (some mouldings are cast from these and it is useful for repairing them) is one form of gypsum plaster and there is a range of slower-drying varieties. Wall plasters are sold in two grades (bonding and finishing coat) or as a one-coat plaster, and come in many colours. Modern plaster powders absorb water and if used after a month or two of storage will dry faster, making work difficult.

Plaster for walls and mouldings can be mixed with powder colours. Follow the instructions on page 333 and only use alkali-resistant colours (these are listed on pp.324–7).

Traditional plaster is made of lime, sand and often horsehair or some other fibre. Old houses that have never had a damp-proof course should be plastered with a traditional lime-based plaster and then painted with distemper (see p.332) to allow for the natural evaporation of moisture.

Drying out

Freshly plastered walls or newly cast decorative plasterwork should be allowed to dry out for several weeks (or ideally several months) before decorating, to allow for the full evaporation of moisture from the surface; otherwise the paint may bubble and flake off.

Preparing bare plaster

Bare plaster that is to be painted with emulsion should be sealed with PVA or a coat of emulsion diluted to half its strength with water. Before painting with oil-based paints, coat the plaster with PVA or an alkali-resistant primer. Shellac is an alternative sealant that can be used before applying both water-based and oil-based paints.

Painting in plaster
Fresco is one of the oldest types of painting; a mixture of powder pigment and water is applied to a coat of half-set, freshly applied lime plaster. As the plaster dries it absorbs the wet paint, bonding it into the top layer. I painted the cherub fresco above in this way using alkali-resistant powder colours (these do not fade in contact with lime).

Gilded plaster *This cherub, cast in plaster of Paris, was sealed with a coat of shellac, sprayed with red oxide spray paint and gilded with metal leaf.*

IMITATION STUCCOWORK

I dipped rope in plaster of Paris to match the tassels and give the appearance of stuccowork.

Antiqued plaster cornice

Antique finish
One of the most effective ways of decorating fresh plaster-work is with shellac and liming wax (see the antiquing technique on pp.272–3). The resulting alabaster-like sheen belies the relative cheapness of the actual materials underneath. The technique is as suitable for large areas of plasterwork, such as the cornice above, as small plaster mouldings. It is important to leave small castings for several days before antiquing, to allow moisture to evaporate.

Casting plaster
Plaster mouldings can be bought in a variety of styles or you can experiment with casting your own. Use plaster of Paris and mould-making materials from craft shops. I made the tassel, below left, and coated the plaster with shellac. When this was dry, it was painted with red and brown French enamel varnishes (see p.225). To show up the highlights I rubbed off some of the dry French enamel varnish with a little methylated spirits. Alternatively, castings can be painted or antiqued like the cornice shown above.

Using other materials
Even wooden or plastic mouldings, like the shapes on the left (which I bought from a decorating supplier) can be paint-finished to look like old plaster. This makes it possible to make really fine ornament (which it is not possible to cast from plaster) fit in with other antiqued features in a room. To extend the warmth of plaster to a whole wall use the pink-tinted paint finish on page 183.

Plastic castings with a pink plaster paint finish

Home-made plaster casting

Corbels and bowl
The technique used on the cornice at the top of the page is just as effective on the corbels and bowl, right (I used the latter as a lampshade on p.63). These mouldings would be at or near ceiling height but the resulting finish is so soft and beautiful and can withstand such close scrutiny that it warrants use on eye-level objects too. So satisfying is the finish that it encourages you to buy castings to hang on your wall, like the panels on page 75.

Antiqued corbels

Antiqued bowl

NATURAL WOOD

WOODS THAT have been treated so that the natural character of the grain can be appreciated (either by varnishing, polishing or oiling with a clear medium) have a friendly and warm appearance. Before applying standard varnishes (see pp.224–5), wood should first be prepared as described, right. Beeswax furniture polish nourishes wood as well as giving it a pleasing, soft finish and a scent of honey.

Choosing wood

The world is being depleted of more natural forest than can be replaced, so buy wood that comes from a renewable source, such as pine from Scandinavia, in preference to Brazilian hardwoods, which come from tropical rain forests.

If you plan to paint wood the standard way or to woodgrain it (the latter is shown on p.239) you will obliterate its natural qualities anyway, so consider using fibreboard, chipboard or hardboard, all of which are products of timber waste.

Most softwoods such as pine and spruce are relatively inexpensive and hence popular in the home. Some have an attractive grain, which you may choose to enhance by giving a clear finish, but often it is not particularly interesting and looks best when painted.

Hardwoods, such as oak, elm, ash, walnut, beech and mahogany are, as their name suggests, harder, and they have subtler and prettier grains. Because of their cost they are more common for furniture and mouldings than large areas, such as flooring and panelling, and they are often polished to beautiful natural finishes rather than painted.

Softwood mouldings

The architrave moulding below is an example of the extensive range of widely available low-relief stamped mouldings. They make an inexpensive alternative to machine-carved mouldings, or the even more superior hand-carved mouldings. Because their finish is often rather coarse they are usually best painted. Use screws or nails to attach them.

Oil-based varnish

Knotting

Preparing and varnishing wood

Use varnish to protect wood and allow the natural grain to show through. I prefer oil-based varnish to polyurethane varnish, which has a tendency to yellow. To prevent resin seeping from knots in the wood, apply knotting (which will darken the wood slightly) or white polish (which is less effective but will not darken the colour). A coat of shellac-based sanding sealer will prevent the varnish from colouring the wood.

Softwood architrave moulding

Narrow mouldings

These are widely available, either simply shaped or patterned. They can be used singly or in combination, as dado rails, to enrich standard skirtings or at picture rail height. Softwood examples look most effective stained, painted or glazed, while mouldings made from hardwoods, such as mahogany and oak, are best polished with wax or varnished so their grain can be fully appreciated.

Stamped softwood moulding

Softwood ogee moulding

Softwood panel moulding

Olive
wood

Turned ash
nutbowl

Hardwoods

*Oak, elm and mahogany
are amongst the most
widely used hardwoods
and are often used to
make highly polished
mouldings. They are ex-
pensive (and mahogany
should be used sparingly
because it is a tropical
wood) but small amounts
look effective in conjunction with softwoods
stained or woodgrained
to match (woodgraining
techniques are shown on
pp.296–301). Sycamore
and fruit woods, such as
cherry, are usually used
for inlay, veneers and
for turning.*

Oak

Mahogany

Qualities of ash *This hardwood is a
popular wood for decorative objects and
furniture veneers because of its attractive
grain pattern, which remains highly
pronounced even when it is stained,
colourwashed (see pp.252–3), limed
(see pp.260–61), or even sprayed black.
It is turned, to make objects like the
nutbowl above; less expensive woods,
like pine, are usually inadequate for
turning because the high number of knots
in the wood catch against the turning
blade and sometimes shatter the wood.*

Darkened oak beam

Old oak

*In the Middle Ages, oak
beams were sometimes pro-
tected with pitch, or whitewashed (so if you paint oak
beams white you will be following an ancient tradition).
But most were left bare and
darkened naturally with time
(over the last 150 years there
has been a vogue for artificially darkening old beams).*

DECORATING WOOD

THERE ARE several techniques for colouring wood that, far from disguising its natural characteristics, serve to enhance them. But standard coats of paint can also be used to great effect, particularly on mouldings and panelling. On page 67, for example, the character of the wood is subjugated, so that the Classical composition of forms stands out.

First steps

Before painting, the knots in resinous woods should be brushed with knotting to prevent the seepage of resin. The knots in the pine that forms the background here, were treated with white polish (see p.225) rather than knotting (which is dark brown) so as not to spoil the

subtle pale-pink colourwashing. Except in the case of colourwashing and ageing paintwork, wood that is to be painted or limed should be sealed with sanding sealer, or primed, lightly sanded (in liming, the wood is wire-brushed instead) and then undercoated. Previously painted wood should be cleaned with sugarsoap first, and gloss paint lightly sanded. Varnished wood should be stripped.

Imitation wood

Cast resin is often less expensive than wood. Some companies make resin panelling that can be used to clad an entire room. Because the moulds are taken from wood originals the reproduction of grain and pattern is realistic.

Colour-washed wood

Colourwashing wood

This simple technique, using thin washes of diluted paint, gives wood a soft, almost milky-looking appearance. The advantages over using woodstain are that you have a far wider choice of colours and can control the amount of grain you see.

Wood-effect flooring

Some types of plastic flooring have a pattern and surface finish that is almost indistinguishable from real wood. This is a suitable alternative to painted and/or varnished wood for bathroom floors because it does not lift or stain.

Cast resin "carving"

Pickled (limed) pine floorboards

Aged paint finish on matchboarding

Plastic wood-effect flooring

Imitation woodgrain

For centuries, paint has been used to imitate different woodgrains, either on non-wood surfaces or on wood, which provides a natural underlying pattern. The paler grain effects, right, were executed on plywood; the dark example is beech with a paint-simulated rosewood grain. Woodgraining (see pp.296–301) can be used to make some woods like pine resemble more expensive hardwoods, and to unify non-wood surfaces with other elements in a room; see the woodgrained bath on page 63, for example.

Dark oak-grain effect on plywood

Plywood painted to resemble light oak

Beech with a painted rosewood grain

The effect of liming on a carved oak panel

Liming wood

Liming is one of the simplest and most stunning ways to treat wood. The wax or paste with which the wood is rubbed, leaves a faint white deposit in the wood's pores, accentuating the natural grain pattern; it can look particularly effective on carved surfaces, where it sticks in the recesses. Woods that have an open grain, like ash, oak and elm, are the easiest to grain; woods like pine, which have a closed grain, need to have their grain artificially opened by vigorous and repeated wire-brushing. The technique is shown on pages 260–61.

Aged paint finish

Wood can be given a peeled and chipped paint finish. The yellow emulsion paint on the matchboarding, left, was applied over blobs of wax, which resisted the paint, allowing it to be rubbed off to reveal patches of wood (see pp.266–7).

PAPER & CARD

FOR MANY centuries, paper decoration has been used in houses and is still very popular today. There are three main ways paper is used, the most obvious being surface decoration on walls and objects, for example wallpapers, borders and *découpage*. Another use is to screen and filter light, for instance when paper is stretched on a frame and treated with oils. Finally, paper can be used as a technical decorating aid, such as in stencilling and tracing.

being lining paper, which can be used either underneath decorated wallpaper or as a base for paint. In the eighteenth century, lining paper was often glued directly over wooden boarding and then painted in imitation of more expensive wallcoverings. The first printed wallpapers also imitated other surfaces, such as tapestry, wall paintings and stretched fabric.

For best results, always use conventional wallpaper pastes (or PVA for *découpage*) when pasting paper.

Wallpaper
The most familiar type of paper decoration is wallpaper. There are many forms, the simplest one

Photocopy decoration
Glue photocopies of unusual designs on to furniture or walls for a cheap form of découpage (see pp.318–9).

Photocopy of a gryphon

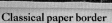
Classical paper border

Paper borders
These are traditionally printed on heavy-duty paper and often come in long rolls. You can easily make your own borders, however, by sticking together repeated photocopies. Placed either at frieze height or dado level, borders can add that extra touch of style.

Stencils
Some modern stencils are cut out from acetate sheet, which is tough as well as being flexible enough to go round corners. But it is slippery, so can be difficult to cut. Stencil card (also called oiled manila card), is the traditional material, and is tough and thick.

Stencil for a frieze

Stencil cut from oiled manila card

Tracing paper with pencil design

Tracing paper
This paper is indispensable for transferring patterns to walls, floors and furniture. Designs are first traced on to the paper and then the pencil outline of the image is transferred to the surface by rubbing the back of the tracing with pencil.

240

Wallpaper with
nineteenth-century
design

Oiled tissue
paper

Tissue paper

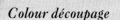

Floral
wrapping
paper

Colour découpage
*Inexpensive gift paper,
though very thin, can be
cut out, glued and then
applied to walls or pieces
of furniture. For repeated
images you can use colour
photocopies. Protect the
découpage with a coat of
clear varnish.*

Oiled tissue paper
*When paper is coated with
varnish, oil or shellac, it
becomes translucent. Use
oiled tissue paper to make
screens for windows; coat
lining paper with shellac
for lampshades (see p.332).*

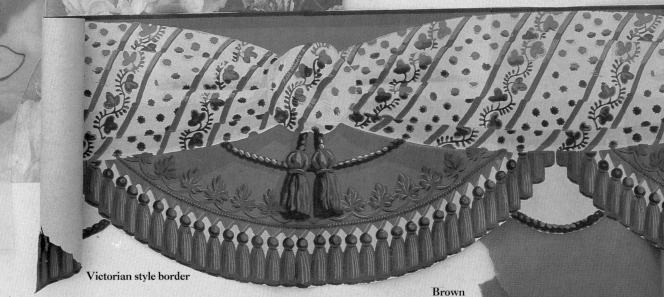

Victorian style border

Brown
paper

Wallpaper
*Although it can be expensive, wallpaper
offers an immense range of patterns.
You can choose between pictorial papers,
like the Victorian frieze above, or flat,
graphic designs like the nineteenth-
century Gothic design, top.*

Brown paper
*This was sometimes used instead of
patterned wallpaper in late nineteenth-
century Arts and Crafts interiors, which
were simply decorated and furnished; see
pages 28–9 and 176–9.*

METAL & SPECIAL FINISHES

IN THE home, metal takes the form of radiators, pipes, and door and light fittings. It looks effective bare, painted or even corroded; the natural decorative patinas of rust, verdigris and gold can be imitated on metal and non-metal surfaces.

Protecting metal

Many metals (gold is one exception) tarnish on exposure to air. Iron and steel turn to rust, and copper and brass tarnish, or turn green to form verdigris. You can prevent rust on bare metalwork with a rust-inhibiting primer, which can then be undercoated and painted over with gloss or eggshell. To appreciate the natural qualities of metals, simply protect with a layer of either varnish or metal lacquer.

To make the most of the highly decorative appearance of chemical change, place differently patinated metals together for stunning visual effects or imitate them on metal, plastic, wood or plaster. The techniques for imitating iron, rust and verdigris are on pages 286–9.

Gold

Because of the cost of solid gold, for centuries it has been beaten into wafer-thin layers, or leaves, and used to gild all sorts of surfaces. The art of gilding (see pp.302–3) is worth mastering, if only because of the sheer pleasure to be derived from handling metal leaf.

Priming metal
Metal must be primed and undercoated before being painted (if the metal has been lacquered, first strip it with a chemical stripper). For iron and steel use red oxide primer, shown on the radiator below; this is a specially formulated oil-based primer.

Rusty fire-tongs

Decorative rust
Why not view rust as a naturally-occurring decorative finish? These iron fire-tongs, once too brash and shiny for the room they occupied, were left outside for a month and then, to prevent the rust progressing, polished with beeswax polish (beeswax has anti-rusting properties).

Gilding
Use gold leaf to bring the shine and richness of gold to metallic and non-metallic surfaces. On carved pieces, like these plastic ornaments, gold leaf really catches the light; the effect here was furthered by gilding over a coloured ground, which shows through the leaf.

Gilded plastic ornaments

Verdigris paint finish on a pipe joint

Red oxide primer

Copper and verdigris
Copper bathroom pipework looks extremely effective unpainted, lacquered with metal lacquer and polished to a shine. Corroded metal, in the form of real verdigris or a verdigris paint finish (like that on the pipe's joint above), looks good with polished metal.

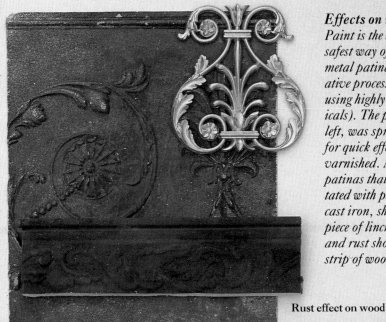

Sprayed plastic anthemion

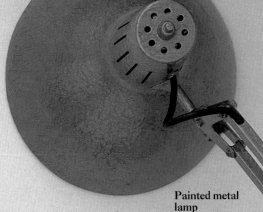

Painted metal lamp

Effects on non-metals

Paint is the cleanest and safest way of emulating metal patinas (alternative processes involve using highly toxic chemicals). The plastic motif, left, was sprayed gold for quick effect and varnished. More complex patinas that can be imitated with paint include cast iron, shown on the piece of lincrusta, left, and rust shown on the strip of wood, left.

Rust effect on wood

Patterned paint finish

There are several specialized metallic paints that give a patterned finish on metals and non-metals, like wood. One such is the hammer-finish enamel paint used on the lamp, above, which gives a beaten metal effect when brushed out. Most metallic paints are tough and quick-drying, but have toxic solvents.

Cast iron effect on lincrusta

Antiqued doorknob

Antiquing metals

New brass, and surfaces gilded with metal leaf, can sometimes look too brash. French enamel varnish can be applied to most metal surfaces for an antiquing effect. Dilute it 1:1 with methylated spirits and sponge it on, as I did on the brass doorknob above, or spatter it, as I did on the gilded urn on the opposite page. The method of antiquing metal leaf and metallic powder is shown on page 304.

Gold and metal finishes

The most unlikely surfaces can be given the appearance of metal. For the lincrusta dado above I used water-based washes and for the verdigris effect, gold powders, and French enamel varnish.

Lincrusta panel decorated with metallic powders and verdigris paint finish

GLASS & PLASTIC

GLASS IS a beautiful and varied medium, with many decorative uses in the home. It is available moulded and pressed, polished, coloured and painted, patterned, etched and sand-blasted. Yet whatever form it takes, glass retains its essential qualities of hardness, brittleness and translucency.

The relationship between glass and light is intrinsic to how glass performs; it is a modifier of light and so its role in the interior is an important one. The positioning of glass in a room should primarily be in response to the light source in that room, so that glass vases are backlit with light from windows, and mirrors repeat the imagery of the windows, in their shape, size, and reflections.

An undervalued material

It might be thought that plastic is a poor substitute material, and in fact the qualities of plastics that are imitative of glass are poor; they scratch, do not refract light into the spectrum colours and are prone to a build-up of static electricity that attracts dust. But there are hundreds of other plastics available, some of which possess unique characteristics; their use should not be dismissed lightly.

The argument against using plastics is that they are fake, cheap and mass-produced, and they are not sympathetic companions to the otherwise "natural" materials used in building. But plasticizers are used today in concrete, plaster and paint. And the pedigree of plastics is an old one: Robert Adam, the eighteenth-century English architect, asked several companies to manufacture component wall decorations in either *papier-mâché* or composition (a mixture of rosin, glue and whiting) that performed the role of more expensive carved wood. Two linseed oil-based products, linoleum and lincrusta, which can also be seen as prototype plastics, followed in the nineteenth century. All these materials have pleasant handling properties.

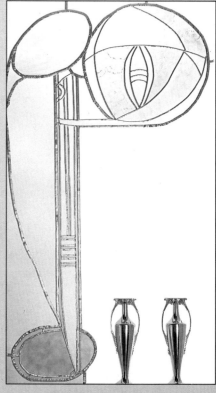

Stained glass effect
One way to control the quality of light in your room is to paint your own stained glass (see pp.308–9).

Cast resin decoration
The use of high-quality silicone rubber moulds ensures faithful reproduction of every detail of the wood-like platerack, right. There should be few qualms about using cast resin decoration, such as this, because even the use of moulds to cast plaster decoration can be seen as a way of imitating carving.

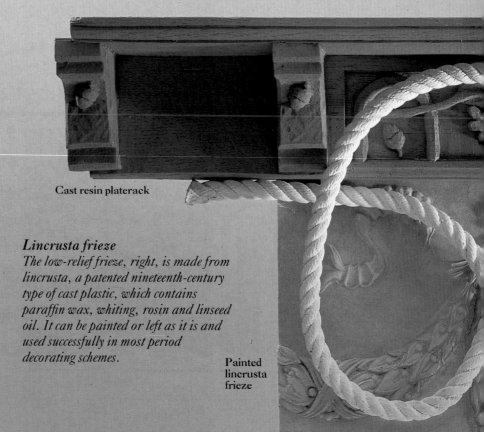

Cast resin platerack

Lincrusta frieze
The low-relief frieze, right, is made from lincrusta, a patented nineteenth-century type of cast plastic, which contains paraffin wax, whiting, rosin and linseed oil. It can be painted or left as it is and used successfully in most period decorating schemes.

Painted
lincrusta
frieze

Imitation terracotta
floor tile

Tiles and ornaments

*Like the imitation wood
flooring on page 63, the
plastic tiles, right, faithfully
reproduce every detail of the
material they imitate.
Decorative ornaments, like
the leaf pattern, right, and the
wreath, below, are still made
in composition by some
fibrous plaster firms, but
these imitations are in
cast plastic and can
be transformed with
special paint finishes or
gold leaf. They become
flexible when steamed,
which allows you to bend
them round curved forms.*

Plastic
anthemion

White cast-plastic moulding

Rope decoration

*When using rope in your
decorating scheme, there is a
choice between polyester rope,
below, which looks beautiful
painted (see p.81), or hemp
rope, which you can dip in
plaster or gesso (see p.67).*

Imitation marble
floor tile

Plastic wreath

Polyester rope
painted blue

245

SIMPLE DECORATIVE EFFECTS

The techniques in this section are mostly used for decorating large surfaces – walls, floors and woodwork, though some, such as spattering and liming, are also suitable for furniture and small areas. They are all easy to master, only slightly more advanced than painting with a flat coat of colour, and the effects are immensely satisfying. Most of the techniques involve "colour building", using a thin wash of paint or a glaze over a background colour. Colourwashing, in particular, lends itself to a wide variety of settings (there are three versions of colourwashing: one for wood and two for walls).

Examples of paint-spattered wood lie on a limed wood panel, left

One of the simplest decorative treatments for bare wood is colourwashing, above (the bottom sample has also been limed)

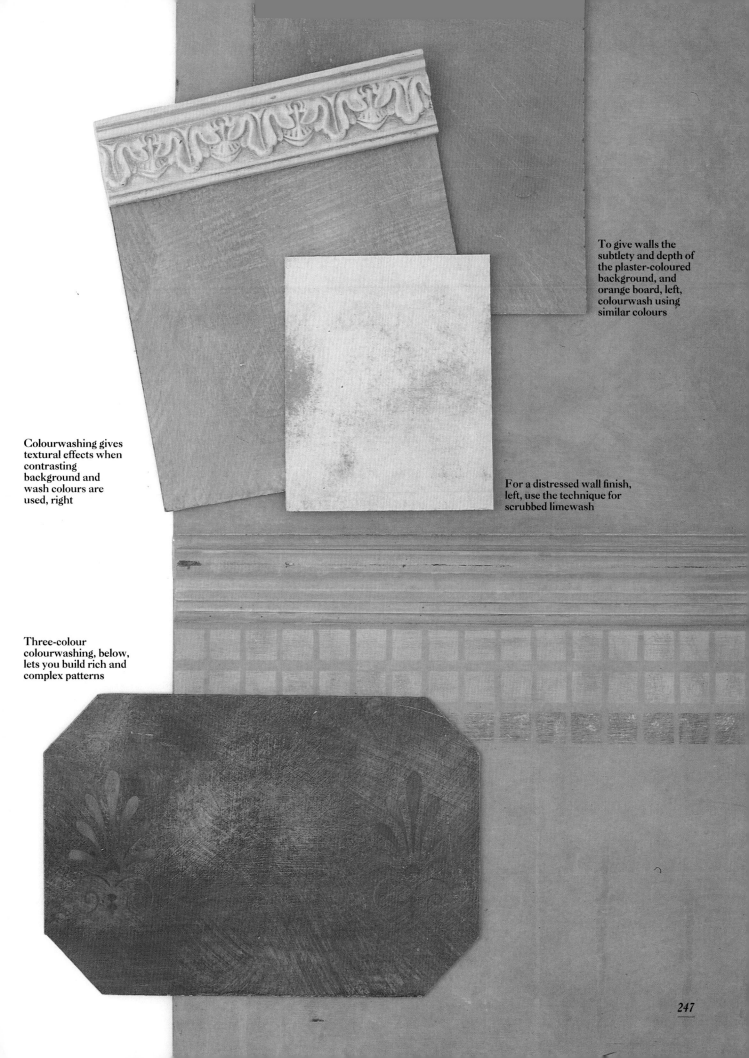

To give walls the subtlety and depth of the plaster-coloured background, and orange board, left, colourwash using similar colours

Colourwashing gives textural effects when contrasting background and wash colours are used, right

For a distressed wall finish, left, use the technique for scrubbed limewash

Three-colour colourwashing, below, lets you build rich and complex patterns

247

COLOURWASHING

This is one of the simplest and most effective techniques for painting walls. It is descended from a long tradition of water-based-paint techniques. Instead of distemper (which was the standard paint in Europe and the USA up until the 1950s), whose poor covering qualities were often craftily disguised with decorative brushstrokes, I use a home-made PVA wash or a wash made by diluting emulsion. These water-based washes are brushed out over a white emulsion background to give smooth walls a softly patterned, subtle translucent finish. Using a slightly different colourwashing method they can be used to colour and flatter the texture of roughly plastered walls (see pp.274–5) and, in a sister technique, sponged.

Large decorating brush   Synthetic sponge

PVA wash

TOOLS & MATERIALS
I made a PVA wash with raw sienna powder colour; I diluted it to make a pale colour for the rough wall. After using the brush to apply the wash (step 1), wipe off excess paint.

THE BASECOAT for colourwashing is white emulsion. If walls are already painted white, ensure that they are dirt-free. A wash is roughly brushed on top of the basecoat; the pattern of brushmarks is then softened with a damp brush and finally rebrushed.

Colours
Soft colours, such as dusty pink (see p.55), yellow ochre, grey, raw sienna, cream and pale beige, give the most subtle results over a large area of wall.

Stronger colours like terracotta are effective for colourwashing dados as you can see from the Venetian scheme above.

Choice of washes
You can colourwash with a home-made PVA wash (as I do here) or diluted emulsion. A PVA wash is easiest to work with because any hard lines of paint that appear when

the wash dries can be dampened with water and rebrushed. To make a PVA wash, mix water, PVA and powder colours or, for small areas, water-based tube colours (artists' acrylics or gouache); see page 333. Powder colours are highly toxic; follow the safety precautions on page 325. To give your wall a washable finish, apply a coat of matt oil-based varnish.

Using emulsion
Colourwashing with an emulsion wash gives a less dramatic finish. To make an emulsion wash, dilute emulsion 1:4 with water. Because emulsion dries to a waterproof finish, hard edges cannot be dampened and reworked. Apply the wash (*step 1*) in areas of no more than a square metre at a time and soften brushmarks (*step 2*) immediately. Practise the technique first on a piece of paper or board until you feel confident.

SPONGING
I dribbled a wall with powder colour washes and water. Once dry, I softened the dribbles with a damp sponge, below, until they became mottled, bottom.

COLOURWASHING

SMOOTH WALL

1 *Apply the wash over a dry white emulsion basecoat. Randomly brush it in all directions. (If using an emulsion wash, paint a small area.)*

2 *A few minutes later (immediately if using an emulsion wash) pass a damp brush lightly over the surface, blurring the brushmarks.*

3 *After a few minutes, when the wash starts to dry, brush with a firm pressure, lifting the remaining paint to make a patchy effect.*

ROUGH WALL

1 *For a mottled, patchy paint finish, brush on the wash in all directions, over a white emulsion basecoat. Be sure to brush plenty into the recesses.*

2 *Soften the brushmark pattern by passing a damp brush lightly over the surface; repeat five to ten minutes later, using pressure.*

3 *As this half-finished wall shows, colourwashing enhances the contrast between the raised areas and recesses of the textured plaster.*

ALTERNATIVE EFFECT

This was painted using steps 1 and 2 for smooth walls. The result is a simpler-looking pattern with more obvious brushmarks and subtler colour contrasts.

THREE-COLOUR COLOURWASHING

Incredible effects of depth and texture can be created by building up washes in three colours. Three-colour colourwashing can even produce an effect redolent of ancient watercolour-painted walls, as in the Greco-Roman Bathroom, left, where cream, yellow and green were applied to the dado. For the rich, bronze wall, I used two home-made PVA washes (one of yellow ochre and one of burnt sienna) followed by a wash of diluted cream emulsion. The first wash was applied as in steps 1–3 *for colourwashing a smooth wall (p.249); the steps opposite illustrate the application of the second and third washes.*

Burnt sienna powder colour

Yellow ochre powder colour

Cream emulsion

Decorating brush

Decorating brush

PVA

THE THREE colours used should be different but related. Choose combinations like tomato red, terracotta and beige, or blue-green, green-blue and pale blue.

The third colour is used to soften the texture and cover the surface with a translucent, mist-like layer of colour so it should be paler than the other colours. It is important to apply it sparingly with delicate brush strokes.

Paint options

I use home-made washes for the first two steps because they have greater purity and intensity of colour than ready-made paints and produce a highly textured result. The quality of colour of the final wash is not important (it should just be pale to give a dusty finish) so I use emulsion for convenience.

Powder colours are highly toxic so exercise particular caution and be sure that they do not come into contact with your skin. If you do use powder colours, follow the safety precautions on page 325.

For the softest finish, omit the PVA from the washes and varnish when dry. Or, for a finish with a slight texture dilute emulsion 1:4 with water for all three washes.

Preparation

As with simple colourwashing, this effect is suitable for smooth and rough surfaces and the best basecoat is white emulsion, applied with a paintbrush, not a roller. Rollers leave a heavy texture that becomes obvious once the wall has been colourwashed.

System of working

When you apply the second colour work on several patches of about a square metre at a time. Apply the wash (*step 1*) and rework patches that are drying (*step 2*) at about five-minute intervals.

In order to avoid making repetitive hard edges, vary the shape of the patches as you go.

TOOLS & MATERIALS

To make the first two washes mix yellow ochre and burnt sienna powder colours respectively (or water-based tube colours), water and five per cent PVA by volume (see p.333). For the third wash, dilute cream emulsion paint 1:6 with water. For an average room you will need about 1–2 litres (2–4 pints) of each. Use high-quality decorating brushes – poor quality ones shed bristles.

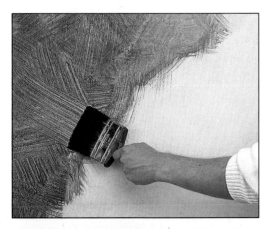

1 Over an already dry colourwash of yellow ochre (follow steps 1–3 for a smooth wall shown on p.249), apply a wash of burnt sienna. Brush the paint out in a random pattern, pulling the brush in every direction. Use a firm pressure for this so that you make visible brushmarks.

2 As with simple colourwashing, subtlety and depth is created by moving the paint about as it dries. Use an almost dry paintbrush and a heavy pressure to brush over previous brushmarks, again pulling the paint about in random directions to produce complex patterns.

3 After some hours, when the surface is completely dry, apply the third, paler wash. Brush a small quantity over the surface so that it forms a thin, smooth veil of colour. Use a light pressure this time so there are no visible brushmarks.

Colourwashed stencil
Before I applied the wash of burnt sienna (see steps 1 and 2) I stencilled this design with gold spray paint. The final, pale wash (see step 3) was applied over the top. When dry, I revealed some of the stencil more clearly by gently rubbing off some of the pale wash with a rag which I had dampened with methylated spirits beforehand.

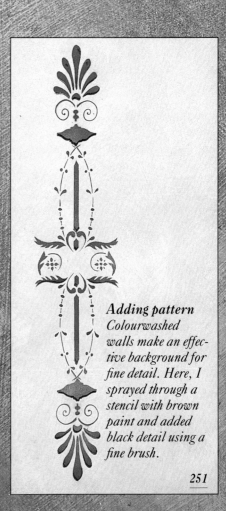

Adding pattern
Colourwashed walls make an effective background for fine detail. Here, I sprayed through a stencil with brown paint and added black detail using a fine brush.

COLOURWASHING WOOD

There is a long tradition of painting wood with water-based paints. But while applying thick layers of paint completely disguises the woodgrain beneath, colourwashing allows the natural qualities of wood to show. In this technique one or two washes of colour are brushed on to bare wood. The paint acts rather like a woodstain, in that it penetrates and colours the wood, whilst allowing the natural patterns to show. Steps 1 *and 2 result in a richer finish than* step 2 *used alone;* step 3 *is used to expose more of the wood. The result of using* step 2 *only is shown in the flooring of the English Baroque scheme above and on page 67.*

Emulsion paint

Raw umber powder colour

Cloth

Decorating brush

TOOLS & MATERIALS

For step 1 *mix raw umber powder colour (or artists' acrylics or gouache) with water. Powder colours are toxic so follow the precautions given on p.325. To make the wash applied in* step 2 *add water to your chosen colour of emulsion paint until it is as runny as milk. You need a decorating brush to apply the paints and a cloth to wipe the wood and expose the grain.*

THE IDEA OF applying a water-based paint directly to bare wood floors or walls is often greeted with horror because water tends to raise the grain and can react against natural resins and oils present in wood.

But bare wood and emulsion paint are perfectly compatible because emulsion contains a polyvinyl binder that binds paint and wood together. If the wood does become furred sand it lightly.

Preparation

Ensure that no traces of paint or varnish are left on wood that has been stripped. Wood that has been chemically stripped or bleached should be washed down with a 1:20 mixture of vinegar and water to neutralize any chemicals. (See also the information on pp.248–9.)

Choosing colours

Pale colours such as soft blue, olive green, white and pink are most compatible with the natural tones of pale wood, such as pine, and slightly stronger colours with darker woods, such as oak. Bear in mind when you choose a colour that it will look much less intense when it is diluted.

To make sure you have diluted the emulsion to the right consistency and to check the colour, test some on a small area of wood first. Left for 20 minutes, a correctly diluted wash will penetrate the wood without obliterating the grain. If necessary, alter the emulsion colour, by mixing in some water-based tube colour, such as artists' acrylics or gouache.

Varnishing

Colourwashed floors, and other areas that need to be hardwearing, should be lightly sanded, brushed with sanding sealer and then varnished. The sanding sealer prevents the varnish from soaking into the colourwashed wood and darkening it. Varnish will make the finish yellow slightly.

1 *For a subtle variation in colour start by brushing the bare wood (in the direction of the grain) with a wash of raw umber. Stir the mixture frequently to prevent the colour settling at the bottom. Leave to dry.*

2 *For a simpler finish start with this step. Using a brush, slop a generous layer of diluted emulsion on to the wood. Brush it on in the direction of the grain. Dilute emulsion penetrates and lightly stains the wood while allowing the natural grain and patterning to show through.*

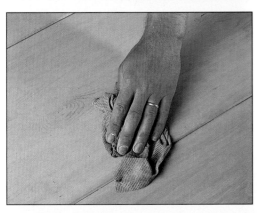

3 *To expose more of the wood's grain wait 15 to 20 minutes and then wipe the surface with a clean cloth. This will remove some of the surface paint.*

Colourwashed wall, *below. Diluted emulsion was painted over stained wood and, when dry, sanded. (See p.95.)*

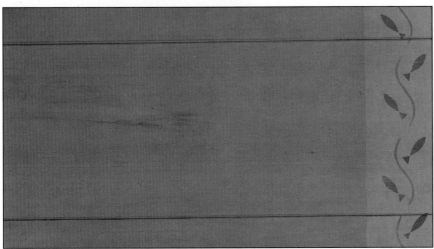

SCRUBBED LIMEWASH

This technique gives walls the appearance of well-scrubbed, old-fashioned limewash (used to paint outside walls) and white distemper (used inside). I evolved the technique, which employs neither a scrubbing brush nor limewash, to give walls an aged appearance sympathetic to distressed wood and the naive wall paintings (shown below) typical of medieval interiors. But a scrubbed limewash wall finish makes an equally effective background in ethnic and country settings, like the Santa Fe Dining Room shown above and on page 99.

A N UNEVEN, distressed appearance is achieved by dry-brushing a layer of water-based emulsion over an oil-based eggshell basecoat. Methylated spirits is used to rub away some of the emulsion resulting in a patchy, scrubbed-looking finish.

Applying the basecoat

Ensure walls are dirt- and grease-free before applying a coat of eggshell, diluted 1:2 with turpentine. There is no need to brush the paint to a smooth finish because only small patches of it will show. Use a neutral colour for an authentic-looking scrubbed limewash finish. I used raw sienna eggshell for the effect shown in the steps opposite; other suitable colours are mid-brown and plaster pink.

Dry-brushing

White emulsion paint is applied using a scenery painters' technique called dry-brushing. It is easy to master, but as with all techniques you are unfamiliar with, experiment on pieces of board first.

Before applying the emulsion to the wall, brush out the paint on a piece of board in order to distribute a small amount of paint evenly through the bristles.

To begin with, apply the paint with the lightest of strokes, just grazing the surface of the wall. As more paint comes off, build up the pressure until you are roughly brushing the paint with an almost dry brush.

Finishing

Emulsion paint dries to a tough finish, so most walls will need no extra protection, but in areas of high traffic, such as a hallway, you may wish to protect the paint with a coat of matt oil-based varnish.

Complementary techniques *The aged finish of red-ochre wall paintings and the hand-painted knight (which I gilded and antiqued with wax) make a complementary accompaniment to scrubbed limewash walls. I used all three of these finishes in the medieval kitchen scheme (see pp.114–5).*

TOOLS & MATERIALS

Use a good quality decorating brush that will withstand the robust dry-brushing shown in steps 1 *and* 2 *without shedding bristles. A black hog-bristle decorating brush (shown, right) is ideal. For a room about 4m (13ft) × 5m (16ft) you may use 5 litres (1 gallon) of emulsion and 2 litres (¹/₂ gallon) of methylated spirits. The latter gives off toxic fumes so open windows and do not smoke; you can wear a respiratory mask (available from DIY shops).*

White emulsion

Cloth

10-cm (4-in) decorating brush

Methylated spirits

1 *Dip the tips of a 10-cm (4-in) decorating brush in white emulsion and distribute the paint through the bristles by brushing them against a piece of board. Loosely brush the whole of the relatively dry bristle surface against the eggshell basecoat, increasing pressure to build up cloudy patches of dry-brushed paint.*

2 *When the paint has dried, patches of the basecoat will show through. If you would prefer a greater amount of texture, brush on more paint, using the same technique as above. Leave the paint to dry. For a more "brushy" effect skip this step and move straight to* step 3.

COLOURFUL ALTERNATIVE

Using two brushes, I concurrently dry-brushed indigo and purple emulsion over a pinky-brown eggshell basecoat and rubbed vigorously with methylated spirits for a highly distressed finish.

3 *Dip a cloth in methylated spirits and rub it over the whole surface. The methylated spirits will soften the dry emulsion paint, exposing the basecoat in some areas and depositing a thin white film over the whole surface. When rubbing a large area wear waterproof gloves to prevent absorption of the spirit by the skin.*

SOFTENED GLAZEWORK

Transparent oil glaze is a truly invaluable decorating material. Using the simplest of techniques, glaze tinted with artists' oil paints will cast a soft veil of colour over a painted surface, and thus impart an unsurpassable richness. Glaze can be blended and softened (see steps 1–4) to give newly painted surfaces, like the wall shown left, a warm, antique glow, add subtle depth to a painted wall (see the Oriental scheme on p.193) and also render colours deeper and more complex (see the deep-blue wall in the medieval scheme on p.123). Painted mouldings, such as dado rails, and carvings, can be highlighted by stippling and wiping glaze.

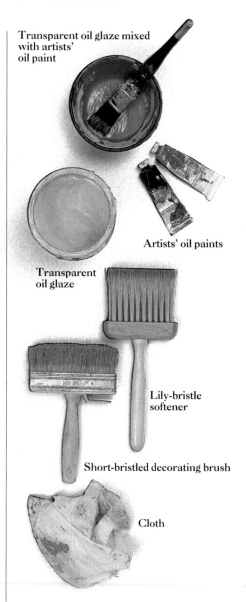

Transparent oil glaze mixed with artists' oil paint

Artists' oil paints

Transparent oil glaze

Lily-bristle softener

Short-bristled decorating brush

Cloth

T RANSPARENT oil glaze is available ready-made, or you can make your own (see the recipe on p.332). It is diluted with turpentine or white spirit to a single cream consistency and mixed with artists' oil paints to produce richly coloured mixtures that have the advantages that they do not run, like paint, or stick, like varnish.

If the diluted glaze seems too treacly when brushed on add more turpentine; if it seems too thin, thicken it with more glaze.

Glaze remains workable for at least half an hour after being brushed on and becomes fully dry within six to ten hours.

Preparation

The standard basecoat for transparent oil glaze is two smooth coats of eggshell paint, but you can also glaze over printed paper as I do in the steps opposite. The surface must be as smooth as possible because glaze will adhere to the minutest nooks and crannies, which will show up as dark marks (the only exception is antiquing, when dark marks are an asset).

Colours for antiquing

Glaze can be tinted with artists' oil paint of any colour but particular colours are used for giving surfaces an appearance of age. These include raw umber (which I used for glazing the patterned wall opposite and the corbel, far right), raw sienna, burnt umber, Vandyke brown, and any of these mixed with grey, white or black.

Varnishing and polishing

Surfaces coated with transparent oil glaze should always be varnished because glaze remains soft, even when dry, and rubs away with time.

For an exquisitely smooth finish, rub the varnished surface with beeswax on the finest grade wire wool (grade 0000). Then polish the surface to a shine with a soft duster.

TOOLS & MATERIALS

You will need two decorating brushes: one for applying the glaze and one for blending it. For step 3 use a lily-bristle softener or a dusting brush. Use artists' oil paints to tint transparent oil glaze, which appears opaque until it is brushed out, when it forms a translucent film. See page 333 for tinting glaze.

1 *Apply the tinted glaze with a decorating brush. At this stage do not worry if the colour is a little patchy because the glaze is rebrushed while still wet.*

2 *With a soft, dry decorating brush, use a light pressure to distribute the glaze evenly, softening out the brushmarks and blending in any patches of colour. As you do this the colour of the glaze will appear less intense. Finish by brushing over the surface with the lightest of strokes imaginable.*

3 *Using the tips of a lily-bristle softener (or dusting brush), stroke the surface of the glaze in all directions until no brushmarks are visible and the surface is faultlessly smooth.*

ANTIQUE PATINA

The dusty, antique appearance of this plaster corbel was produced with transparent oil glaze and eggshell paint. First it was stippled with oil glaze tinted with raw umber artists' paint and wiped (using the technique shown below, left). Then the surface was brushed with white eggshell paint (diluted 1:4 with turpentine) and the raised areas were wiped with a cloth.

STIPPLING & WIPING

To give painted mouldings depth and shade, use the time-honoured technique of stippling and wiping. Apply the glaze. Then, holding a firm decorating brush (or stippling brush) at 90 degrees, lightly jab at the glazed surface, to produce a finely speckled impression. Wrap a cloth around your fingers and wipe the raised areas to reveal the colour beneath.

PATTERNED GLAZEWORK

Transparent oil glaze coloured with artists' oil paints has a drying time and flow properties that make it the ideal medium for brushing over a basecoat of colour and working and manipulating into broken patterns. Different effects can be produced by "dragging" a brush through wet oil glaze, gently texturing it with a sponge, bag or rag, or combing it to create patterns. These techniques are equally suitable for furniture as for large areas (the wall in the French Empire scheme, above left, and on p.59 was dragged).

Transparent oil glaze

Dusting brush

Decorating brush

Turpentine

Dark-blue artists' oil paint

Red universal stainer

Flogging brush

TRANSPARENT OIL glaze has the translucency, brilliance and depth of watercolour, and yet (unlike watercolour) is simple to use because it is slow-drying. It can be worked and manipulated with a brush, rag or bag for between half an hour and an hour, which gives you plenty of time to break up the surface into remarkable, delicate patterns.

Surfaces for decorating

Dragging and texturing are effective treatments for walls, doors, dados and furniture. Combing is a dramatic way of enlivening old pieces of furniture, and using a sponge instead of a plastic bag or rag (which create a lively pattern) lends a soft, muted tone to any surface, especially walls.

Choosing colours

In the French Empire Study scheme, above and on page 59, I painted the wall with a basecoat of mauve eggshell paint. I then brushed on dark-blue oil glaze (see p.333 for how to mix colours with oil glaze), and dragged a flogging brush through it to expose the underlying paint. For the ragging and "bagging" technique, I used red glaze over a red basecoat.

With any of these techniques the colour combinations you choose depend largely on the mood of your room and the character of the piece you are decorating, but it is advisable to avoid glaring contrasts between the colour of the basecoat and that of the glaze.

"Bagging" *A plastic bag makes lively patterns when dabbed on wet glaze. For a more dramatic result, dampen the bag with turpentine.*

TOOLS & MATERIALS

You can buy transparent oil glaze, or make your own using the recipe on page 332. To mix it with colour (either artists' oil paint or universal stainer), see page 333. For dragging use a flogging brush or other long-haired brush. A dusting brush can be used instead of a more expensive lily-bristle softener for step 2 of ragging.

PATTERNED GLAZEWORK

1 Using a decorating brush, apply a mixture of transparent oil glaze and dark-blue artists' oil paint over an eggshell basecoat, in a thin, even layer.

2 Brush the glaze in vertical strokes with a dusting brush (or a softening brush), to soften it out and distribute it more evenly over the surface.

3 Hold a spirit level up to the wet glaze and either push the edge of it in, or score the glaze lightly with a blunt pencil, to establish vertical guidelines.

4 Following the lines, slowly drag a flogging brush or long-haired decorating brush through the glaze, holding the bristles against the surface.

RAGGING

1 Brush on glaze over dry eggshell paint. Dab or roll a rag (leather can also be used) through the wet glaze to make a "broken" finish.

2 Leave the glaze to dry for half an hour. Then, using just the tips of a lily-bristle softener, stroke the pattern to a soft blur.

COMBING

Pull a metal or rubber comb through wet glaze to make striped patterns. Cross-comb at right angles, or at very acute angles, for a pattern that resembles woodgrain.

LIMING WOOD

Limed wood has a mellow white sheen and subtle, grainy appearance that suits furniture and small objects as much as larger surfaces, like the panelling shown here (and on p.103). Liming originated in sixteenth-century Europe when furniture and panelling were cleaned and protected from worm with a caustic paste containing slaked lime. The white pigment left in the pores of the wood suggested a decorative finish and by the seventeenth century liming was in vogue – but to the horrific detriment of limers. The paste ate away their nails and fingers and the fumes dramatically reduced their life span – we are lucky to have less noxious materials around today.

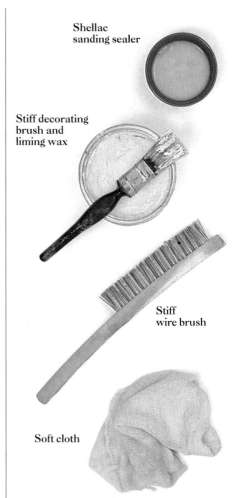

Shellac sanding sealer

Stiff decorating brush and liming wax

Stiff wire brush

Soft cloth

THE MIXTURE most commonly used to lime wood is a harmless wax and pigment paste – liming wax. You can make your own from beeswax furniture polish and white pigment (see p.333) or buy it ready-made.

Preparation

Only bare wood can be limed and as preparation it should be sealed with shellac sanding sealer. Varnished or stained wood must first be stripped or bleached, washed with a 1:10 mixture of vinegar and water, sanded lightly in the direction of the grain and then sealed.

Suitability of woods

Only certain woods can be limed effectively. Open-grain woods (which have scratch-like pores in patterns that follow the grain) are the most suitable. Of these, oak, like the panels here, is the most responsive, followed by ash. Though pine is not open-grained it can be limed if you first make artificial indentations in the wood with a wire brush, using much more pressure than in *step 1*, where the oak's existing pores are simply being opened up; then follow *steps 2 and 3*. It is also possible to lime carved or distressed pine.

Beech is too hard and close-grained to prepare with a wire brush but white eggshell diluted 1:4 with methylated spirits can be washed on and then rubbed off moulded areas to create limed or pickled beech.

Alternative technique

As it is not possible to put a coat of protective varnish over liming wax, areas subject to heavy wear, such as floors and worktops, should be limed with a water and white pigment mixture (see p.333). Using this, follow *steps 1-3* and when dry, brush on another coat of shellac sanding sealer, followed, when dry, by varnish.

TOOLS & MATERIALS

Quick-drying shellac sanding sealer is used to seal the raw wood before the grain is opened with a stiff wire brush. A decorating brush is used to apply the shellac (clean the brush with methylated spirits) and the liming wax (clean the brush with turpentine). You can buy liming wax ready-made or make it yourself (see p.332). You will also need some soft cloths to remove surplus liming wax and to buff the limed surface.

1 *Wire-brush the prepared wood, using a firm pressure so that you open up the grain. If you find later that you have not brushed sufficiently hard and not enough paste has taken into the wood simply brush it again. Always work in the direction of the grain; if you do not, scratches across the grain will show up white and spoil the effect.*

2 *Apply the liming wax with a stiff decorating brush, using a circular motion so you rub the wax into the grain; you will soon see where the open pores pick up the white wax. Work an area of about half a square metre at a time and do not worry if the effect is patchy at this stage.*

3 *Leave the wax for about 10 minutes so that it hardens slightly. Stretch one thickness of cloth across your fingers and polish off the surplus paste, using a circular movement. (Stretching the cloth prevents it from reaching the grain and lifting the paste out.) After 15 minutes buff with a clean cloth.*

Limed pine *These new pine floorboards (like those on p.95) were colourwashed (see pp.252-3) and then limed with a water and pigment mixture.*

SPATTERING

With a little practice spattering is easily mastered and can be used to decorate walls, furniture and small objects with dots of paint. A loaded paintbrush is knocked against a stick to spatter furniture and other large areas. The paint flies off the brush and lands on the surface as tiny dots. The more paint that is flicked, the richer the final look, especially when more than one colour is used. The tomato-red wall of the scheme shown above, was spattered with black oil glaze and then gold paint for an exotic appearance. Paint can also be densely spattered to simulate porphyry (a purplish rock) and granite, both shown far right.

Oil-based varnish   Gold paint   Artists' paintbrush

Large brush

Stencilling brush

Toothbrush

Transparent oil glaze

"Spatter" stick   Artists' oil paints

IN ADDITION to paint and glaze, ink and varnish can be spattered and a wide range of effects created according to the type of brush used and how heavily it is charged. Use a toothbrush or stencilling brush for small objects and thin the media you use to the consistency of milk.

For a granite effect, spatter grey, then white emulsion over a dark-grey basecoat; for porphyry, spatter purple, black, and pink paint over a rust-red basecoat.

Controlling the dots

As paint is knocked off the brush the dots become finer. Every time that you reload the brush with paint knock some off on to a rag until you get the size of dot you want. Then spatter the surface and repeat. To reduce the vibrations cover the stick with fabric.

Preparation and varnishing

Painted, unpainted, smooth and textured surfaces can be spattered.

The technique is messy so ensure you cover everything with dust sheets, and wear a mask, eye protection and, especially if you have sensitive skin, gloves. Only surfaces spattered with transparent oil glaze need be varnished. To disguise any unevenness in the finish use matt varnish; for a polished finish use gloss varnish.

"Antique" paper To give this new wallpaper an antique appearance it was glazed, spattered and given a craquelure finish (see pp.268–9).

TOOLS & MATERIALS
You need brushes (old ones that you are happy to be bashed about a bit) and a "spatter" stick (a piece of wood against which to knock the brush). To colour oil glaze mix it with artists' oil paints (see p.333). Gold paint is available from artists' suppliers. For small objects use a small brush with stiff bristles (a toothbrush is ideal) and oil-based varnish tinted with artists' oil paint (which I am using, right), ink, tinted glaze or paint (diluted if necessary).

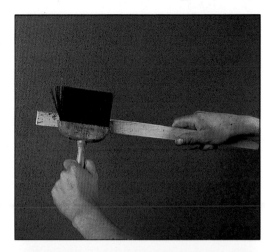

1 *Before starting, load a brush with glaze and, aiming it at a rag, flick off the excess paint. Then hold the brush parallel to the wall and hit the ferrule of the brush against the "spatter" stick. The glaze will fly off the bristles in a rain of dots. Repeat until the wall is covered with equally distributed dots; respatter any areas that are too sparsely covered with dots.*

2 *When the black glaze has dried use a smaller brush to cast a loosely distributed pattern of tiny gold paint dots. As in step 1, each time you recharge the brush, flick off the excess paint on to newspaper or a rag, before beginning to spatter the wall.*

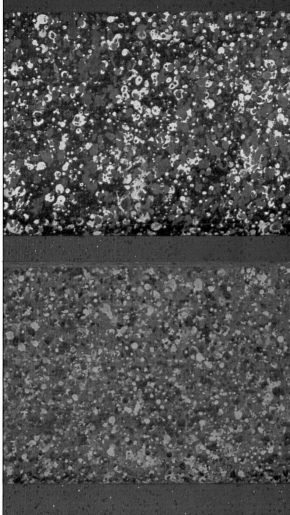

Small-scale spattering *Dip the tips of a toothbrush or stencilling brush into tinted varnish or paint and draw your finger towards you across the brush.*

AGEING & ANTIQUING

The techniques of ageing and antiquing all produce finishes that imitate the effects of time on paint, wood, plaster, plastic, metal and even paper. Although it may at first seem odd to want to give a worn look to fresh new paint or plasterwork, an antique finish gives a friendly, mellow feel to a decorating scheme and helps tie in new materials with the genuinely old. This section includes how to use wax or glaze to give surfaces an antique patina; how instantly to age new paintwork, plasterwork and plaster walls; and how to create a web of cracks on paintwork. The first three techniques in this section can be used independently or, for a complex effect, in the sequence in which they appear.

This new plaster casting was given an antique patina with shellac and liming wax

The resin knights were aged following the technique on pages 266–7 and antiqued with wax as on pages 270–71

Crackle varnish was used to produce the web of tiny cracks and dark-brown ink was spattered to resemble fly-spotting

A fine spatter of brown-tinted varnish was used to give the rocking horse an antique finish

Antiquing waxes were used to tone down the colour of the wooden candlestick and piece of painted lincrusta

Aged paint on wood, left, and a cracked paint finish, below

265

AGEING PAINT ON WOOD

A scheme that is designed around old furniture, or combines old with new, often fails to establish a visual link between the older elements and the paint treatment of architectural features in the room, such as doors, dado rails, skirting boards and panelling. Often the sympathetic solution is to give a worn, faded look to such features (and furniture), so creating a room in which all the elements look unified. The formula for a faded look is simple: wax is used in combination with a process of building up and wearing back layers of paint. The colour combination used here is the traditional blue-green that is typically Scandinavian (see pp.86–9), but there are more vibrant alternatives (see pp.108–11).

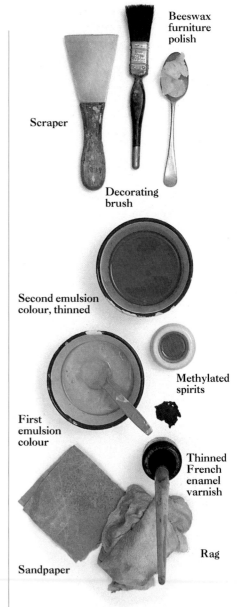

Beeswax furniture polish

Scraper

Decorating brush

Second emulsion colour, thinned

Methylated spirits

First emulsion colour

Thinned French enamel varnish

Sandpaper

Rag

TOOLS & MATERIALS
Use beeswax furniture polish or vaseline as the resist medium to create a chipped and peeled look, and have plenty of old rags and sandpaper (100 and 220 grit) at hand. Dilute the French enamel varnish with methylated spirits.

T HE GREAT joy with this technique is that it can be applied to both new and old wood. You will, however, need to prepare wood that has already been treated: on old pine furniture, first remove any build-up of wax polish by scrubbing with turpentine or white spirit and then with a strong detergent cleaner. If the piece is varnished or painted, sand it well to remove most of the finish and key the surface. Even better, strip off the finish entirely.

Using water-based paints
The technique here uses water-based emulsion paint (rather than an oil-based paint) – not the most obvious choice for wood today, but one that is nevertheless traditional. In the past, furniture was mostly painted with water-based paints, vinegar- or beer-based washes, paints bound with casein (a latex-like milk derivative), or gesso paints (pigments bound in a chalk and glue mixture).

The complex appearance of this finish belies the simplicity of the technique and the materials used. There is no need to worry about the grain in the wood being furred or raised by the water in the emulsion paint, since the technique involves sanding at a later stage.

Finishing treatments
This technique will give the impression of wood that is chipped, peeled and faded, but to prevent any real deterioration protect the surface with varnish. Or use beeswax furniture polish, which will give the paint a sheen.

The steps opposite provide a finished treatment for wood, but you can develop the effect further by following the techniques shown on pages 268–9.

1 *Darken the wood to an aged colour with a coat of mid-brown French enamel varnish (thinned 1:2 with methylated spirits). Avoid using wood-stain as this may penetrate the paint.*

2 *Once the French enamel varnish has dried, apply blobs of beeswax polish or vaseline with a small brush. Use your little finger to elongate some of these in the direction of the woodgrain.*

3 *Leave the wax to dry for at least 12 hours before applying a liberal coat of emulsion paint. Use light press-ure so you do not remove any wax.*

4 *Leave the paint to dry thoroughly – this can take up to a day when it is applied over wax or vaseline. Then apply the second colour, diluting the emulsion paint 1:3 with water.*

5 *Half an hour later you can begin to expose the layers of paint and French enamel varnish beneath. Use a scraper for obstinate blobs and a rag to remove as much of the wax or vaseline as possible.*

6 *To soften the edges, remove more paint and "tie" together the patches of exposed wood, sand care-fully with 100 grit and then 220 grit sandpaper.*

SUBTLE ADDITION

You can end with step 6 *or go on to create a more subtle effect by covering the whole area with a wash of the original green colour, as here (diluted 1:4 with water), or experimenting with a completely different colour.*

CRAQUELURE

Most newly painted furniture and objects, mouldings and even some painted antique pieces (like the bedhead, left) can benefit from a little faded glory in the form of a craquelure (delicately cracked) finish. Craquelure was invented in eighteenth-century France, inspired by the lacquer finish of imported Oriental ceramics and Japanese Raku pottery. To enhance further the antique patina of a craquelure finish, first add softly speckled fly-spots, as I did to the wallpaper that forms the background to these pages. For a more open cracked finish, see page 192.

T WO VARNISHES, which are sold in a pack, interact to produce the cracks. A flexible, slow-drying varnish is applied first, followed by a brittle, quick-drying water-based one. The skill lies in judging exactly when to apply the second varnish, This should be done at a point when the first varnish is very slightly tacky. The cracks produced by the interaction of the two different varnishes are so fine that they are almost imperceptible until dirt gets into them or, in this case, a colourant, like tinted oil glaze, is rubbed into them, as shown in *steps 3* and *4* opposite.

Crackle varnish is not suitable for deeply carved surfaces because it tends to pool and will not dry at a constant rate.

Cloth

Two-part crackle varnish

Water-based ink

Cloth

Fitches

Terra verde artists' oil paint

Transparent oil glaze

Raw umber artists' oil paint

Stencilling brush

TOOLS & MATERIALS

Ready-made crackle varnish comes in two bottles (see p.224). One contains an oil-based varnish (often called antiquing varnish), the other a water-based varnish. To make your own highly effective version see page 332. Mix transparent oil glaze 1:1 with earth colours (here terra verde *and raw umber) artists' oil paint to colour the cracks. Use water-based ink and a toothbrush for the fly-spot effect.*

FLY-SPOTS

1 *To imitate fly-spots on a craquelure finish (or any painted surface) spatter ink from a stencilling brush over the surface.*

2 *After two minutes dab the ink spots without smudging with an absorbent cloth to leave softly speckled rings of colour.*

1 *Apply the oil-based crackle varnish with a soft brush (a fitch is ideal). Establish a really smooth, thin and even layer of varnish to ensure the drying time is constant for the whole surface. Let the varnish dry until it is slightly tacky; then follow* step 2 *without delay. (You might like to test the varnish's drying time before starting* step 1*).*

2 *Brush on a generous coat of the water-based varnish with a fitch. Ensure you cover the first coat of varnish entirely. Leave to dry (this should take about an hour). Cracks will appear; if necessary, you can accentuate the cracks by heating the varnish with a hairdryer.*

3 *To show up the cracks and antique the varnish rub coloured oil glaze all over the surface. Use your fingers or a cloth. Earth colours make the best antiquing colours for this step. I used a mixture of* terra verde *and* raw umber *artists' oil paints, but you can experiment with brighter colours.*

4 *Rub off most of the glaze with a cloth, taking care not to lift it from the cracks. Leave to dry for several days. The second coat of varnish is water-soluble so either protect with a coat of oil-based varnish or wipe it off with a damp sponge, so that you leave traces of colour in the cracks only.*

ANTIQUING

In this process a translucent antiquing medium (either a glaze or a wax) is used to cast a spell of age on painted surfaces. Glaze or wax is coloured with a neutral, dull coloured pigment (usually brown), which represents the gradual deposit of dirt and dust on a surface that has been cherished by many years of polishing. By toning down colours and highlighting areas of wear and tear, painted wood is given the mellow beauty that occurs naturally with time. The new pine dado on the opposite page was given an aged paint finish (see pp.266–7) and then antiqued with glaze; the woodgrained panelling above was antiqued with wax.

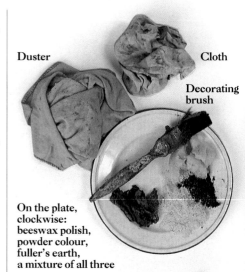

Duster   Cloth

Decorating brush

On the plate, clockwise: beeswax polish, powder colour, fuller's earth, a mixture of all three

Raw umber artists' oil paint

Transparent oil glaze

Long-bristled fitch

CONTRARY TO the usual rules of preparation, the rougher the surface, the better. This is because the antiquing medium looks most effective when it lodges in scratches, knocks and open woodgrain. If a surface is new, sand or wire-brush it, or give it a chipped or cracked appearance (pp.268–9).

To antique smooth surfaces use the softened glazework technique on pages 256–7.

Wax versus glaze

Your choice of medium will depend on the finish you prefer and practical considerations. Waxed surfaces can be polished to a shiny, antique patina. Beeswax polish can be coloured with artists' oil paints or powder colours, smells pleasant and offers some protection.

Antiquing glaze, on the other hand, gives an unsurpassable translucent finish. But it will require a protective layer on top because it does not dry very hard. For areas of high wear and tear use oil-based varnish, and for added depth of colour tint it with artists' oil paints.

Other antiquing methods

For a more opaque, dusty appearance, cover painted surfaces with a thin wash of emulsion diluted 1:4 with water, or eggshell paint diluted 1:4 with white spirit.

"Old" paint *This dado was painted with blue eggshell and then diluted sage-green eggshell for an old, dusty look.*

TOOLS & MATERIALS

The colours that best represent dust and dirt are raw umber and raw sienna. For antiquing glaze make a 1:8 mixture of artists' oil paint and transparent oil glaze. Add the glaze slowly to the oil paint (see p.333). For antiquing wax mix a little artists' oil paint, powder colour, and fuller's earth or powdered rottenstone with beeswax furniture polish and a little turpentine (see p.228). Powder colours are highly toxic (follow the safety advice on p.325). Use a stiff brush, such as a long-haired fitch, to fidget the antiquing medium into all of the recesses.

USING GLAZE

1 *Apply the antiquing glaze. Take care to brush it out in a thin layer over the whole surface as well as to work it into every crack and crevice. Use a long-bristled fitch or small decorating brush.*

2 *Delicately wipe the wet glaze. Use a circular movement and constantly reshape the cloth to present a clean surface. Your aim is to leave just a hint of colour on the surface but to leave behind the glaze in the recesses.*

Finishing off *To protect the glazed surface when dry, apply a layer of matt oil-based varnish or beeswax furniture polish. To antique the surface further, tint the varnish or wax with artists' oil paints before applying it.*

USING WAX

1 *Brush on the antiquing wax, just as you would with the antiquing glaze, filling every recess and covering the entire surface.*

2 *After 10 minutes rub off most of the wax on the surface leaving only a thin veil behind. Take care not to disturb the wax in the recesses.*

3 *A day later, polish the thin layer of wax remaining on the surface with a duster to give a shiny, antique patina. (This technique can be used on its own as well as over dry antiquing glaze, to add depth of colour.)*

ANTIQUING PLASTERWORK

White plaster mouldings can have a powdery and unyielding quality that cries out for a sympathetic treatment. The transformation of a fresh cornice, niche, panel, or casting like the one being antiqued opposite (which is hung as a lampshade in the Biedermeier Bathroom on p.63) is quick and easy. With a few simple materials you can create a delicate antique patina and a surface finish redolent of fine crystalline marble or alabaster. So good are the results that they actually encourage you to hunt out more pieces of plasterwork to transform and display on your walls as decorative artefacts in their own right.

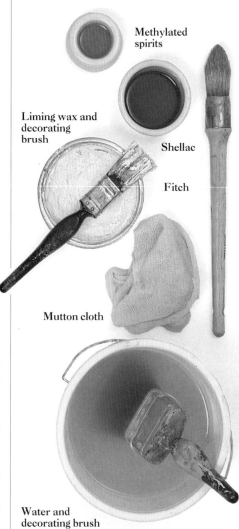

Methylated spirits

Liming wax and decorating brush

Shellac

Fitch

Mutton cloth

Water and decorating brush

W HEN PLASTER is cast in a plaster mould, shellac is used as a mould-releasing agent. Here, it is used to add colour and textural interest to new, unpainted plaster.

How the materials work
The joy of working with the materials for this technique is their quick drying time. Shellac hardens in minutes and liming wax in half an hour. Shellac is part soluble in water so a porous surface, like plaster, that has been dampened, will absorb the shellac, to produce a soft, matt finish. If you apply a second coat of shellac a few minutes after the first one (see *step 2*) it will dry to give a strongly-coloured surface gloss.

Technique options
Shellac comes in colours ranging from brown to orange. Alternatively, use French enamel varnish (see p.225), or tint liming wax with artists' oil paint.

Plaster that has been painted must be stripped before using the technique shown here. This is time-consuming but you can instead work on top of emulsion paint to create a finish that is similar to the one here. Mix a 1:2 solution of shellac and methylated spirits and apply sparingly, as in *step 2*. Follow *steps 3* and *4* but do not expect to create the same lustre and depth of colour.

Transforming plaster *Follow steps 1-4 to give new white plaster, left, the mellow sheen of antique plaster, right.*

TOOLS & MATERIALS
Liming wax can be bought ready-made or you can make your own (see p.332). Shellac comes in several grades; choose a treacly brown one and dilute it 1:1 with methylated spirits to make it more workable and a little paler. Apply the shellac with a pointed brush such as a fitch (see p.208).

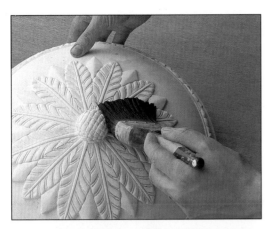

1 Unless your plaster is very fresh, and therefore very damp, you must wet it to prime the surface for the shellac. Soak the plaster by brushing water over it several times – it is amazing how quickly the water is absorbed. For a cornice, treat one whole side of the room at a time; remember to protect the room with plastic sheeting.

2 While the plaster is still damp use a stiff-bristled brush to stipple and fidget the dilute shellac into the carving (avoid using broad strokes, as these will show up later). Apply one coat for a mottled, matt surface and a second, a few minutes later, if you want a richer, glossier colour.

3 Leave the shellac to dry for about 10 minutes and then work in the liming wax. Make sure you penetrate every nook and cranny, otherwise you will have ugly, dark "holes" in the finish. Keep the coverage of wax even by transferring any excess on the brush to new areas, or diluting the mixture on the surface with turpentine.

4 Immediately, take an absorbent rag, such as mutton cloth, and rub the raised areas of the moulding to take off some of the wax and reveal the shellac beneath. Where there are expanses of plain surface, use the cloth to dab a pattern into the wax, taking most of the wax off. Leave to dry for at least half an hour before polishing to a sheen.

AGEING PLASTER WALLS

Although it may seem slightly perverse to want to damage and distress a perfectly smooth, flat wall, the effect can be charming, adding texture and character to a room. The crumbly plaster wall of the balcony, left (see also p.167), gives a sense of decayed grandeur, which is perfect for the setting. (See also the French Medieval Bedroom on p.123 and the Venetian Studio on p.145.) If your home is not blessed with the texture of decay then consider using this technique to introduce it as a theatrical gesture in a dining room, bedroom or hallway.

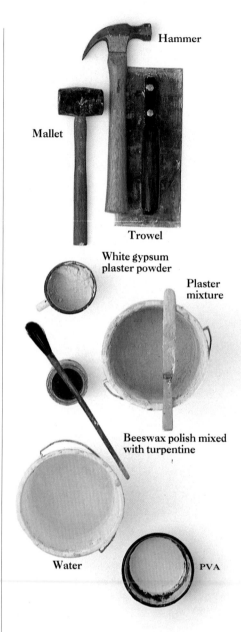

Hammer

Mallet

Trowel

White gypsum
plaster powder

Plaster
mixture

Beeswax polish mixed
with turpentine

Water

PVA

THIS TECHNIQUE uses wax in a "resist" method similar to that used on pages 266–7. Wax that has been heated is applied in patches before plastering, preventing adhesion of the plaster coat. The dry plaster can then be chipped away in random-looking crumbly shapes.

Wall preparation

Plaster can be applied to an unpainted or painted plaster wall. The colour of the paint will show through the chipped areas, so for a neutral effect paint the wall the same colour as the plaster. Before you brush on the wax, coat the wall with PVA mixed 1:1 with water.

Choice of plaster

For this technique use white gypsum (finishing coat) plaster. Its advantages are that its setting time is slower than other plasters and, being white, it can be tinted with powder colour when being mixed (see p.333) or colourwashed when dry (see pp.248–51). Mix up the plaster with water according to the manufacturer's instructions and add one per cent PVA – this will help the plaster adhere to the surface.

Applying plaster

The plaster coat need only be a few millimetres thick and so it is relatively easy to apply. If you have ever tried plastering you will know how difficult it is to achieve a really flat surface free of bumps and pits. The joy of this technique is that blemishes actually contribute to the finish. The trick when using a trowel is to keep it angled slightly off the surface so that only the trailing edge touches as you move it.

Alternative finish

Instead of plaster you can use a PVA-bound, smooth-texture coating (available from DIY stores). This is much easier to work with than decorator's gypsum plaster. Use a brush to apply it and then smooth it with a trowel when it is nearly dry. This smooth-texture coating will peel rather than chip away when dry, giving a slightly less ragged texture.

TOOLS & MATERIALS

PVA is used to seal and protect the surface, and one per cent by volume should be mixed with gypsum finishing plaster and water. The trowel is used for plastering; if you are plastering large areas you may also want to invest in a hawk (a hand-held tray for the mixed plaster). It is advisable to wear eye protection for step 5 as plaster can fly off the surface in all directions.

AGEING PLASTER WALLS

1 *Seal the surface with PVA mixed 1:1 with water and allow it to dry. I started with a coloured background but this is not essential.*

2 *Gently heat equal quantities of beeswax polish and turpentine in a bain-marie; brush on the cooled mixture in random patches.*

3 *While the wax is still soft, trowel on the plaster in broad, arc-like movements, until the whole surface is covered with a thin layer.*

4 *Once the plaster has begun to set, splash plenty of clean water on it with a brush and remove ridges and obvious marks with a wetted trowel.*

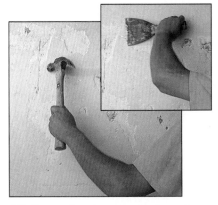

5 *Leave the plaster to dry for a day. Then knock the wall with a hammer or mallet to loosen the plaster over the waxed areas, and scrape this away.*

6 *Sand the surface lightly to soften the edges and remove any unwanted tool marks. Apply a protective coat of PVA diluted 1:4 with water.*

FAUX EFFECTS

False, or faux effects transform the appearance of a surface and so deceive the eye into thinking that it is something else. The techniques for creating the effects of stone, marble, wood, rust, gold and even leather are all given in this section, together with ideas on where to apply them. As well as "tying in" ordinary materials, like plastic and hardboard, with a rich decorative scheme, faux finishes can be used to provide rooms with an unexpected element, such as walls with a dark lead finish, or skirting boards that look like dusty terracotta.

Metal leaf, shown on a wood moulding and plastic ornament, can be laid haphazardly to reveal the colour of underlying paint

Sand is used to give *faux* rust, below, a gritty texture

An example of a stone finish executed in emulsion, above, and woodgraining done using a simple home-made wash, left

These hardboard shapes with a leather-like texture executed in unusual colours can be seen as wall panels on page 133

The yellow Siena marble, below, and the brown fossilstone marble, bottom, are sophisticated finishes

Plastic ornament with plaster finish

The effects of terracotta, above, and verdigris, right, are achieved by the accurate representation of colour and the random building of layers

PIETRA SERENA

There is nothing to equal the texture of stone for adding power and weight to an interior. But it is not necessary to have the real thing – it can be convincingly imitated on all kinds of materials, including wood, plastic and plaster (see the Florentine room, left, and on p.137). The type of stone imitated here, is pietra serena, *which is rough-cut marble that over the years turns from grey to a mellow, raw-umber brown. Once the main building material for the great Renaissance buildings of Florence, its distinctive colour (which is often copied by decorators for exterior stucco and stonework) can add Italian panache and historical significance to interior schemes.*

T HE characteristics of this stone – its mellow colour, varied texture and pale veining – can be simulated using simple materials.

To reproduce the colour of *pietra serena* start with a dark, grey-brown eggshell basecoat. If you cannot find a suitable colour add dark-grey eggshell paint slowly to umber-brown eggshell paint (if you do this

the other way around you will end up with a colour that is too cold and blue). Eggshell paint can be applied to most surfaces, provided they are correctly primed (see the section on surfaces on pp.232–45). Eliminate any surface texture before you apply the primer.

Stone texture

To imitate the stone's worn and textured surface, start by applying a thick layer of a paste made from pale grey emulsion paint and whiting. Once dry, rub with methylated spirits. This slightly softens some of the roughest areas of paste and completely removes others to reveal patches of the smooth eggshell basecoat, which resemble the exposed or raised parts of stone that have become highly polished through wear. Finally, add thin lines to imitate the white veining characteristic of the stone. Protect the finished surface with a coat of matt, oil-based varnish.

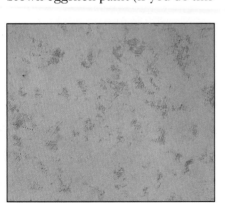

Imitating limestone *Follow* steps 1–4, *but use a creamy-beige texturing paste for a limestone colour.*

Diluted white emulsion and swordliner

Methylated spirits

Texturing paste

Eggshell basecoat and decorating brush

Decorating brush

Whiting

Rag

TOOLS & MATERIALS

Eggshell paint is used for the basecoat and emulsion diluted with water for the veined lines. The texturing paste is made from emulsion paint and whiting; add whiting until the mixture begins to look bitty and solid, like congealed butter icing (you should be able to make it peak). Use a decorating brush to apply the basecoat and the paste and a swordliner or lining brush (see pp.208–9) for the veining.

1 Apply a thick layer of texturing paste over the dark, grey-brown eggshell basecoat. Pull the brush away from the paste sharply to create a stippled texture with little peaks. Leave the paste to dry – this may take up to two days in damp conditions.

2 Dip a rag into methlyated spirits. With the rag in a tight bundle, rub the surface firmly, using a circular motion. The methylated spirits will soften the peaks of the paste to resemble worn, rough-cut stone. In places it will also expose the smooth grey-brown eggshell basecoat.

3 Draw a swordliner (or a lining brush) across the surface to create fine, fractured veins. Use white emulsion, diluted 1:1 with water.

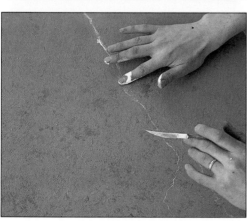

4 The swordliner will naturally deposit small puddles of paint in some areas; immediately blot some of these with your finger. Blot others when they are half dry, to leave rings and outlines of white paint. This occasional softening of the line will make it appear as if it runs right through the depth of the stone.

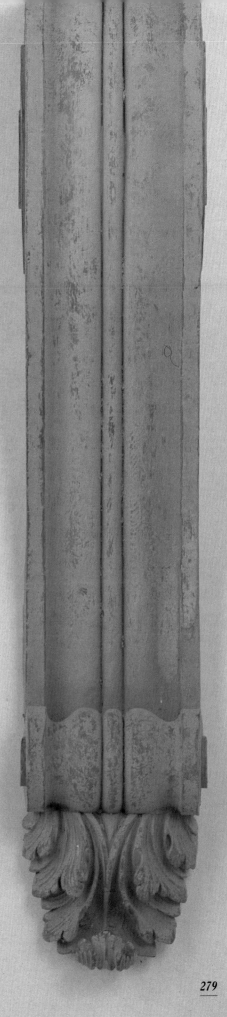

SANDSTONE

This technique follows in the eighteenth-century tradition of using paint to imitate exterior finishes indoors. But whereas early methods were aimed at suggesting materials such as sandstone in the enormous hallways and echoing stairwells of grand homes, this technique results in a more subtle finish that will withstand close scrutiny in rooms of

a modest size. The result of the steps opposite is a dusty and granular finish that both looks and feels like the material it apes. I used this technique for the wall in the Scottish setting shown above and on page 155. Not only is the effect fun to produce but the theatrical result will add atmosphere.

FIRST PAINT the wall with a basecoat of white emulsion. If it is already painted white, ensure that it is clean and that none of the paint is flaking.

If you are applying a new basecoat you can brush on the paint in a reasonably rough-and-ready manner because most of it will be obscured by the emulsion paint and glaze applied in *steps 2* and *3*.

Texture and colour

Like the leather effect on pages 282–3, the sandstone effect is created by building up texture with thick layers of paint. The texture is "heightened" with coloured transparent oil glaze.

Diluted eggshell paint is used to add a thin veil of colour that tones down the previous colours and makes the effect more realistic. The surface is then lightly sanded so that some of all the colours beneath are exposed.

Protection

The diluted eggshell paint applied in *step 4* will protect the oil glaze beneath and this is suitably durable for most rooms. However, in a hallway, for example, you may wish to protect it with matt varnish.

Special tips

Stipple on a very thick layer of the emulsion paint (*step 2*). If the surface does not look textured enough, stipple the paint again five minutes later. Rather than stipple the whole wall at once, stipple each stone-shaped area separately; this way each stone will have a slightly different character.

Include one or two curved as opposed to right-angled corners of mortar but avoid having too many or the wall might look like something from a Walt Disney cartoon.

Sandstone and mortar *This "sandstone" wall is as subtle and realistic when viewed from nearby as from afar. Emulsion paint was used for the lines of mortar.*

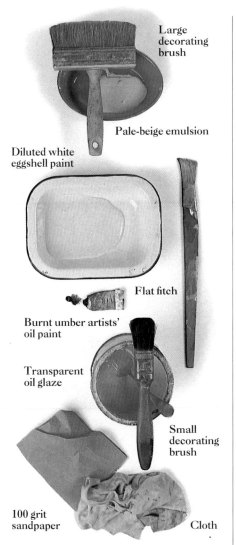

Large decorating brush

Pale-beige emulsion

Diluted white eggshell paint

Flat fitch

Burnt umber artists' oil paint

Transparent oil glaze

Small decorating brush

100 grit sandpaper

Cloth

TOOLS & MATERIALS

The tools you need are two decorating brushes (one large, one small), a flat fitch (or similar-shaped artists' brush), a cloth and 100 grit sandpaper. Mix the transparent oil glaze with brown artists' oil paint (see p.333 for instructions) and dilute white eggshell with a little turpentine. You can experiment with applying more than one colour of emulsion in step 2 *for different effects.*

1 *Draw irregular stone shapes on a dry, white emulsion basecoat; leave space between the stone shapes in which to paint in the mortar (*step 6*).*

2 *Use a large, stiff-bristled decorating brush to stipple on the pale-beige emulsion paint. Paint almost up to the pencil lines.*

3 *When dry, brush on transparent oil glaze mixed with brown artists' oil paint. Wait five minutes. Then wipe the glaze with a cloth.*

4 *After the glaze has dried (this may take a day), apply diluted white eggshell. Brush it out to make a thin, even layer of colour and leave for a day.*

5 *When the paint is dry, sand the whole area with 100 grit sand-paper. This will reveal the pale-beige emulsion applied in* step 2.

6 *Following the gaps between the "stones", use pale-grey emulsion and a fitch to paint freehand the mortar lines between each of the individual rect-angles of "sandstone".*

LEATHER

The rich, textural quality of medieval worked leather adds theatrical grandeur to a room. The techniques for faux *leather can achieve the same sumptuous effect, as shown on the right, as well as the more subtle leather effect on the blue and pink wall panels of the Tudor decoration, shown left, and on page 133. The technique was developed from an accidental discovery made by a pupil of mine when learning how to antique a textured paint surface. Rather than brushing on the paint she "fidgeted" it, making swirling patterns which revealed themselves when antiqued (steps 3–5). Adapted and refined, this provided a starting point for an effective imitative finish.*

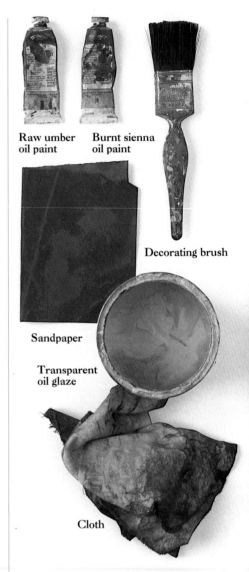

Raw umber oil paint

Burnt sienna oil paint

Decorating brush

Sandpaper

Transparent oil glaze

Cloth

THE TECHNIQUES of leather finishing can be applied to any clean and grease-free surface. Both the finishes here are suitable for walls and furniture.

"Stamped leather"

An obelisk-shaped mask was used to make the "leather" on the opposite page look as if it has been stamped. (The same mask was used in a different technique for the frieze in the Tudor scheme above.) To pattern leather, make a card shape. Use it to make a guide for painting and to shield the first colour of emulsion (*step 1*) from the second, in which the brush is "fidgeted" to make swirling, leathery patterns.

Your choice of colours can vary according to how fantastic you want the leather to look. To convey a realistic sense of the material use light tan, and brown emulsion paints, together with a mixture of raw umber and burnt umber or burnt sienna artists' oil paints to colour the transparent oil glaze.

For leather with no "stamped" pattern follow *steps 1–5* opposite, without using a mask, painting and texturing the whole surface.

Subtle effects

The softer finish of the Tudor panels, which can be seen in more detail on page 133, was achieved by applying brown artists' oil paint mixed with glaze over pink and blue emulsion basecoats, textured as in *step 2*.

Finishing touches

Either finish can be left semi-matt or, for a sheen, rubbed with beeswax furniture polish. Protect surfaces with semi-matt varnish.

Making a mask This mask was cut from oiled manila card (see pp.214–5).

TOOLS & MATERIALS

Use a small decorating brush to apply the two shades of emulsion paint. The paint must be thick enough to allow you to build texture into it. If you think the paint will fall back on itself mix in a little whiting. Mix a little raw umber and burnt sienna artists' oil paint 1:1 with transparent oil glaze. Some artists' oil paints are toxic and can be absorbed through the skin, so should be applied with gloves if you are working on a large area (see the table on pp.324–7). Use cartridge paper or the back of a piece of sandpaper for step 5.

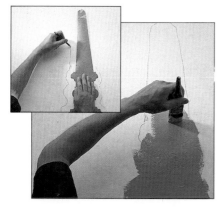

1 *Loosely draw round the mask; remove it and stipple the outlined area with tan emulsion to make a peaked texture. Leave to dry for a day.*

2 *Secure the mask in its original position. Apply a thick layer of brown emulsion, "fidgeting" the brush all over the surface around the mask.*

3 *Remove the mask and leave the paint to dry for a day. Then rub artists' oil paints mixed 1:1 with transparent oil glaze over the surface.*

4 *Using a cloth, gently wipe off the glossy excess of the glaze mixture, leaving the rest in the recesses of the textured emulsion.*

5 *To reveal patches of the emulsion colours beneath, gently rub the raised areas (including the obelisk shape) with the back of a piece of sandpaper.*

6 *The obelisk shape, which was not painted with the brown emulsion in step 2 will appear lighter. To give the shape a sharper outline draw round it with a pencil.*

TERRACOTTA, PLASTER & LEAD

The weathered patina of old lead, the salty bloom of terracotta and the dusty surface of raw pink plaster have something in common. They are all mineral finishes that result from chemical changes on raw materials, and they can all be imitated with a brush, a sponge and emulsion paint. The simple and quick technique shown opposite is for a terracotta finish; just use different colours of emulsion paint to imitate plaster and lead.

THIS TECHNIQUE relies for its effect on broad, random marks made with a sponge and paintbrush, so it is only effective on fairly large surfaces. The odd run of paint is part of the effect, so work on vertical surfaces or objects that you can turn upright.

The wall and skirting board in the scheme above, and the large frame, far right, have a terracotta finish; see page 183 for the plaster-effect finish and page 127 for lead.

Terracotta, plaster and lead all have a dry dustiness that can only be imitated with water-based paints such as emulsion, which dry to a matt finish.

Areas prone to scuffing, such as a hallway dado, or water splashes, such as a bathroom wall, should be protected with one coat of oil-based extra matt varnish or matt acrylic varnish. Do not use gloss varnish because it will destroy the required dusty effect.

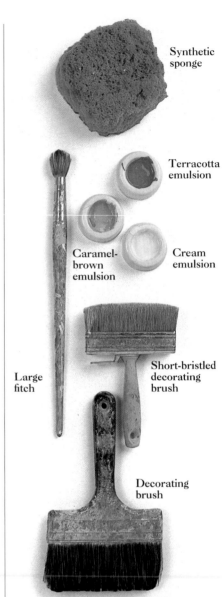

Synthetic sponge

Terracotta emulsion

Caramel-brown emulsion

Cream emulsion

Large fitch

Short-bristled decorating brush

Decorating brush

LEAD & PLASTER

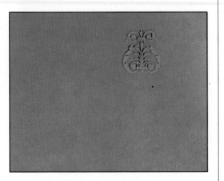

Lead effect *Apply dark-grey emulsion, skip* step 1 *and follow* steps 2–4, *using light-grey paint.*

Plaster effect *Follow* steps 1–4, *simply substituting a pinky-brown colour for the terracotta paint.*

TOOLS & MATERIALS

You can use a decorating brush of any quality for brushing on the basecoat and the paint in step 1, *as any faint brushmarks will be disguised by the subsequent sponge marks. Natural sponges have the best configuration of holes but an excellent alternative is a synthetic sponge, ripped to give it a random shape. Use emulsion paint, diluting it as indicated in the steps opposite.*

TERRACOTTA, PLASTER & LEAD

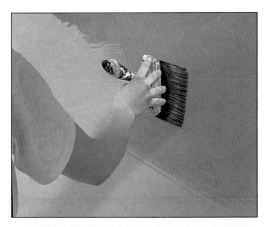

1 Brush on terracotta emulsion (diluted 1:1 with water) over a dry basecoat of caramel emulsion. Keep brushing the paint (even as it dries) to leave a soft and patchy layer, allowing cloudy patches of basecoat to show through here and there. For a plaster effect, use pinky-brown emulsion diluted 1:1 with water.

2 When the paint is completely dry (one to five hours later) use a clean decorating brush to dampen the surface (this makes the paint applied and sponged in the next steps more workable). Dampen areas of a square metre at a time. For plaster and lead, dampen the pinky-brown or dark-grey paint.

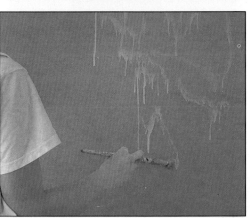

3 Apply cream emulsion (diluted 1:2 with water) with a large fitch or 2.5-cm (1-in) decorating brush to make a random pattern of blobs and lines; use enough paint for it to run slightly. Follow this step, using the same colour for plaster, and light grey for lead.

4 Dab and smudge the blobs and lines with a slightly damp sponge. The thin film of water on the wall (applied in step 2) will cause the sponge marks to soften into gentle blurs and the paint to run. At intervals of about a minute, sponge the area for 10–15 seconds; continue this until the sponge marks become clearer.

THE EFFECT

You can clearly see how the water applied in step 2 causes the sponge marks to blend into a wispy blur and how the odd run of paint is allowed to remain after being sponged as in step 4.

285

VERDIGRIS

Patinated metals have a rich variety of colours and textures that are fascinating reminders of the passage of time and the action of the elements. Verdigris, with its green, crumbly saltiness, is the result of naturally-occurring corrosion and affects brass, copper and bronze. The decorative appeal of verdigris is such, that metalworkers reproduce it with acids and heat in a highly toxic process. You can create authentic-looking verdigris – safely – using simple materials and following the steps shown opposite. The brand-new metalwork in the bathroom above (and pp.158–61) was transformed using this technique.

Whiting

Verdigris paste, ready to apply

Pale-blue emulsion

Artists' paint-brush

Mint-green emulsion

Diluted deep blue-green emulsion

French enamel varnish

Methylated spirits

Yellow-ochre spray paint

THIS technique is suitable for any metal or plastic surface that you can work on horizontally. The verdigris paste will not adhere to vertical surfaces but you can produce a verdigris effect (like the wall on p.173 and the background here) using a slightly different method, which is shown below.

This depends on achieving a random effect. Apply all the layers on top of the first coat of paint (thick pastes, spray paint and powder) in random patches rather than even layers so as to achieve a natural-looking result. You can seal the powdery finish with diluted PVA, followed by matt varnish to produce a hardwearing surface.

Application

If you are not working on bronze, copper or brass you can create a suitable base colour by painting your surface with bronze powder colour or spray paint (use gold for a brighter effect). If your surface is silver, like the metalwork here, simply paint it with brown French enamel varnish (see p.225).

Like marbling, woodgraining, and ageing and antiquing paint-work, the aim of this technique is to imitate a naturally-occurring phenomenon and to trick the eye into believing that no human hand has had any part in the process.

Vertical surfaces *To verdigris vertical surfaces apply diluted emulsion paint in the colours of verdigris and flood water through the damp paint layers.*

TOOLS & MATERIALS

You need two verdigris pastes, one that is pale blue and one that is mint green. To make verdigris paste make a 1:2 mixture of methylated spirits and emulsion paint, then sieve in whiting until the mixture is the consistency of butter icing. Methylated spirits evaporates quickly, so you may need to add more as you go along to keep the mixture workable.

1 Brush a 1:4 mixture of deep blue-green emulsion paint and water over the bronze- or gold-coloured basecoat and leave to dry.

2 Work the pale-blue and the mint-green verdigris pastes over the surface together. Vary the thickness and texture to create a random effect.

3 Whilst the verdigris pastes are drying, use a yellow-ochre spray paint to apply small, light patches of colour haphazardly across the surface.

4 Flood the surface with water to expose the underlying colours. Just let the water wash over the top of the mixture – do not work it in.

5 Take some whiting or plaster powder and lightly sprinkle it across the surface, pressing it into the damp and sticky mixture. Pay special attention to recesses.

6 When the mixture is half dry, wipe some – not all – of the raised areas with a rough cloth to expose patches of underlying colour. When dry, seal with diluted PVA.

IRON & RUST

Metal finishes can be exploited to great decorative effect in an interior scheme. In the Spanish Baroque Bedroom, left, and on page 45 the door, treated to resemble iron, has a silvery metallic sheen, lightly dribbled with rust. On the skirting board, architrave and door studs, metal is imitated in its more heavily corroded state as dark rust. Both of these simple techniques are demonstrated here, and they can be applied to any surface.

THESE SIMPLE metal techniques use materials that are built up in separate layers to give naturalistic metallic finishes. In the rust technique, see *steps 1–4* below left, a wood surface is given texture with a mixture of glue and sand. This will also cover any imperfections on the surface. The final coat is French enamel varnish (see *step 3*), mixed with methylated spirits and highlighted with emulsion paint. In the iron process, diluted black emulsion is applied over a dry coat of oil-based paint.

Random effects

The success of these metal finishes depends on the randomness of the surface pattern. In the final stages, water is used to break up the basecoat of paint on the "iron" door, and, in the rust technique, methylated spirits is applied on the varnish, to emulate the texture of metal. To "randomize", when using rags and brushes, constantly change the angle at which you hold them, the direction in which you work, and the pressure you apply.

Protecting the "metal"

Although the rust effect is very durable (the glue, sand and paint form a sort of cement), it is still worthwhile protecting it with a coat of matt oil-based varnish. This will give the surface a really hard finish.

The silver metallic paint used for the iron technique contains metal powders. These are likely to be aluminium, in which case no protection is needed. But sometimes paints contain other metals; the air causes these to darken and they need protection. Check the ingredients of your silver paint, and if you are unsure whether it contains aluminium, protect it with semi-matt polyurethane varnish.

IMITATING RUST

1 *Coat the surface generously with undiluted PVA and throw sand at it. On vertical pieces hold a board beneath to catch the excess.*

2 *Leave to dry thoroughly and brush on deep brown emulsion, fidgeting the brush to work the paint well into the texture of the sand.*

3 *When dry, brush on a coat of rich brown French enamel varnish, diluted 1:1 with methylated spirits.*

4 *After 10 minutes brush on methylated spirits and touches of rust-coloured emulsion. Make patterns with more methylated spirits.*

TOOLS & MATERIALS

Basic tools – decorating brushes, a dusting brush, an artists' brush and a cloth – are needed for imitating iron and rust. The brown emulsion is used for the rust, and the brighter, rust-coloured emulsion is used for highlights in both of the finishes. Methylated spirits is used to work on the paint and French enamel varnish, in the technique on the left, producing random patches, which suggest the texture of rust.

French enamel varnish

Cloth dipped in black emulsion

Decorating brush

Decorating brush

Brown emulsion

Methylated spirits

Artists' brush

PVA

Rust-coloured emulsion

Sand

Dusting brush

IMITATING IRON

1 *Paint the surface with silver metallic paint. Dilute black emulsion 1:4 with water and add a drop of detergent. Apply with a damp cloth to produce random patterns. The mixture dries fast so cover only a small area of the surface at a time.*

2 *As the mixture dries, soften it with a dry dusting brush, or a lily-bristle softener, to make the marks of the cloth less obvious. Soften out the paint more in some areas than others, to lend a randomness to the texture.*

3 *When thoroughly dry, brush water over the surface and dribble rust-coloured emulsion (diluted 1:2 with water) through it. The water brushed on the surface will dilute the "rust" further, making it dry pale and translucent over the silver as the large example on the left shows.*

CARRARA & SERPENTINE MARBLE

The decorative technique of simulating marble dates back to Roman times and there is a wealth of different styles. White Carrara and green serpentine marble are quite easy to paint and can be applied successfully to different surfaces, from floors and skirting boards to small objects. Painted well, marble adds style and a certain classic quality to a room, as can be seen in the Florentine Hallway, shown above left and on page 137.

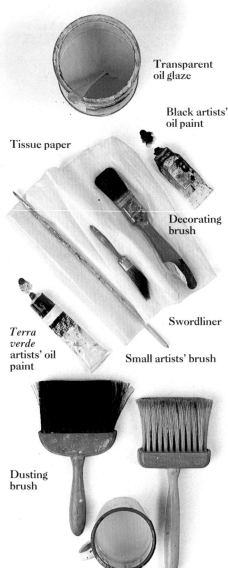

Transparent oil glaze

Black artists' oil paint

Tissue paper

Decorating brush

Swordliner

Terra verde artists' oil paint

Small artists' brush

Dusting brush

Turpentine   Lily-bristle softening brush

F{OR CENTURIES} marbling was carried out in distempers and gesso paints. But the nineteenth century saw a desire for a new realism and in Britain the new and cheap medium adopted was transparent oil glaze, which was used as a vehicle to extend expensive artists' oil paints.

Transparent oil glaze is still used for marbling today. Buy it ready-made or follow the recipe on page 332 to make your own.

The best surface preparation for transparent oil glaze is two coats of white eggshell paint. This gives a degree of slip whilst presenting a reasonably smooth surface. Oil glaze rubs away with time so always coat with semi-gloss varnish when dry and wax for a reflective sheen.

Oil glaze attracts dust like a magnet so work in a draught-free area and vacuum it before you begin. Always shake your brushes free of dust before using them.

TOOLS & MATERIALS

Use artists' oil paints to colour transparent oil glaze (for mixing instructions turn to p.333). Black is used to tint the glaze for Carrara marbling, terra verde *and white for the first serpentine glaze and* terra verde *only for the second. Artists' oil colours are toxic so always clean your hands after using them. For information on dusting and softening brushes see pages 210–11 and for the swordliner, turn to page 208.*

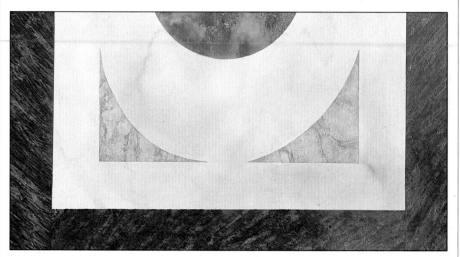

Marbled floor *I used a combination of different coloured marbles to make a striking pattern; the method for the yellow marble is overleaf.*

CARRARA MARBLING

*1 Using a soft cloth, rub some trans-
parent oil glaze into the eggshell
background to give the surface a greater
degree of "slip".*

*2 Dip a thin brush in black-coloured
glaze and use it to paint a few very
rough veins on the surface, adding the
occasional dot and spatter.*

*3 Using a dusting brush or softening
brush, stroke at the veins with the
tips of the bristles, to spread them
slightly in all directions.*

*4 Dip a swordliner in turpentine
and use it to paint the odd wet line
over the glazed surface, following some
of the softened veins.*

*5 Soften the surface again, brushing
the wet lines made in step 4 in one
direction only, to make feathery crack-
shaped veins.*

*6 Stroke the surface in all directions
with the tips of a lily-bristle softener, to eliminate all brushmarks and
create a hazy blur.*

SERPENTINE MARBLING

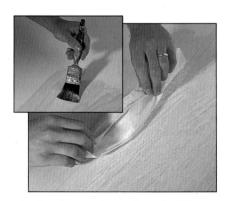

*1 Brush on a glaze coloured with
terra verde artists' oil paint. Dab
at the surface with a pleated piece of
tissue paper to add pattern.*

*2 Leave the surface to dry for at
least a day and then thinly brush
on a much deeper terra-verde coloured
glaze over the entire area.*

*3 Dab the surface with tissue paper
as before, ensuring you present a
clean surface to the wet glaze each time.
Vary the pressure you use.*

Siena Marble

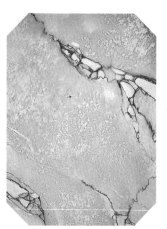

Although simply executed marbles, such as Carrara and serpentine, convey a cool, elegant beauty, the most effective use of marbling with paint is to divide a surface up realistically into blocks and inlays, and incorporate small amounts of rich and complex marble in a design, as in the marbled and varnished flooring shown on page 290. Siena marble has long been favoured by Italian masons for this type of decoration as it possesses a strong concentration of colour and pattern, and might look too intense and overpowering over a large area. As well as decorating floors, Siena marble can be used in patterns on box lids or table tops.

T HE TECHNIQUE for Siena marble is more time-consuming than other marbles, but it pays dividends when you see the final results. Study original examples or pictures of Siena marble – the more you notice about it the more life-like your copy will be.

Preparing and varnishing

As a marble finish should be faultlessly smooth, sand down your surface if necessary and paint it with two coats of cream eggshell. Oil glaze attracts dust so clean and vacuum the day before you start. Ensure brushes are dust-free and do not wear wool clothes. When the glaze is completely dry, protect it with a coat of hard varnish, otherwise it will gradually wear away.

Making patterns

Use masking tape as an aid to marbling neat shapes. Stick on the tape before painting with the cream eggshell and remove it while this is still wet, carefully wiping off any glaze overspill with a cloth as you work.

If the colour of Siena marble does not appeal use the same technique but a different coloured glaze, a sumptuous red or emerald green, for example. For Brescia marble (which forms part of the marbled floor on p.290) mix a browny-red glaze.

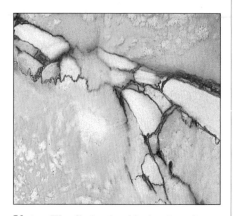

***Veins** The distinctive black veins of Siena marble are drawn with a black wax crayon dipped in turpentine.*

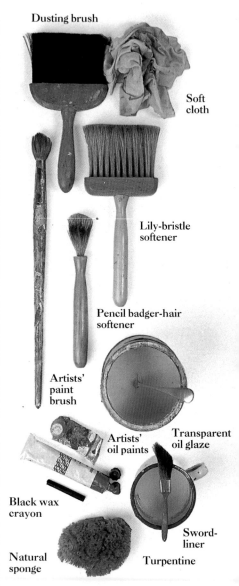

Dusting brush

Soft cloth

Lily-bristle softener

Pencil badger-hair softener

Artists' paint brush

Artists' oil paints

Transparent oil glaze

Black wax crayon

Sword-liner

Natural sponge

Turpentine

TOOLS & MATERIALS

Buy or make some transparent oil glaze (see p.332). Mix the glaze with a little raw sienna artists' oil paint (see p.333). As some artists' oil colours are toxic, always clean your hands after using them, and make sure there are no paint deposits under your nails. A fine artists' brush can be used instead of a swordliner, and an artists' sable brush instead of a badger-hair softener. For information on brushes see pages 206–11. Turpentine or white spirit can be used for step 4.

1 *Wipe a layer of transparent oil glaze over the surface. Then dab on patches and streaks of raw-sienna coloured oil glaze.*

2 *Roughly soften the patches and streaks with a dusting brush, pulling the glaze across the surface in all directions as you do so.*

3 *Using a softener, stroke the patches with the tips of the bristles, to remove any brushmarks and soften the glaze further.*

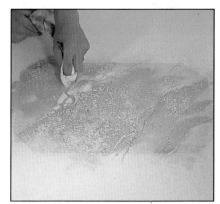

4 *Dip a swordliner or fine artists' brush into turpentine and then use it to paint a few wet veins across the surface of the glaze.*

5 *While the veins are opening up, use a sponge to dab some turpentine very sparingly on the surface. This will create a mottled effect.*

6 *To prevent the turpentine from opening up the glaze further, dab the sponged areas with a cloth, or soften or stipple them with a brush.*

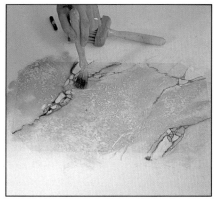

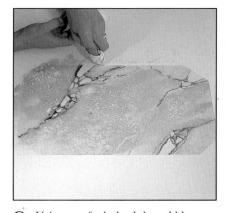

7 *Dip a black wax crayon into some turpentine to soften it and then use it to draw a few veins in the wet glaze in "boulder and pebble" formations, which are typical of the marble.*

8 *Let the surface dry for about 10 minutes, by which time the turpentine will begin to evaporate. Then gently soften the veining with a badger-hair softener or sable artists' brush.*

9 *Using a soft cloth, dab and blur some of the black veining so that it "recedes" into the stone, and wipe out some of the "boulders and pebbles" to make cream-coloured stone chips.*

FOSSILSTONE MARBLE

Some of the most effective mineral finishes are those created when a brush hardly touches the surface, and all the pattern is created in a random fashion by mixing different media. Fossilstone marble is an excellent example of this type of decorative finish and the results are quite beautiful, as can be seen in the decoration here. If possible, lay the surface to be decorated flat on the floor so that the solvent can form pools (for vertical surfaces, see below). Use either a water-based wash as I did, or an oil-based glaze.

PVA

Burnt sienna
wash

Raw umber
wash

Fitch

Methylated
spirits

Lily-bristle softener

Decorating
brush

FOR MARBLING to look real, it requires the smoothest possible basecoat. Sand the surface if necessary and apply two coats of pale-beige eggshell paint, taking care to avoid visible brushmarks.

Media

The traditional medium for marbling is oil paint, or coloured oil glaze. However, for fossilstone marble, nothing beats the variety of patterns obtainable with a home-made water-based wash. This is made from powder colour, water and a little PVA, which is added to bind the mixture.

Before applying the wash add a drop of detergent; this prevents it from opening into patches when applied over the basecoat.

Drying times

In *steps 2* and *4* the wash is manipulated whilst drying. The difficulty with using a water-based wash is that it dries so quickly (10 minutes on a warm, dry day) that only areas under one square metre can be tackled at a time. Oil-based glazes take upwards of two hours to dry.

If you are concerned that you may not be able to work fast enough use an oil-based glaze – the results are good but not as spectacular. To tint the glaze, mix transparent oil glaze with raw umber artists' oil paint (see p.333).

Both PVA water-based washes and oil-based glazes remain soft when dry, and so you will need to protect them with a coat of oil-based varnish.

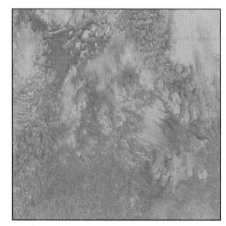

Vertical surfaces *Follow* steps 1–4, *using a sponge instead of a brush to apply the methylated spirits, water and coloured wash in* step 3.

TOOLS & MATERIALS

To make the water-based washes, slowly add 0·5 litre (1 pint) of water mixed with 1 tablespoon of PVA to 2 tablespoons of powder colour (mixed with a little water), stirring all the time. Add a drop of detergent. If the colour does not look right add more powder colour or more water and PVA. Powder colours are highly toxic; follow the safety precautions on page 325. Protect your eyes with goggles when spattering with methylated spirits as in step 3.

FOSSILSTONE MARBLE

1 *If you are using a water-based wash, rub a small amount of fuller's earth into the dry eggshell basecoat to absorb any grease. Brush the raw umber wash on in criss-cross strokes, covering under one square metre; continue with steps 2–4 and then start on a new area. If using oil glaze, cover the whole surface in one go.*

2 *Using a decorating brush, roughly stipple the surface to break up the coarse pattern of brush-marks. Work quickly if you are using a water-based wash; the advantage of oil-based glazes is that they give you much more time to complete this step.*

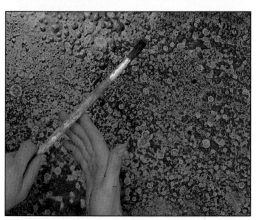

3 *This is the magical part. Spatter methylated spirits on to the water-based wash to make it split. Then flick on a little water here and there to make rivulets and pools of liquid, and (this is optional) spatter on spots of the burnt sienna wash. The overall effect should be random. (On oil-based glaze, use turpentine and then methylated spirits.)*

4 *Allow the surface to dry partially so that only the pools and rivulets remain wet (you can speed up the drying process of oil glaze with a hairdryer). Then, using a lily-bristle softener or dusting brush, soften these wet areas, stroking away the brushmarks and carrying the wet, coloured liquid over the surface in all directions.*

CLAIR BOIS

This easy and effective technique for a clair bois *(pale wood) finish is the first to experiment with when learning to woodgrain. Using a simple home-made wash and a flogging brush you can convey the impression of the fine, polished finish of pale woods (such as maple and satinwood) on surfaces ranging from inexpensive wood furniture and doors, to dados and floors. Biedermeier-style furniture is traditionally made from pale woods so this technique is particularly suitable for a Biedermeier-style room scheme (see p.63); I used it to decorate the exterior of a bath and then protected the wash from water with a coat of varnish.*

Small decorating brush

Water-based wash brushed out

Water-based wash

Raw sienna powder colour

Flogging brush

T HE WATER-BASED wash used here dries quickly and can be brushed into feather-edged forms and crisp shapes. Surprisingly, it is easier to work with this than the oil-based glaze (used for the woodgraining techniques shown on pp.298–301) and it can be dampened and reworked after it has dried. If you can work quickly enough, you may be able to complete all the steps before the wash dries. If not, work on just one area at a time, swapping between *steps 1* and *2*. Alternatively, work on the whole area at once, brushing any of the wash that has dried with a little water to make it workable again.

Choice of finish

Steps 1–2 for a burr wood finish create a pattern that looks like a knotted wood veneer (see the close-up on the top half of the page and the "Biedermeier" bath). A subtler effect can be created by applying less pressure on the brush. A grainy effect can be achieved by following *steps 1–2* for an elongated grain (shown on the bottom half of the page).

Preparation

The smoother the surface you are going to give a *clair bois* finish, the better. As preparation, carefully apply two coats of cream eggshell paint. When dry, rub the surface with a little whiting or fuller's earth to absorb any surface grease.

Finishing touches

When the glaze has dried apply a coat of oil-based varnish. Brush it on swiftly and lightly so as not to disturb the pigment in the glaze. I use goldsize (see p.224), which is quick-drying or, where necessary, a tough oil-based varnish.

To give the "wood" a shiny and smooth finish redolent of French polish follow this decorator's trick: when the varnish is completely dry polish it first with beeswax furniture polish on some grade 0000 wire wool, and then with a duster.

TOOLS & MATERIALS

Water and raw sienna pigment in the form of powder colour are needed for the wash (see p.333). If you are covering a small area, you may wish to use gouache instead of powder colours. (If you use powders follow the precautions on p.325). A flogging brush provides the best clair bois *finish.*

BURR WOOD FINISH

1 *Apply the glaze with a decorating brush. It does not matter what brushmarks you leave as long as the whole surface is covered with an even layer of wash. The wash dries within minutes; if it dries before you move on to step 2 dampen it with a wet paintbrush.*

2 *Hold a flogging brush at 90 degrees to the surface and firmly push the bristles into the wet wash. The long bristles will "splay" outwards, making wild, knotty shapes, which look like the burr patterns of some wood veneers. For a more subtle effect and texture repeat with a lighter pressure.*

ELONGATED GRAIN

1 *Push a flogging brush through the wash, so the bristles splay outwards. This will give the effect of a very coarse but lively woodgrain. Work fast so you can go on to step 2 before the wash starts to dry. If the wash does dry dampen it with a wet brush.*

2 *Hold a flogging brush flat against the surface and pat the wash while pulling the brush towards you. This softens the wilder patterns made in step 1.*

OAK GRAIN

Apply the wash as in steps 1 and 2, below. Soften out the brushmarks with a softening brush, and run a checking roller charged with black paint over the surface (see p.212).

GRAINING WITH A BRUSH

Woodgraining is the technique used to imitate the beautiful, random patterns of natural woodgrains. It reached the height of sophistication in the nineteenth century, when highly skilled artists emulated every known configuration of woodgrain. The comparatively simple technique opposite, is for a non-specific but effective woodgrain finish shown on the door of the Scottish Sitting Room, above. See pages 300–301 for a more pine-like woodgrain and pages 296–7 for a clair bois *(pale wood) finish.*

ANY SMOOTH surface that can be painted with eggshell paint can be woodgrained. Standard modern doors, like the ones here, can be transformed to blend in with a room's decoration and expensive dark woods, like mahogany, can be imitated on inexpensive woods and those that come from renewable resources (see pp.236–7).

Other suitable candidates for woodgraining include skirting boards, furniture and floors.

Glaze and surface preparation

For woodgraining I use transparent oil glaze, coloured with artists' oil paints and diluted to a single cream consistency with turpentine (see p.333 for tinting glaze). Glaze does not form a hard, protective surface so varnish over the top.

Prepare the surface for wood-graining by applying two coats of eggshell paint. This provides a smooth working surface.

Woodgrain colours

The final wood colour results from the colour of the eggshell basecoat and the colour of the glaze. For the door shown on the opposite page, I used glaze tinted with burnt umber artists' oil paint, over two different eggshell basecoats (brown and soft yellow) to give the impression of two sorts of wood.

For different-coloured wood-grains, experiment with other colours of eggshell paint and glaze mixed with any of the earth-colour artists' oil paints.

Transforming a door *This once green door was sanded down and painted with eggshell basecoats of ochre-cream and pink. Once grained (using the glaze colour and technique shown in* steps 1–6*), the panels were stencilled with emulsion and outlined in black.*

Dusting brush

Flogging brush

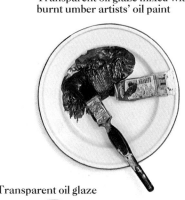

Transparent oil glaze mixed with burnt umber artists' oil paint

Transparent oil glaze

Cloth

TOOLS & MATERIALS

Any clean decorating brush can be used to apply the tinted glaze. You also need a flogging brush, the long hairs of which can be pushed, pulled and patted in the glaze. Use a dusting brush to soften the glaze. (For specialist decorating tools see pp.212–3.)

1 *Brush a coat of glaze on to the panel mouldings. Then jab the glaze with a flogging brush to create a random woodgrain pattern.*

2 *Apply glaze to the panels, and push the flogging brush upwards, to produce the whorls and scratches typical of woodgrain.*

3 *Wipe away any odd marks with a cloth. Then lay the flogging brush almost flat against the surface and pat it to soften the previous marks.*

4 *Push the flogging brush through the glaze on the door frame (as in step 2). On narrow areas use the edge of the brush.*

5 *Using the flat side of the flogging brush, gently pat the glaze as in step 3. Take care to work the brush slowly towards you.*

6 *If you want a subtle effect wait 10 minutes and then stroke the glaze in the direction of the grain with the tips of a dusting brush.*

GRAINING WITH A ROCKER

If you are wary of attempting woodgraining because you feel it may be too complicated, try your hand at this simple technique that uses a little-known "wonder" tool, called the rocker. It creates pine-like patterns and is particularly effective if used in small quantities in a room, on doors, for example, or skirting boards, as in the scheme above, which is also featured on page 95. For a realistic-looking woodgrain use only natural colours over wood or a painted wood-coloured background. Fantasy variations using unnaturalistic colours also look effective; I have seen old farmhouse beams with rough-and-ready blue and red graining that gave them an original and naive charm.

Dusting brush

Decorating brush

Woody-coloured
artists' oil paints

Rubber rocker

THE WORKING surface of the rubber rocker is curved and ribbed in semicircles to make the woodgrain pattern. The medium I use is artists' oil paint, either thinned with a little turpentine (for an intense pattern), or mixed with transparent oil glaze (for the subtle effects shown here).

For faultless graining the paint or glaze should be applied to a smooth, non-absorbent surface. Any bumps will interfere with the pattern, which is only an advantage if you want a rough-and-ready effect. When the paint or glaze is dry (this takes a day or two) apply a coat of oil-based varnish.

USING A ROCKER

Hold the rocker so that the curved surface is touching the wet glaze or paint and then pull the rocker gently towards you, slowly altering the angle
you hold it at as you go (left to right, above). As the rocker moves, its sections of ribbing scoop up the glaze, as in step 3 opposite.

TOOLS & MATERIALS

A rubber rocker is indispensable for this technique. Although virtually any brushes can be used to apply the glaze and soften the pattern, I prefer to use a dusting brush for the latter job, because its bristles are strong enough to work with the sticky glaze, while the bristle tips are fine and soft. Experiment with woody-coloured artists' oil paints, such as raw umber or raw sienna, mixing them 1:3 with transparent oil glaze and a spot of turpentine (see p.333) or, for a bolder pattern, diluting them with just a few drops of turpentine.

1 Using a small decorating brush, paint the glaze over the surface, brushing it out to make an even layer. On pitted surfaces or on grooved surfaces like the matchboarding here, push the glaze into the crevices because it is better for the overall effect that these show up later as dark rather than light.

2 Decide on which direction you want the wood-grain to go and, using a dusting brush, gently brush the glaze layer in that direction, using just the tips of the bristles. Aim for a soft, overall grainy look at this stage.

3 Take the rocker and pull it slowly through the glaze, as described on the opposite page. Keep changing its angle as you pull it along, but do not jerk it or rock it too wildly as movements like these will leave unpleasant marks. Clean the rocker repeatedly with a rag to prevent a build-up of glaze in the rocker's grooves.

4 Soften the grain pattern with a dusting brush to blend it into the background and remove any thick deposits of glaze that the rocker may have left. Drag the brush through the glaze for a "pulled" look (as I am doing), or open up the glaze by patting the surface with the flat side of a flogging brush (shown on p.213) to create oak-like pore marks.

GILDING – METAL LEAF

Gold has a magical, seductive quality, reflecting colours of intense warmth and variety. For centuries, water-gilders have practised the highly skilled art of laying loose sheets of gold over layers of damp glue. But there is a much simpler, quicker method, known as oil gilding, which is illustrated here. Transfer gold leaf (which comes on waxed tissue paper) is laid on top of goldsize, an oil-based varnish. The leaf can be applied directly on to any hard surface including wood and sealed plaster, or, for a silky-smooth finish, over gesso. The three celestial shapes, far right, were gilded directly on to painted plaster.

GILDING WITH transfer leaf (either real gold or inexpensive Dutch metal leaf) gives a richer and more lustrous finish than gold paint or metallic powders. Once you are confident of gilding flat surfaces, move on to carved mouldings and accessories, such as lamp bases. New gilding can be antiqued (see p.304).

Optional gesso preparation

For a perfect, silky-smooth finish, gild over gesso, which is a thick, tough paste that is applied in layers. On a flat surface, the slightly convex shape formed by gesso makes gold leaf look even more reflective and shimmering.

Gesso comes in various forms but rabbit-skin and PVA versions are easy to scrape and polish (*step 2, far right*). To highlight any eventual holes and imperfections rub with fuller's earth; then sand and polish further. Gesso dust may cause asthma so always wear a mask when sanding large areas.

In imitation of the coloured clays sometimes used under gilding, use ready-coloured gesso, colour your own with powder colours, or paint dry gesso with gouache.

Technique tips

Transfer leaf sticks to grease, so before starting clean your hands and rub around the area to be gilded with whiting.

The key to a smooth finish is to lay the leaf when the goldsize is almost dry, but just tacky enough for the leaf to adhere. The drier the goldsize the better the finish.

The drying speed of different brands varies from one to twelve hours, so check the drying time before starting to gild.

Finishing

Dutch metal leaf oxidizes and in time turns black. To prevent this, brush with goldsize several days after gilding, by which time the underlying goldsize will be dry. Real gold leaf needs no protection.

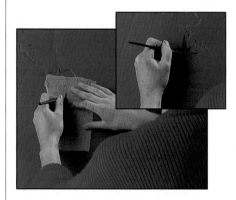

1 *Draw the outline of the design; you may like to use a cutout as a guide. Paint on goldsize (tinted with artists' oil paint so that it is visible).*

2 *When the goldsize is almost dry but slightly tacky, gently press on a sheet of transfer leaf (I am using Dutch metal). Carefully peel away the tissue.*

3 *Several hours later (drying time varies) gently rub off the loose leaf with a soft cloth or cotton wool. Then polish the gilded area with a cloth.*

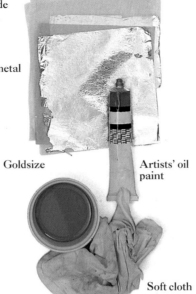

Ready-made rabbit-skin gesso

Dutch metal leaf

Artists' paintbrush

Home-made rabbit-skin gesso

Goldsize

Artists' oil paint

Soft cloth

TOOLS & MATERIALS

Goldsize is the adhesive for transfer leaf. The traditional type of gesso (used here) is made from rabbit-skin glue. It is gently heated in a bain-marie *(double boiler) and applied warm. To make your own traditional gesso or a modern* PVA *version, see page 332. Gilding materials are covered in detail on pages 230–31.*

GESSO PREPARATION

1 *Paint on three or four layers of gesso until the surface is slightly raised. If you are using rabbit-skin gesso, leave to harden overnight after the last coat.*

2 *When the gesso is dry, scrape with a craft knife and polish with silicone carbide paper and grade 0000 wire wool until the finish is smooth.*

3 *Apply one coat of coloured gesso or gouache. Let it dry and then polish to a shine with grade 0000 wire wool. This step is optional.*

4 *To gild over the gesso, apply leaf as shown, left. The gesso provides a build-up of relief which makes the gold glow even more brightly.*

GILDING – METALLIC POWDER

Shimmering and brilliant, the effects that can be achieved with metallic powder are superior to those of gold paint, and from a distance much decorative work in metallic powder is mistaken for gold leaf. Gilding with powders is inexpensive and quicker than gilding with metal leaf, making it suitable for small and fairly large areas, like the Art Nouveau frieze here. For added drama, metallic powder can be patinated (see pp.306–7).

METALLIC POWDERS are available in many colours, including the gold used here. The powder is brushed or shaken on to a surface coated with a thin layer of goldsize. As metallic powders are highly toxic they should not be inhaled. It is important to wear a mask over your nose and mouth, and goggles over your eyes. Ventilate the room when applying the goldsize but not when handling the powder.

The only requirement for gilding with powders is that the surface is reasonably smooth and non-absorbent. Absorbent surfaces, such as bare wood and plaster, should first be primed with paint or sealed with sanding sealer.

Protective coating

Leave the gilded surface to dry for three days before applying white polish or shellac (see pp.224–5) diluted 1:1 with methylated spirits.

Duster

Camel-hair mop

Dusting brush

Mask

Metallic powder

French enamel varnish

Artists' oil paint

Artist's paint-brush

Goldsize

Cloth

Soft brush

TOOLS & MATERIALS

Goldsize is an oil-based varnish. Its drying time ranges from one to twelve hours (see Technique tips on p.302). Apply the metallic powder with a pad of cotton wool, a camel-hair mop or soft make-up brush (see specialist brushes on p.212). For antiquing use French enamel varnish (a shellac-based varnish) diluted with methylated spirits.

ANTIQUING GOLD

1 *To antique metallic powder or gold leaf liberally brush with French enamel varnish (diluted 1:1 with methylated spirits).*

2 *Dab off some of the French enamel varnish to reveal the gold beneath. Alternatively, spatter with more varnish (see p.262).*

1 Tint some goldsize by mixing in a little artists' oil paint; this will enable you to see where you have brushed it. Using a soft brush apply the goldsize, brushing it out into a thin, even layer. Wait until the goldsize is nearly dry but still tacky.

2 Protect your mouth and nose with a mask and your eyes with goggles. Dip a camel-hair mop (or make-up brush) into a small pot of metallic powder. Shake off excess powder, inside the jar, and then gently stroke the tacky goldsize with the brush to leave a thin layer of metallic powder.

3 Leave the goldsize to dry completely hard (preferably wait for 24 hours). Wearing a paper mask and goggles, dust off any loose powder with a dry dusting brush; vacuum up the loose powder. Gently polish the gilded area with a soft cloth or cotton wool until it is really gleaming.

"Gold" ornament Gilding with metallic powder is a quick and inexpensive way of transforming an ornament, like this plastic leaf, into a rich, lustrous decoration. Follow the steps shown above using gold, bronze or silver metallic powder.

PATINATED GOLD

This technique is used to give surfaces that are painted gold, or gilded with metal leaf or powder, added decorative interest in the form of a dramatically patinated finish. (It can even be used directly on cast metals.) The complex appearance of the patina belies the simplicity of the technique. French enamel varnish, methylated spirits and spray paint are built up in opaque and translucent layers of colour. The technique is suitable for surfaces that can be worked on horizontally, ranging from furniture to mouldings, like the gold-sprayed skirting board and the hardboard frieze above. The frieze was given extra pattern with colours sprayed around a triangular template.

Methylated spirits

Diluted French enamel varnish

Gold spray paint

Pointed fitches

French enamel varnish

H ISTORICALLY, a variety of methods have been used to patinate metals. Today, chemical patination is the most common process but it is highly toxic and ineffective on real gold.

The technique here is much safer and, used over copper-coloured paint, gives surfaces the appearance of antique bronze. To give gold leaf or metallic powder a more subtle antique patina use the simple method shown on page 304.

Importance of varnishing

On exposure to air any metal finish, other than pure gold, will become dull. It is, therefore, important to protect the finish with a coat of oil-based varnish. This also serves to harden the rather brittle French enamel varnish, which is used as part of the technique.

Do not use an alcohol-based varnish (consult pp.330–31) as this will dissolve the methylated spirits used to dilute the French

enamel varnish (which is applied in *steps 2* and *3*), and the whole effect will be ruined.

Alternative materials

French enamel varnish is available from specialist suppliers. If you are unable to obtain it, make some from woodstain and white polish, using the recipe on page 332.

Alternatively, colour oil-based varnish with artists' oil paints and dilute it 1:1 with white spirit. Using this mixture, follow the steps opposite, substituting turpentine for methylated spirits.

Safety advice

When you spatter the methylated spirits (or turpentine) in *step 3* protect your eyes from splashes with a pair of goggles. The fumes of methylated spirits are narcotic and sometimes stimulate reactions in asthmatics; if you use it in any quantity wear gloves and a respiratory mask as well as goggles.

TOOLS & MATERIALS

French enamel varnish is available from specialist suppliers (see p.340); if you find it difficult to obtain, follow the recipe on page 332. Ready-made French enamel varnish should be diluted 1:1 with methylated spirits. You need three to four different colours, including at least two shades of brown. Have two pointed fitches (or pointed artists' brushes) to hand: one for applying the French enamel varnish, the other for the methylated spirits.

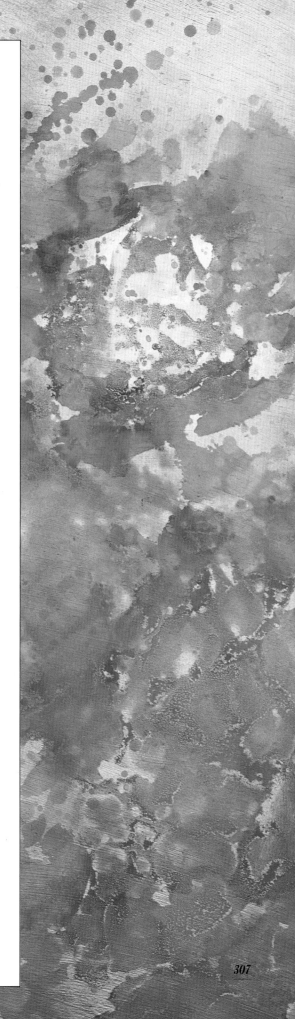

1 Dilute several colours of French enamel varnish with methylated spirits. Apply each colour, daubing some in loose patches and spattering others by knocking the loaded brush against your fingers. (The technique of spattering is shown in detail on pp.262–3).

2 Dip a clean brush into methylated spirits (this will dissolve the French enamel varnish) and work it among the patches of colour, joining some of them up and completely covering others (to make them almost translucent). Work quickly and make as random an effect as possible. Leave for five minutes to allow the methylated spirits to evaporate.

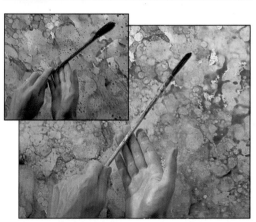

3 Take a little undiluted French enamel varnish on the brush and gently knock it against your fingers to spatter the whole surface with little dots of colour. Try to distribute the dots evenly. Then spatter the surface with methylated spirits in the same way. This will dissolve some of the varnish, breaking it into a variety of complex pool-like patterns.

4 Lightly spray the surface with gold paint, applying it just here and there, where the methylated spirits is still wet. The paint and methylated spirits will react to make a broken pattern. This softens the effect, so you may wish to omit this step if you are working over a background of gold leaf, which is more reflective and lustrous than gold paint.

STAINED GLASS

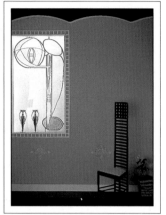

Though the true art of stained glass is not a very complicated one, it does require specialist training and equipment. This lively theatrical imitation, on the other hand, can be done simply, and apart from the fact that it scratches easily, it is almost indistinguishable from the real thing. Imitation stained glass is achieved by painting coloured varnishes on glass and then sticking on lead strips. The stained glass in the steps opposite was based on a Charles Rennie Mackintosh design. This, together with the window design, above, was taken from a furniture inlay detail.

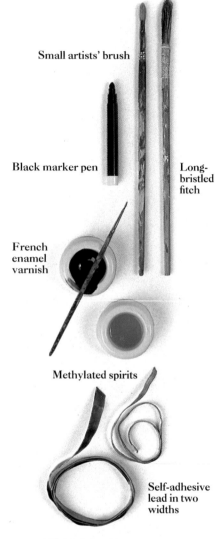

Small artists' brush

Black marker pen

Long-bristled fitch

French enamel varnish

Methylated spirits

Self-adhesive lead in two widths

TOOLS & MATERIALS

Soft, pliable brushes (long-bristled fitches, for example) are essential for this technique, plus some small artists' brushes. French enamel varnish is the colouring medium (see p.332 to make your own). Methylated spirits, which is used to dilute the French enamel varnish brushed on in step 1, *and is applied in* step 2, *should always be used in a well-ventilated area. Self-adhesive lead is obtainable from* DIY *stores. Lead is poisonous so keep your fingers away from your mouth after handling it and wash your hands.*

FRENCH ENAMEL varnish, the medium used to paint the glass, is available from specialist suppliers, in a range of colours. To make any colour subtler, dilute the varnish with methylated spirits, but avoid mixing different colours together – the resulting combinations often turn out to be rather dull and muddy.

Useful tips

To help the varnish stick to the glass, clean the glass thoroughly with methylated spirits before beginning painting. Try to avoid getting the varnish on your skin because the dyes stain heavily. French enamel varnish becomes brittle when

dry, and will scratch and wear away easily, so you may wish to protect your design by covering it with another sheet of glass, or perspex. It is also a good idea to use this decorative technique in areas that are out of reach of small children.

Decorative uses

It is easy to get carried away and overdo things with this technique, thus spoiling the effect, so be judicious. Stained glass works best in discreet quantities, for example on glass panels over a door, on skylights or on mirrors, rather than decorating every window! Abstract designs or patterns are generally much easier to produce than naturalistic ones.

Design ideas All kinds of contrasting sources (not just stained glass designs) can provide inspiration; this is a medieval tile pattern.

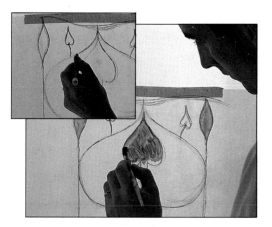

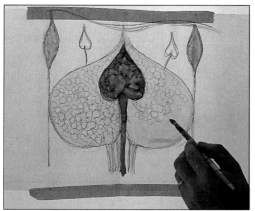

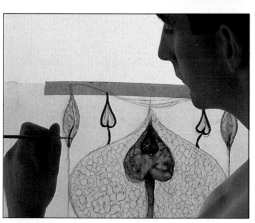

1 Draw out your design on tracing paper, then tape this on to the reverse side of the glass. As an extra guide, trace the outline of the design on to the front of the glass with a black marker pen. Using a very soft brush (I am using a long-bristled fitch), paint on the French enamel varnish (diluted 1:1 with methylated spirits).

2 Since French enamel varnish quickly dries to a transparent finish, obvious brushstrokes are usually difficult to avoid. To disguise them and make a decorative mottled pattern, dab a small artists' brush dipped in methylated spirits over the surface. This dissolves the varnish even when it is dry, creating rings and patterns.

3 Using undiluted black French enamel varnish and another small artists' brush, paint in any details on the design, like the veining on the leaves, here. You can also use undiluted varnish to outline any parts of the design that are too small to outline with lead.

4 When the varnish is dry, carefully press some self-adhesive lead around your design. Stretch it around shallow curves and, to make it fit around tight bends, snip little cuts into the inside edge of the lead with heavy-duty scissors. The lead will hide the black guidelines drawn in marker pen.

PAINTED PATTERN

Although there is no quick method for transforming the decorator into a fine artist with a practised eye, there are a number of straightforward and highly effective techniques you can employ to create painted patterns, and these are explained in this section. Stencilling is perhaps the most versatile of such techniques, and even the simplest design can be treated to look like the freehand work of an artist. Découpage, *the old tradition of pasting up cut out engravings, was my model for hand-colouring photocopies, which can be used for occasional interest or as part of a grander scheme. Finally, come the sister techniques of* grisaille *and* trompe l'oeil, *which will set you on the path to more ambitious illusionism.*

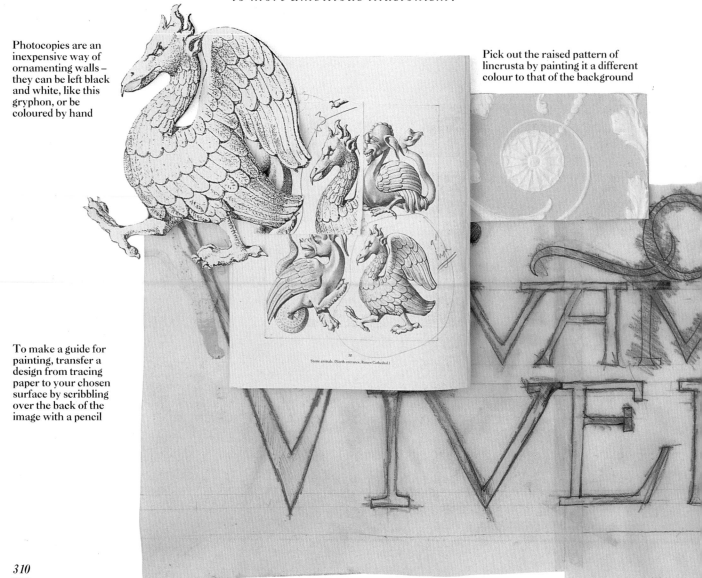

Photocopies are an inexpensive way of ornamenting walls – they can be left black and white, like this gryphon, or be coloured by hand

Pick out the raised pattern of lincrusta by painting it a different colour to that of the background

To make a guide for painting, transfer a design from tracing paper to your chosen surface by scribbling over the back of the image with a pencil

Different stencil effects can be created with spray paints, below left, and by stippling with a brush, below

Use colour photocopies for highly detailed colour imagery, especially for repeat patterns

Applying a complex stencil to a patterned surface creates the impression of painstaking freehand work

An intricate floral stencil, below

Painted ornament and mural

MAKING STENCILS

Designing and making your own stencils can be an exciting and very rewarding process. Although it may take some time and considerable patience, you will achieve real pride and satisfaction as you see your design take shape. The blue stencilled wall, on the left (see also page 141), is an example of the designs it is possible to create. Of course, you need not start with anything quite so ambitious – try a fairly simplified design to begin with and then progress from there. Once you have mastered the technique, you will be limited only by your imagination.

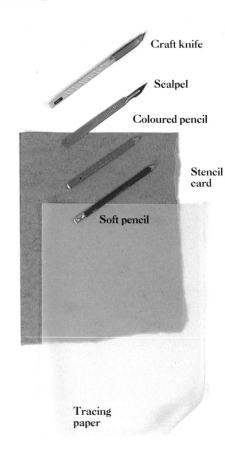

FOR CENTURIES, stencils have been cut from either brass or tin plate, or, more commonly, made out of stencil card, which you can still buy today from artists' suppliers. It is made from stout manila card soaked in either shellac or linseed oil. (To make your own, see p.332.)

Once you have cut out your stencil, spray both sides lightly with spray paint. This will prevent the card from curling when you use it with water-based paints.

Islands and bridges

The art of making a complicated pattern lies in how you "bridge" the various parts of the pattern together. Floating "islands" of card in the middle of a cut area need to be tied across to the edges to hold the stencil in one piece.

The bridges should occur at regular intervals otherwise the stencil will fall apart. With practice you can incorporate these bridges into the design of the stencil. In a delicate pattern try to make the bridges fairly thin. Most simple patterns, like the fish design on page 317, need no bridges at all.

If you have cut out a particularly intricate pattern, glue a sheet of fine dressmakers' netting on to the back of the stencil. This will also help to hold the stencil together when you are using it. Use waterproof masking tape to repair stencils that become damaged.

Reference materials *The stencil design shown in the steps opposite was taken from this book on nineteenth-century ornament (you can see the area of the design enlarged). Patterned papers and fabrics are also a rich source of ideas.*

Craft knife

Scalpel

Coloured pencil

Stencil card

Soft pencil

Tracing paper

TOOLS & MATERIALS

The essential tool for cutting out is patience, plus a sharp craft knife. If you use a scalpel, do not apply too much pressure as the blade might snap and fly off. If you plan to do a lot of cutting, consider investing in a cutting mat.

VISUALIZING THE PATTERN

Here you can see the pattern (top) that a stencil design (bottom) makes when it is painted. It is always worth checking the results of your stencil on a piece of paper before you actually begin decorating.

1 Draw a grid over the original design, and number and letter the horizontal and vertical axes. (If you are taking a design from fabric, draw or photocopy it for this step.) Decide what size stencil you want and draw up a new grid on tracing paper. Copy the original design, square for square, on to the tracing paper.

2 Turn the tracing over and tape it on to the stencil card. Pencil over the reverse of the outline, pressing down firmly. This will transfer the original tracing you made in soft pencil on to the card. (A short cut to steps 1 and 2 is to copy the design using an enlarging photocopier, then glue the copy directly on to the card and cut out the design.)

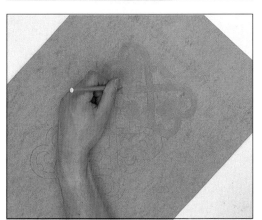

3 It is a good idea to colour in your design on the card at this stage to give an idea of what it will look like as a solid pattern. With a coloured pencil, draw in a system of bridges to link up any floating islands of card in the middle of the design. These bridges will also serve to strengthen the stencil.

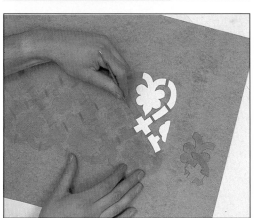

4 Cut out the coloured parts of the stencil, taking care not to cut through any bridges. Do take your time when cutting, as it pays to be accurate and you run less risk of cutting yourself. If you do make a mistake or tear the card, stick it back together with masking tape.

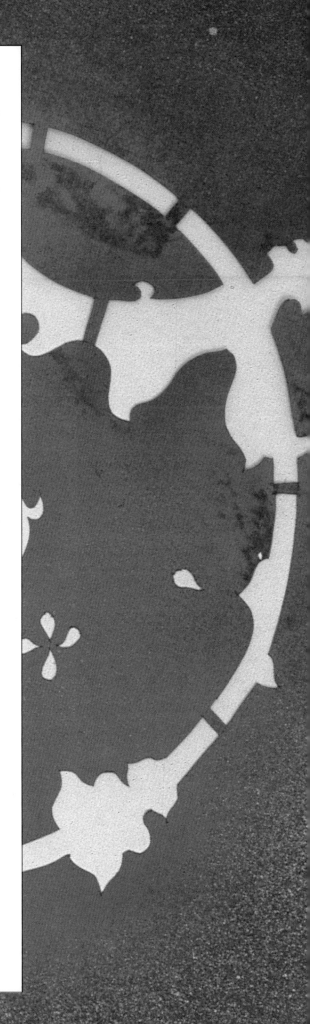

USING STENCILS

Stencilling is one of the most effective and inexpensive ways of adding pattern and ornament to a room. It is also one of the simplest – paint is stippled through a manila card stencil (see the tools and materials on pp.214–5) to create an image with a charming softness that manufactured borders and wallpapers cannot imitate. The fleurs-de-lys *here, were stencilled on the rough plaster wall of the French kitchen scheme shown on pages 90–93. Add freehand details, as I have done, to make your stencils look like impressive pieces of freehand painting, lightly sand them for a faded look or blend them into the background with a thin wash of paint.*

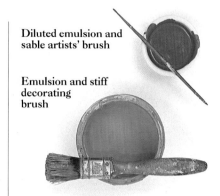

Diluted emulsion and sable artists' brush

Emulsion and stiff decorating brush

TOOLS & MATERIALS

Use a stiff decorating brush or a stencilling brush for stencilling and a sable artists' brush or lining brush for painting freehand detail.

SPECIAL EFFECTS

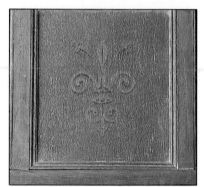

The plaster wall, top, was stencilled as in steps 1–4 and then painted with diluted emulsion; the small fleur-de-lys, *above, was stencilled on a panel, which was then limed (see pp.260–61).*

M Y STANDARD stencil-ling paint is emulsion because it comes in a wide range of colours, dries fast and can be used on many surfaces (see the table on pp.328–31). Other types of paint, including spray paint, can also be used for stencilling; the effects are shown overleaf.

You only need a little paint on your brush, so before starting, dab off any excess on to waste paper. To add freehand details use a sable artists' brush or lining brush and diluted emulsion (this flows on easily). For the medieval *fleurs-de-lys* designs here, I used two typi-cally medieval colours: deep apple green and russet.

Combination techniques

The stencils were lightly sanded to give them the same aged, faded quality as the cracked plaster wall. Sanding is also an effective way of giving stencils on wood the same

rough graininess as their back-ground and stencils on a sponged or colourwashed background a similar soft unevenness. To blend a stencil even more closely with its back-ground, paint over both with a thin wash of diluted emulsion, as I have done, above right.

Stencilling can also be combined with the technique of liming wood. The design, right, was stencilled on to a panel, which was then rubbed with liming wax.

Patterns and repeats

If you are using your stencil to make a border, frieze or regular pat-tern, measure up and mark the pos-ition for each image. If you skip this step you may find that images are slightly out of line, meet badly at the corners of a room or are chopped in half where they meet the ceiling. Use a spirit level for accurate horizontal alignment and a plumb line for vertical alignment.

1 Work out where you want each stencil and mark the position lightly with a pencil. Use a long ruler for measuring, a spirit level for horizontal alignment and a plumb line for vertical alignment.

2 Secure the stencil with low-tack masking tape and/or low-tack adhesive spray. Put a little emulsion paint on the brush (dab off any excess before starting) and stipple it on with a quick, dabbing action. Use a stiff decorating brush (I am using one here) or a stencilling brush.

3 When the paint has dried, remove the stencil. For outlining and adding detail use a sable artists' brush (as I am) or a long-haired lining brush, and emulsion paint diluted 1:1 with water so that it flows off the brush easily.

4 To age and fade the newly stencilled image (shown in the inset), wait for the paint to dry and then lightly sand it with 100 grit sandpaper. This produces pleasing results on textured surfaces such as plaster and bare wood and smooth surfaces that have been sponged or colourwashed (see pp.248–53) and have soft variations of colour.

STENCIL EFFECTS

Decorative borders of stencilled patterns on a plain background have become a familiar sight in homes, restaurants and hotels. But many people are unaware of the wide variety of effects that can be achieved with stencils and their versatility as a decorating aid. The secret is to think of a card stencil not simply as a decorative emblem to be transferred to a surface, but as an elementary template to be used to complement and elaborate other special paint techniques. The pattern of the stencil itself may be extremely intricate and original and executed in unusual colours, or it may be used in subtle and interesting ways, perhaps on a patterned or perforated background.

T HE SIMPLEST use of stencils is to repeat them to form a running border. For a more complex effect the stencil pattern can be overlapped and the position of the stencil shifted slightly each time (see the oak leaf stencil on p.317). Some all-over designs can even be made into excellent "wallpaper", such as the intricate stencilling on page 141.

Different emphases

A stencil design can be given extra subtlety and depth by setting it against a surface with a textured paint finish, such as colourwashing, spattering or woodgraining (see the marquetry-like thistles on the door on the opposite page), or even a perforated screen. Bare plaster walls make an unusual background.

Or, you can give a stencil more interest by applying paint over it, in the form of a pale wash of diluted emulsion or spattered paint, glaze or even varnish.

Paint types and colours

As well as stippling emulsion paint through with a stiff brush (see pp.314–5) you can use eggshell paint or artists' oil paints. With oil-based paints like these it is easier to blend colours for soft shading as the paint stays wet longer. You can also use spray paints to achieve beautiful soft edges by varying the pressure on the nozzle.

Stencils sprayed in gold and silver paint will add lustre to a scheme. The gold colour of the floral design on page 189 added to the glamour of the decor.

STENCIL CARD GUIDES

Card stencils and masks make useful guides for other techniques. Here I used the stencil to draw a pencil guide before applying metal leaf, shown on page 302; on page 283 I used a mask to shield separate applications of paint.

Effects of background
Here it can be seen how different painted backgrounds have different effects on a stencil pattern. One design is sprayed on a grey background, the other is on a red background. Colours can soften or accentuate different parts of the stencil. On the grey background the border is emphasized; on the red background the central part stands out most.

Repeating stencil patterns

*Single images can be repeated to create
an all-over pattern, or to fill a
particular space, as with the thistle
design, below, which was designed to fit
the woodgrained door panels. Repeats
can also be used to create a border
around a room. The early American oak
leaf design, right, overlaps where the
gold colouring of the leaf fades to
nothing. The second stencil, used to add
the black veins on the leaves, is cut with
registration holes to line up the card with
the gold leaves. Traditionally, this
technique of gold colouring is done by
shaking metallic powders on to tacky
goldsize. An easier method is to stipple
on gold paint, as I did here.*

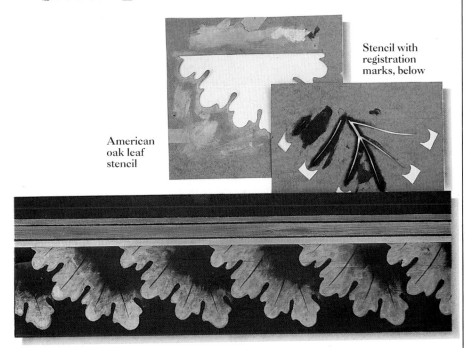

American
oak leaf
stencil

Stencil with
registration
marks, below

Stencilled frieze stippled
with gold paint

Subtle stencil effects

*In complex stencils obvious "bridges" of
card that link the cut out areas together
can be camouflaged for a subtler effect if
the stencil is executed on a perforated
surface, like the wooden screen, below.*

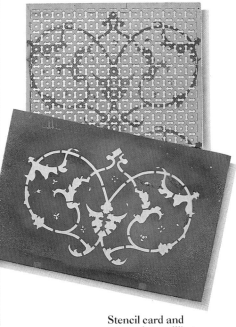

Stencil card and
sprayed stencilling
on a wooden screen,
above

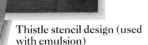

Thistle stencil design (used
with emulsion)

COLOUR VARIATIONS

*A simple stencil constructed from
one piece of card can be partly taped
over or masked so that different
colours can be stippled or sprayed
on separately. In this way colours
can be used to emphasize different
parts of the pattern, and their
qualities balanced to suit the colour
of the background. This fish pattern
can also be seen on page 95.*

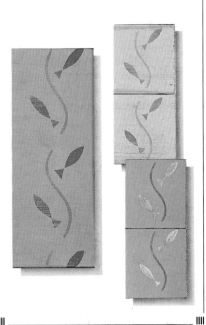

USING PHOTOCOPIES

The art of using paper cutouts (découpage) has a historical background of high pedigree. In the late eighteenth century, for example, there was a vogue for découpage *engravings, which were pasted on to walls and coloured. The black and white lines of engravings reproduce well on a photocopier. I take copies from books on historical ornament and use them as an integral part of a room's decoration, either in black and white, as in the bathroom scheme above, or hand-painted. Colour photocopies are also effective (see the French Empire Study on p.59).*

PAPER CAN be glued to any hard surface that has been painted or wallpapered, as well as bare wood, plaster and stiff leather. PVA diluted 1:1 with water is the best all-purpose glue for pasting paper; wallpaper paste is a suitable alternative.

I used diluted emulsion paints for colouring the photocopy shown on the opposite page, but acrylic paints, gouache, artists' watercolours and artists' oil paints can be used instead.

Protecting paper

Paper will discolour and may become damaged if it is not varnished. A coat of diluted PVA is perfectly adequate for protecting cutouts on walls, unless they are likely to get wet, in which case you should use a waterproof varnish, such as EVA or acrylic varnish (see pp.224–5 and pp.328–31). Use a tough oil-based varnish to protect paper glued to surfaces where paper needs to be hardwearing.

To antique your image in the style of Victorian *découpage* apply a coat of amber French enamel varnish and to give it a delicate, cracked appearance apply crackle varnish (see pp.224–5).

Timesaving

There is no need to cut out an intricate design accurately if you are going to paste it to a painted surface because any unwanted areas of photocopy can be painted to match the background colour.

***Trompe l'oeil effect**, left. This painted photocopy forms part of the* trompe l'oeil *decoration shown in the scheme on page 75. It is much quicker to handcolour photocopies than to paint complex designs from scratch.*

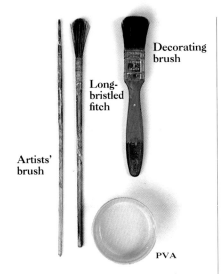

Decorating brush

Long-bristled fitch

Artists' brush

PVA

Scalpel

Craft knife

TOOLS & MATERIALS

Use a scalpel or craft knife to cut out photocopies and a decorating brush to paste and varnish them. PVA is the best all-purpose glue and varnish for paper. For painting, use a small brush like an artists' paintbrush or fitch.

COLOURED DÉCOUPAGE

I coloured these photocopies of eighteenth-century engravings with artists' watercolours, so they blend in with the tones of the authentic eighteenth-century green of the walls (for the overall effect of this technique, see p.71).

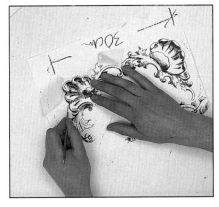

1 Place the photocopy on a smooth, hard surface and carefully cut it out with a craft knife or scalpel while steadying the paper.

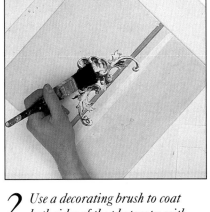

2 Use a decorating brush to coat both sides of the photocopy with PVA (diluted 1:1 with water). Position it and brush it flat.

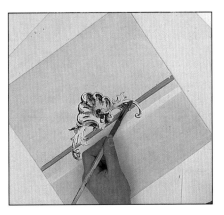

3 The paper will shrink flat on drying. Paint the photocopy with emulsion (diluted 1:1 with water) the same colour as the background.

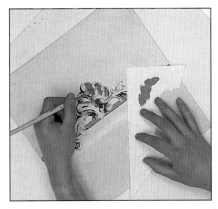

4 When dry, use an artists' brush to paint the shadows. Use the dark areas of the photocopy as a guide and blend the paint with your finger.

5 Paint the highlights with white paint; use the areas of the photocopy that appear to be raised as a guide. Take care to be as neat as possible with the paint.

6 Soften the division between the highlights and the background colour by smudging the white paint with your finger. When dry, seal the photocopy with PVA or varnish.

GRISAILLE

Popular throughout the history of decoration, grisaille *is the simplest and one of the most effective forms of* trompe l'oeil *(visual trickery). Shades of black, white and grey paint are used to imitate three-dimensional subjects, such as stone ornaments and cartouches, and architectural features, like the door frame in the scheme shown, left. In the steps opposite, I demonstrate how to imitate a panel moulding in monochrome on a textured plaster wall; turn to page 322 to see the same moulding painted in colour (a more complex process) and refer to page 75 to see it employed as part of an exuberant and entertaining* trompe l'oeil *scheme for a dining room.*

Pointed fitches

Long-haired lining brushes

Black, white and grey emulsion

Straight edge

FOLLOWING IN the tradition of using water-based paints for *grisaille*, I use water-based emulsion, which is easy to work with and dries fast. Other suitable paints include artists' oil paints diluted with turpentine, which can take up to 24 hours to dry, and home-made gesso paint (see p.332 for how to make this), which dries fairly fast.

Preparation and finishing

Non-absorbent surfaces painted with emulsion are the most suitable for *grisaille*. Surfaces that are already painted with an oil-based paint, such as eggshell, should be rubbed with fuller's earth or whiting (see pp.228–9) to absorb any grease. Protect *grisaille* that is likely to be damaged with a coat of matt oil-based varnish.

Opposite, I show how to imitate a panel moulding, using a logical system of painted lines, which represent light and shadow.

Use a length of moulded dado rail or moulded picture frame as an aid to painting smudge-free straight lines. Place the rail or frame so the ridged edge lies just above the wall. Then, resting the ferrule of your brush on the ridge, paint the line. There is no danger of paint leaking beneath the rail or frame, as it would if you were using a ruler, because the bristles will come into contact only with the wall.

If, after *step* 7, the painted lines look too stark, soften and blend them by lightly brushing over the surface with a decorating brush dampened with water.

Painted picture frame

To imitate a moulded picture frame, use the system of painted light and shadows shown opposite. Redraw the cross-section of a real picture frame four times; indicate the light raised areas and dark recessed areas by each one. Remember to paint mitred corners.

TOOLS & MATERIALS

The most suitable brushes for painting lines are lining brushes and pointed fitches. Use a piece of moulded picture frame (or moulded dado rail) as a straight edge. Dilute the emulsion paints 1:5 with water (except for step 6 *when the dilution should be 1:4).*

The system

Choose a piece of panel moulding to imitate, and sketch it on the wall in cross-section. Hold the moulding flat against the wall and decide on a source of light (I decided on a source above). Use different colours to mark alongside the cross-section where light falls on the raised areas and where shadows occur in the recesses; I used yellow and black here.

1 In pencil, draw lines that correspond to the areas of light and shade indicated beside the cross-section.

2 Apply pale-grey emulsion over the whole area. This will give the moulding body.

3 Use a fitch and black emulsion to paint broad lines to represent the lightest shadows.

4 To suggest the curve of the moulding, soften the edges of some of the shadows with a damp brush.

5 Using a very thin lining brush, paint dark lines to represent the deep recesses and shadows.

6 Paint white lines where the moulding would catch the light. Dilute the paint 1:4 with water.

7 Paint a "cast" shadow (with raw umber emulsion) over the bottom part of the moulding and the wall.

TROMPE L'OEIL

*Effects that trick the eye (*trompe l'oeil*) can be used to provide incidental ornament or the subject of a whole wall's decoration, like that shown on the left (see also p.75). The techniques I use include using paint and painted photo-copies. Unless you are fairly confident in the art of painting perspective, forget the demands of landscapes and figures and depict architectural features such as low-relief mouldings and columns, using a system of shadows and highlights (copy from other sources if you like), to make the painted image look three-dimensional.*

Paper option *Ready-made paper designs like this are a time-saving alternative to painted* trompe l'oeil. *Blend in the paper by painting it with a diluted version of your wall colour, in this case pale-grey emulsion.*

FOR THE *trompe l'oeil* moulding below I used the *grisaille* technique shown on pages 320–21, replacing the grey background with pale pink and choosing lighter and darker versions of the same colour for highlights and shadows. As with *grisaille* choose an unrelated colour (blue in this instance) for the "cast" shadow. Similarly, for other features, start with an all-over background colour and build up highlights and shadows.

The most useful reference for architectural *trompe l'oeil* is prints of artists such as Piranesi and Leonardo da Vinci. These clearly show areas of light and shade. Look first at the background colour and note how this and other colours are built up. Observe also the two types of shadow: modelling shadows, which describe the shape of an object, and cast shadows, the shadows it casts.

The traditional media used are distemper and gesso paint (see p.332) but you may find it easier to work with artists' oil paints mixed with a little turpentine or transparent oil glaze, or emulsion.

Colour moulding This is a colour version of the panel moulding depicted using the monochrome version of trompe l'oeil, *known as* grisaille, *which is shown on pages 320–21.*

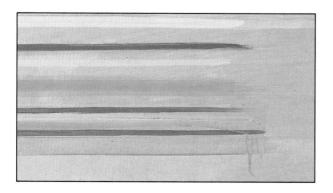

PAINTED WALL DECORATION

I smudged pencil shading to make a three-dimensional-looking frame for the painted ivy-leaf frieze above. The graphic image below, which I scaled up from a poster design, was simple to paint because there was no shading or blending of colours. I painted it on the wall on page 189.

Decorator's Reference

PIGMENTS & COLOURS

MANY OF THE paints that I use are ready-coloured paints, such as emulsion and eggshell. Some techniques, however, call for home-made paints coloured with pigments (concentrated natural or synthetic colours), which are available as powder colours, or are present in tube colours, such as artists' oil paints, artists' acrylics and gouache, each of which has a different binder. These can also be used to alter the colour of different types of ready-coloured paint, and to tint varnishes. Artists' oil paints and universal stainers can be added to transparent oil glaze to colour it.

Colour characteristics

On the right and overleaf is a selection of colours, shown in the form of artists' oil paints. Identical colours, with the same names, can also be obtained as artists' acrylics, gouache, powder colours and universal stainers.

The characteristics of different pigments vary enormously. Some are opaque, others almost transparent; some have good covering power, others very little. Whiting, for example, is translucent when mixed with oil-bound media, but opaque in water. *See overleaf for a key to the table headings.*

Matching colours

Alongside the artists' oil paints are a paint manufacturer's swatches, which show just how closely many of the tube colours can be matched with proprietary paints. Because of this I frequently refer to proprietary paints like emulsion by the names of the pigments they match. However, a proprietary paint does not have the same properties as the tube colour or the powder colour it matches.

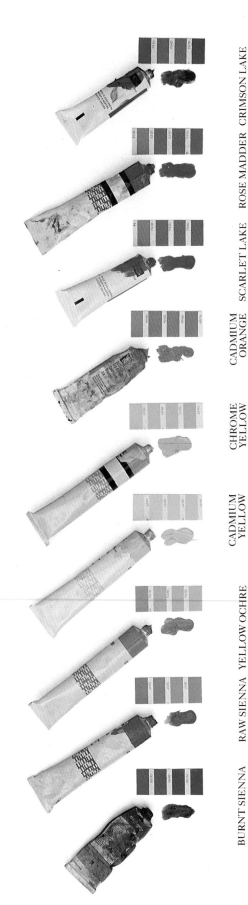

CRIMSON LAKE
ROSE MADDER
SCARLET LAKE
CADMIUM ORANGE
CHROME YELLOW
CADMIUM YELLOW
YELLOW OCHRE
RAW SIENNA
BURNT SIENNA

QUALITIES/USES

Originally made from cochineal, lake colours are now manufactured chemically. See also scarlet lake. Lake colours are intense and brilliant but they tend to fade in light.

A soft, translucent red. Originally produced from the madder plant, this pigment is now manufactured synthetically. Mixes with white to give beautiful pinks.

A similar pigment to crimson lake (above): an intense pigment suitable for all decorating purposes.

Cadmium-based pigments, though toxic, have good covering power, are intense and stable over long periods of time. Also available in red, which can be used as an alternative to scarlet lake.

One of a range of powerful, intense colours derived from chromates of lead.

See also cadmium orange (above). Good covering power; intense, stable colour.

One of the earth colours: a beautiful, warm, brownish-yellow used under gilding. Heated yellow ochre produces purply red ochre.

An ancient, brownish-yellow earth colour from Italy, useful for toning down colours, antiquing and mixing with raw umber.

An earth colour, produced by heating raw sienna. A good terracotta-brown, producing delightful pinks when used in washes.

Table continued overleaf

STAINING POWER	OPACITY	ALKALI RESISTANCE	LIGHT PERMANENCE	COMPOSITION	TOXICITY
****	□□□	✗	2 bulbs	Dyes precipitated on to alumina.	2 skin, 2 inhalation, 2 swallowing
***	□□	✗	4 bulbs	Madder plant extracts; chemical dyes.	1 skin, 1 inhalation, 1 swallowing
****	□□□	✗	2 bulbs	Dyes precipitated on to alumina.	2 skin, 2 inhalation, 2 swallowing
***	□□□□	✗	3 bulbs	Cadmium sulphide, cadmium selenide.	1 skin, 5 inhalation, 5 swallowing
*****	□□□□	✗	3 bulbs	Lead chromate.	5 skin, 5 inhalation, 5 swallowing
***	□□□□	✗	3 bulbs	Cadmium sulphide.	1 skin, 5 inhalation, 5 swallowing
****	□□□□□	✓	4 bulbs	Iron oxide.	1 skin, 1 inhalation, 1 swallowing
***	□□□	✓	4 bulbs	Clay containing iron oxides and aluminium oxides.	1 skin, 1 inhalation, 1 swallowing
***	□□□	✓	4 bulbs	Clay with iron oxides.	1 skin, 1 inhalation, 1 swallowing

Symbols

This table makes use of a system of pictorial symbols for grading the various properties of pigments.

Low staining power, for example, is marked *; good staining power ***** and so on.

Similarly, the toxicity level of the pigments increases from 1 to 5 (extremely toxic) in the following three categories:

✋ skin contact

🫙 inhalation

🥄 swallowing

Pigments with 5 skin contact symbols should be handled wearing gloves. Alkali-resistant colours are marked with a tick, non-alkali-resistant colours, with a cross.

Powder colours

When using powder colours exercise particular caution because in this form the pigments can be very dangerous. Always wear gloves (pigments can be absorbed through the skin and accumulate beneath fingernails), and a paper dust mask, which is essential to avoid inhaling small particles of dust. Pigments that have five inhalation symbols should *never* be used in powder form.

KEY TO TABLE HEADINGS

Qualities/uses
Characteristics of the pigment and its applications.

Staining power
The pigment's ability to penetrate a surface and stain it. If the staining power is high you will need a comparatively small quantity of pigment relative to a given area.

Opacity
Opacity is a good indication of covering power. Yellow ochre, for example, is opaque and covers most background colours in one coat, while others, like rose madder, dry to a translucent finish, making them suitable for tinting transparent oil glaze. The opacity of whiting varies according to whether it is bound in oil or water.

Alkali resistance
Lime is an alkaline compound capable of bleaching colours. To tint plaster that contains lime, or gypsum plaster, use powder colours that are alkali resistant.

Light permanence
Some pigments fade on exposure to natural light; their permanence is indicated here. Manufacturers of artists' oil paints also have a rating system given on the side of the container.

Composition
The chemical formulation of the pigment, excluding its particular oil or water binder.

Toxicity
Many pigments are highly toxic; some are even carcinogens. Never swallow or inhale pigments and do not allow highly toxic ones to touch the skin, specially powder colours. Store all pigments out of the reach of children. Read the chemical formulation of all the pigments you use, and take particular care if they have a five-symbol toxicity rating or are in the "highly toxic" list on the opposite page.

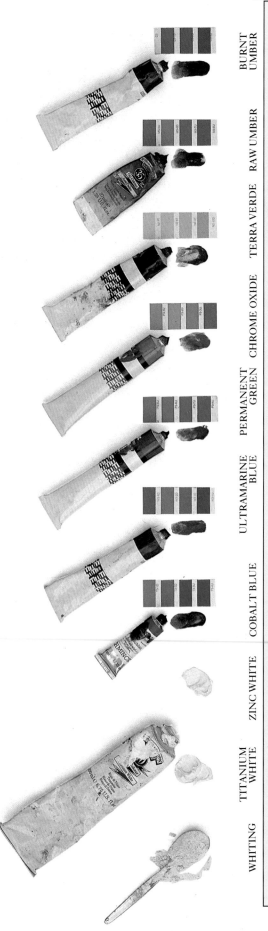

	QUALITIES/USES
BURNT UMBER	A rich, chocolatey-brown earth colour, which is manufactured by heating raw umber pigment.
RAW UMBER	A slightly green/grey-brown earth colour. An extremely useful neutral pigment, good for toning down other colours.
TERRA VERDE	An Italian earth colour, "green earth" is a pleasant green with a bluish-grey tinge.
CHROME OXIDE	A soft pigment, with a pleasant organic shade of green. Extremely opaque. Good mixing qualities, and so frequently used in water- and oil-bound paints.
PERMANENT GREEN	This versatile green (also known as guignet's green) is resistant to acid, alkali and light, but is only moderately enduring when applied in a thin wash. As it does not discolour it is good for solid colour.
ULTRAMARINE BLUE	Meaning from "across the sea", this ancient, beautiful, deep blue pigment was originally very costly as it was made from lapis lazuli.
COBALT BLUE	An ancient pigment, valued for its brilliance and purity of tone. Ideal for solid work and flat areas of detail. Works well in oil glazes, as it has a good degree of translucency.
ZINC WHITE	Also known as Chinese white. Used in some undercoats. Excellent covering power. Has a hardening effect when used in oil glaze.
TITANIUM WHITE	Effective, very white pigment. Used in liming pastes. Slightly chalky, and so is usually hardened with zinc oxide.
WHITING	Ingredient of distemper, whitewash and gesso. Good opacity in water; poor opacity in oil-bound media and wax.

STAINING POWER	OPACITY	ALKALI RESISTANCE	LIGHT PERMANENCE	COMPOSITION	TOXICITY
***	☐☐	✓	🔆🔆🔆🔆	Clay containing iron and manganese silicates and oxides.	(1 hand, 4 bottles, 4 droppers)
***	☐☐	✓	🔆🔆🔆🔆	Clay with iron and manganese silicates and oxides.	(1 hand, 3 bottles, 4 droppers)
**	☐☐	✓	🔆🔆🔆🔆	Natural silicates of iron and magnesium.	(1 hand, 1 bottle, 1 dropper)
***	☐☐☐☐☐	✓	🔆🔆🔆🔆	Chromic oxide.	(2 hands, 4 bottles, 4 droppers)
****	☐☐	✓	🔆🔆🔆	Viridian (an oxide of chromium), mixed with zinc chromate and barites.	(3 hands, 5 bottles, 5 droppers)
*	☐	✓	🔆🔆🔆🔆	Sodium silicate, plus aluminium and sulphur.	(1 hand, 1 bottle, 1 dropper)
***	☐☐☐ (in water) ☐ (in oil)	✓	🔆🔆🔆🔆	Cobalt oxide, aluminium oxide.	(1 hand, 2 bottles, 1 dropper)
	☐☐☐☐	✓	🔆🔆🔆🔆	Zinc oxide.	(1 hand, 2 bottles, 2 droppers)
	☐☐☐☐☐	✓	🔆🔆🔆🔆	Titanium oxide.	(1 hand, 1 bottle, 1 dropper)
	☐☐☐ (in water) ☐ (in oil)	✓	🔆🔆🔆🔆	Chalk (calcium carbonate), ground washed and dried.	(1 hand, 1 bottle, 1 dropper)

Other highly toxic pigments: handle with extreme caution; (avoid in powder form)

Antimony pigments
Lead-based pigments
Chrome-based pigments
Cadmium-based pigments
Phthalo-based pigments
Barium yellow
Cobalt yellow
Emerald green
Carbon black
Lemon yellow
Naples yellow
Scheele's green
Strontium yellow
Vermilion

Other toxic pigments: handle with care

Alizarin crimson
Alumina
Cerulean blue
Cobalt green
Cobalt violet
English red
Indian red
Ivory black
Mars black, brown, red, orange, violet, yellow
Prussian blue, Paris blue
Terra rosa
Ultramarine blue, green, red, violet

PAINTS, VARNISHES & SOLVENTS

THIS TABLE shows the composition, properties and uses of the various types of paint and varnish used for the techniques demonstrated in this book.

Solvents

Paints and varnishes can be diluted with particular solvents, which are also used for cleaning brushes. See the column headed "Solvents" in the table for further information. In addition, some solvents can be used in association with various paints and varnishes for decorative effects (see pp.226–7).

Toxicity

Great care is needed when handling paints and varnishes. While some of their ingredients are poisonous, the solvents used in conjunction with them are, for the most part, highly toxic, the obvious exception being water. Such solvents as well as paints and varnishes can be absorbed into the body in three ways, denoted in the table by three symbols, used on a scale from 1 (mildly toxic) to 5 (highly toxic).

skin contact

inhalation

swallowing

The poisonous effects of solvents depend on how they enter the body.

Safety precautions

When using paints, varnishes and solvents, work in well-ventilated areas. Label containers carefully, and keep them out of the reach of children. Never eat, drink or smoke when working. When using some substances it is also advisable to wear gloves and goggles. A respiratory mask protects against the inhalation of fumes and a dust mask against powder colour particles.

TYPE	USES	MIX WITH
EMULSION PAINT (matt and vinyl silk)	Water-based paints for general interior decorating: ceilings, walls and wood. May be diluted for colourwashing or thickened with whiting for textural effects. Vinyl silk has a greater degree of sheen.	Water (for diluting), universal stainers, powder colours, water-based tube colours e.g. gouache and artists' acrylics.
EGGSHELL, GLOSS PAINT & OIL-BASED UNDERCOAT	Oil-based paints for general interior painting. Can be diluted for hard-wearing washes. Eggshell is the perfect basecoat for oil glaze. Oil-based undercoats can be tinted for a very matt finish.	Univeral stainers, artists' oil paints, transparent oil glaze.
GESSO, DISTEMPER & BUTTERMILK (casein) PAINTS	Traditional water-based paints, which all have similar properties, for walls and furniture. Now less fashionable but gesso is still widely used to prepare surfaces, for relief work and as a ground for gilding.	Gouache, powder colours.
LIMEWASH	Traditional paint used on the exterior of buildings. Was also used on interior walls to give a distinctive, chalky, matt finish, instead of white distemper.	Alkali-resistant powder colours.
SPRAY PAINTS	Convenient way of applying paint for some techniques, such as stencilling, basecoats for gilding, and imitation verdigris.	Nothing.
PVA & EVA	PVA is a good binder for home-made paints (made with powder colours) that are used for colourwashing. It is useful for sticking down and protecting paper from dirt. EVA is similar but waterproof.	Emulsion paint, universal stainers, powder colours, gouache, artists' acrylics, water-based inks.
ARTISTS' OIL PAINTS	These are the paints used in oil paintings. Excellent for colouring transparent oil glaze, varnish and eggshell paint. Mix with beeswax furniture polish and turpentine to make good antiquing colours.	Transparent oil glaze, eggshell paint, gloss paint, beeswax furniture polish and oil- and resin-based varnishes that are soluble in turpentine.
POWDER COLOURS	Use to make home-made paints for colourwashing and freehand detail. Also useful for tinting proprietary paints, varnishes and plaster.	Water, emulsion, PVA, transparent oil glaze, oil-based and polyurethane varnishes.

Table continued overleaf

ADVANTAGES	DISADVANTAGES	SOLVENTS	COMPOSITION	TOXICITY
Inexpensive. Relatively clean. Quick-drying (1–3 hours). Can be tinted to the shade you require. Waterproof finish. Enormous range of colours.	Dark colours lack depth and richness. Finish may need protection as dirt cannot be easily washed off.	Water. When dry can be softened and removed with methylated spirits.	Pigment, synthetic resins and PVA (or polyacrylic binder suspended in water).	
Hard, durable finish with good depth of colour. Enormous range of colours.	Eggshell and gloss need an undercoat and, on an absorbent surface, an initial coat of primer. Slow-drying (6–12 hours). Unpleasant fumes, which are dangerous in quantity.	Turpentine, white spirit.	Pigment, synthetic drying oils and synthetic alkyd resin. Traditional drying oils (such as linseed) and natural resins have been superseded by synthetic compounds.	
Soft texture and chalky colours. Gesso and casein may be highly polished, giving great character to a finished surface. Allow the passage of moisture.	May deteriorate in the container. Poor covering power. Adhere only to porous surfaces. Not waterproof. Soft and liable to rub off when wetted. Not widely available.	Water.	Pigment (often chalk) in water, natural binder, such as animal gelatin or casein (a by-product of cheesemaking) and, in some cases, a water-proofing oil.	*
Disinfectant and insecticidal properties. Good for old walls, which need to "breathe", because it allows the passage of moisture.	Highly caustic when wet. Only semi-waterproof when dry. Rubs off easily.	Water.	Water, slaked lime (calcium hydroxide) and a water-proofing agent, such as tallow.	
Quick-drying to a hard and perfectly smooth finish. Adhere to most surfaces. Fast to apply. Can be reactivated when dry with solvent.	Highly toxic substances with an unpleasant smell. Spray "fallout" can be considerable, coating all surfaces in the immediate vicinity. Often contain hazardous propellants: avoid these.	Xylene, acetone and toluene.	Pigment, nitro-cellulose lacquer (or acrylic lacquer in petroleum distillate) and propellant.	
Versatile media with excellent sealing and binding properties. Quick-drying. Cheap and widely available.	Often dries slightly glossy and remains soft. PVA is not waterproof.	Water.	PVA: polyvinyl acetate dispersed in water. EVA: ethylene vinyl acetate.	
Intense, concentrated colours that tolerate much dilution. Good for mixing with other oil-based media. Slow-drying therefore workable. Wide range of colours.	Degree of translucency and covering power variable. Some colours are expensive, which makes it prohibitive to use them over large areas.	Turpentine, white spirit.	Finely ground pigment, linseed oil and drying oils.	*
Powder colour washes have a particularly pleasing quality. Can be mixed together dry for accurate colour matching. Cheap and widely available.	The properties of different powder colours vary enormously. Generally need protection to prevent colour rubbing away. Many are extremely toxic.	Water.	Finely ground pigment (naturally occurring or chemically manufactured).	*

* Toxicity varies according to colour. See pages 324–7.

COMMONLY USED SOLVENTS

Protection is advised when using any of the solvents below in large quantities. People with sensitive skin or allergies are sometimes affected by turpentine and white spirit even when used in small quantities.

Methylated Spirits

Contains: methanol, wood alcohol, denatured alcohol, methyl violet. Inflammable.

✋ *Can lead to unconsciousness and organ damage. Wear gloves.*

☗ *Can lead to unconsciousness and organ damage. Wear mask.*

⬗ *Fatal; can cause blindness.*

Turpentine

Contains: pure turpentine, gum spirits, gum turpentine. Inflammable.

✋ *Causes skin allergies. Wear gloves.*

☗ *Irritant vapours. Wear mask.*

⬗ *Fatal.*

White Spirit (turpentine substitute)

Contains: petroleum distillates. Cheaper than turpentine, and has the same properties. Inflammable.

✋ *Wear gloves.*

☗ *Irritant vapours. Wear mask.*

⬗ *Fatal.*

Acetone

Contains: acetone (one of the ketone compounds). Highly inflammable.

✋ *Irritant. Wear gloves.*

☗ *Can cause unconsciousness.*

⬗ *Causes nausea and abdominal pain.*

TYPE	USES	MIX WITH
GOUACHE/ARTISTS' ACRYLICS	Concentrated tube colours in a water-soluble base used for solid colour work and washes. Gouache traditionally used on gesso for decorating furniture.	Water, emulsion, PVA.
UNIVERSAL STAINERS	Versatile, intense colours, in a liquid form, that can be combined with virtually all types of oil- and water-based paints and glazes to produce a wide range of colours.	Water, emulsion, eggshell, transparent oil glaze, oil-based varnish and polyurethane varnishes, woodstain.
TRANSPARENT OIL GLAZE	Used with artists' oil paints or universal stainers to make a coloured glaze, which can be used for woodgraining, dragging, antiquing and stippling.	Artists' oil paints, oil-based (alkyd) paints, universal stainers, oil-based varnish and polyurethane varnish (for a glossier finish).
SHELLAC & FRENCH ENAMEL VARNISH	Shellac is used as a sealing varnish, for antiquing, and to coat stencil card; French enamel varnish is used to stain glass.	Shellac products can be mixed with each other and readily accept woodstains soluble in methylated spirits.
SANDING SEALER & KNOTTING	Sanding sealer is used to seal wood before painting and varnishing to prevent discoloration. Knotting seals knots in resinous wood.	Other shellac-based products and methylated spirits.
GOLDSIZE	Used as an adhesive base for applying gold leaf and metal powders, and for sealing Dutch metal to prevent oxidation. Also useful as a quick-drying varnish for small areas.	Oil-based paints, artists' oil paints, powder colours, transparent oil glaze.
GENERAL-PURPOSE OIL-BASED VARNISHES	Traditional varnishes, such as copal varnish and decorative varnish, for protecting all manner of paint finishes. Now superseded by widely available polyurethane varnishes.	Oil-based paints, artists' oil paints, powder colours, universal stainers, transparent oil glaze.
POLYURETHANE VARNISH	All-purpose varnish, which is hard and durable, for coating many interior surfaces. Available in matt, semi-gloss and gloss finishes.	Oil-based paints, artists' oil paints, powder colours, transparent oil glaze.
ACRYLIC VARNISH	Excellent, new generation of quick-drying water- or petroleum distillate-based varnishes. Suitable for all types of decorative varnishing.	Water-based version mixes with universal stainers and powder colours.
BEESWAX FURNITURE POLISH	Used to polish paintwork or furniture. Can be coloured for use as antiquing wax or liming wax.	Artists' oil paints, powder colours, powdered rottenstone, fuller's earth, shoe polish.

ADVANTAGES	DISADVANTAGES	SOLVENTS	COMPOSITION	TOXICITY
Strong colours with excellent staining powers. Tolerate dilution to make vividly coloured washes. Artists' acrylics are waterproof when dry.	Expensive. Artists' acrylics dry very rapidly (1 hour). Gouache does not dry waterproof.	Water.	Concentrated pigments in a water-soluble base.	Hands: 1–3 *; Bottles: 1–4; Cans: 1–4
Colours are very strong and so can be diluted. Good mixing qualities. Inexpensive and adaptable.	Limited range of colours available. For colour variation mix with ready-coloured paints, such as emulsion and eggshell.	Turpentine, white spirit.	Dyes bound in a solvent base.	Hands: 2; Bottles: 3; Cans: 4
Cheap and effective way to extend colour. Dries in 6 hours. Good workability for up to half an hour.	Tends to form skin in tin. Yellows significantly if exposed to sunlight. Protect with a coat of varnish as it dries soft.	Turpentine, white spirit.	Whiting (chalk), linseed oil (or a synthetic alkyd resin), drying oils and white spirit.	Hands: 2; Bottles: 2; Cans: 5
All shellac products are quick-drying. Shellac: several grades available including standard brown, fine-grade orange shellac (button polish) and bleached shellac (also called white polish).	All brittle and yellow (except for white polish). Need to work quickly as they dry rapidly but can be dissolved in alcohol.	Methylated spirits.	Flake shellac (crystals of resinous substance secreted by the lac insect) and alcohol. French enamel varnish is shellac-based and is available in several colours containing aniline dyes.	Hands: 3; Bottles: 3; Cans: 4
Quick-drying; provide effective barrier on wood.	Brittle; knotting is dark-coloured, so unsuitable for use under pale washes (use white polish instead).	Methylated spirits.	Flake shellac (see "Shellac", above) and alcohol.	Hands: 3; Bottles: 3; Cans: 4
Quick-drying, hard, glossy varnish with excellent flow properties.	Slightly brittle. Liable to form skin and partially oxidize in can. Does not dry to as hard a finish as polyurethane varnish.	Turpentine, white spirit.	Traditionally made of linseed oil, resin and drying oils. Often a blend of natural oils and resins, with a high resin content to induce fast drying.	Hands: 2; Bottles: 3; Cans: 4
Extremely high-quality finishes. Can be sanded.	Often slow drying times, due to the low resin content. Sometimes brittle.	Turpentine, white spirit.	Natural oils and resins, with drying oils.	Hands: 2; Bottles: 3; Cans: 5
Cheap, widely available and easy to use. Dries in 4–6 hours to produce a hardwearing, strong finish.	Sometimes yellowish and brittle. Liable to flake when sanded down.	Turpentine, white spirit.	Synthetic resins and oils.	Hands: 2; Bottles: 3; Cans: 4
Water-based version is quick-drying, tough and very clear. Pleasant to work with.	Petroleum distillate-based version is highly toxic. Use water-based where possible. Toxicity rating here is for water-based version only.	Varies according to composition.	Tough acrylic resins dispersed either in water or petroleum distillate solvent (xylene or toluene).	Hands: 1; Bottles: 1; Cans: 1
Flexible and versatile. Easily removed with solvent. Waterproof. Polishes well. Pleasant to work with.	Needs regular applications to maintain finish as it is soft. If overheated, emits toxic fumes and degrades.	Turpentine, white spirit.	Soft beeswax and other waxes, such as hard carnauba wax or synthetic silicone wax in solvent (usually turpentine substitute).	Hands: 1 **; Bottles: 5; Cans: 5

* Toxicity varies according to colour.
** Toxicity risk from inhalation only if overheated.

RECIPES

THE FOLLOWING recipes are for making your own decorating materials. In some cases the recipes I have included are for products not readily available from decorators' suppliers or DIY stores; in other cases they are for techniques that use a preparation that is not available commercially. See also page 335 for calculating the quantities of paint, varnish or glaze you will need.

STENCIL CARD/OILED PAPER

If you are unable to obtain stencil card (oiled manila card) make your own following this recipe.

What you need

| Thick cartridge paper or manila card |
| Linseed oil or shellac or knotting |

Brush both sides of the paper or card with linseed oil and leave it to dry for a week. The oil makes it pliable, which is important if you intend to stencil a curved surface. Alternatively, brush the card with shellac or knotting, to soften and seal it. These techniques can also be used to strengthen decorative papers to make lampshades or screens.

TRANSPARENT OIL GLAZE

This is used in many techniques. If you have difficulty obtaining it, follow this recipe. When dry, protect the glaze with a coat of matt varnish.

What you need

| 0.5 litres (1 pint) turpentine |
| 0.3 litres (12 fluid ounces) ready-boiled linseed oil |
| 0.2 litres (8 fluid ounces) dryers |
| 1 tablespoon whiting |

Mix the ingredients together using a balloon whisk. Store the glaze in an airtight jar or can.

LIQUID GUM ARABIC (CRACKLE MEDIUM)

A commercial crackle medium can be used for a cracked paint effect like that shown in the scheme on page 193, but gum arabic is an excellent substitute.

You can buy this from artists' suppliers as gum water, ready dissolved, or as crystals, which can be dissolved in boiling water to a single cream consistency at the ratio of 0.5 kilogram (1 pound) crystals to 1–1.5 litres (2–3 pints) water.

CRACKLE VARNISH

Crackle varnish is used to produce a delicate, cracked finish called craquelure; see pages 268–9. You can buy it ready-made or make your own. Both have two parts: an oil-based varnish and a water-based varnish. For the first varnish use goldsize, and for the second, liquid gum arabic, the crackle medium described above, adding a drop of washing-up liquid to prevent it from splitting open.

FRENCH ENAMEL VARNISH

To 0.5 litre (1 pint) of white polish add 1 eggcup of alcohol-soluble woodstain to the required intensity.

TRADITIONAL GESSO

Gesso (see p.228), is applied in layers to create a smooth surface on which to gild. Rabbit-skin gesso is applied warm. It cools quickly to a firm jelly, allowing a rapid build-up of layers. When using warm gesso, remove the skin which forms and add a little water.

What you need

| $\frac{1}{3}$ cup rabbit-skin glue powder |
| 0.35 litres (14 fluid ounces) boiling water |
| 0.25 kilograms (8 ounces) whiting |

Place the glue powder in a *bain-marie* (double boiler). Slowly pour on the boiling water, stirring until all the granules are dissolved (to make glue). Sift in whiting ($\frac{1}{3}$–$\frac{1}{2}$ of the total volume) until you have a thick paint.

If you buy the glue as coarse granules, soak them overnight in 0.35 litres of cold water. They will swell into a jelly; heat this in a *bain-marie*.

Gesso can be coloured with powder colours; traditional gesso colours are red and yellow ochre.

MODERN GESSO

Modern PVA gesso has all the qualities of rabbit-skin gesso, but dries more slowly. I use this in preference to commercial acrylic gesso, which is difficult to scrape and polish.

What you need

| $\frac{1}{3}$ cup PVA |
| $\frac{1}{3}$ cup water |
| Whiting |

Dilute the PVA 1:1 with water and mix thoroughly. Sift in whiting ($\frac{1}{3}$–$\frac{1}{2}$ total volume) until you have a thick paint.

GESSO PAINT

This can be used instead of emulsion in grisaille work, *see pages 320–21. Make the paint by adding powder colour to gesso. Follow the recipe for traditional gesso, but instead of whiting, add a 1:3 mixture of whiting and powder colour. When dry, the gesso can be polished with wire wool and beeswax polish.*

DISTEMPER

This ancient paint, which is still available commercially, allows the passage of moisture, so is useful for painting the walls of old houses where dampness may occur. Here is a simple home-made version.

What you need

| 10 kilograms (20 pounds) whiting |
| 4.5 litres (1 gallon) water |
| Powder colour (or universal stainers) |
| Hot rabbit-skin glue (see Traditional Gesso) or PVA |

Sift the whiting into the water until a peak appears above the surface. Leave to soak overnight. The following day discard the top 5 centimetres (2 inches) of clear water. Add 5–10% of glue by volume. Tint with powder colour or universal stainers mixed with water.

LIMING WAX

Liming wax is used to lime open-grain woods (see pp.260–61) and to antique plaster (see pp.272–3). It is widely available ready-made, but is inexpensive and easy to make.

What you need

1 tin beeswax furniture polish
Titanium white powder colour

Heat the beeswax polish gently in a *bain-marie* (double boiler) until liquid. Add ⅓ of its volume of titanium white powder colour and stir. Pour into a pot, and allow to set.

SAFETY NOTE Always heat the wax gently. If over-heated, it produces highly toxic fumes.

LIMING PASTE

Use liming paste instead of liming wax when the surface you wish to lime needs to be varnished. Wipe off any residue on the surface with a damp cloth.

What you need

1 tablespoon titanium white powder colour
0.5 litres (1 pint) water
Hot rabbit-skin glue (see Traditional Gesso) or gum water (see Liquid Gum Arabic)

Mix the titanium white powder colour with water to the consistency of single cream. For every pint of this mixture, add 6–7 tablespoons of rabbit-skin glue (heated in a *bain-marie*: see Traditional Gesso) or 3–4 tablespoons of gum water.

MAKING WASHES

There are various ways of preparing washes (thin paints) for use in colourwashing techniques and for painting a thin wash of colour over a different coloured basecoat. The following recipes are the three you need for the techniques used in this book. (See also pp.248–53).

Emulsion wash

This is a very versatile wash and one that I use most frequently.

What you need

Emulsion paint
Water

Put the full-strength paint you wish to dilute in a bucket. Add a little water, stirring to remove lumps.

Dilute 1 part paint with between 1 and 10 parts water for colourwashing. Note the proportions you use. This is important when working on a large project as emulsion washes separate out and need to be mixed to the same strength on a daily basis.

Water-based wash

This wash can be reworked with a damp sponge or brush when dry, but needs to be protected with an oil-based varnish because it can be rubbed off.

What you need

Powder colour
Water

Mix the colour with a little water to a creamy consistency. As a rough guide, 3 tablespoons of powder colour mixed with 1 litre of water will be sufficient for colourwashing a room. Stir the paint continuously as you work.

PVA wash

For painting small areas you may wish to use writing ink, artists' acrylics or gouache instead of powder colours, but these are expensive to use on large areas.

What you need

Powder colour
PVA or rabbit-skin glue (see Traditional Gesso)
Water

Mix the colour with a little water to a creamy consistency. Add 5–10% glue by volume as a binder. (If you use hot rabbit-skin glue, mix the colour with hot water so that the glue does not cool rapidly to jelly).

Dilute this mixture to the consistency you need: add approximately 8 parts water for colourwashing or for half tones in *grisaille* and *trompe l'oeil* work.

The thinner the paint, the more quickly the powder colour will settle to the bottom. You will need to stir it back into the paint continually as you work.

TINTING MEDIA

A useful decorating practice is to tint various media with colour. The following recipes explain how.

Tinting emulsion

Use powder colours, artists' acrylics, gouache or universal stainers.

What you need

Powder colour, artists' acrylic, gouache or universal stainers
Water
Emulsion paint

Mix the colour with a little water first. If using universal stainers, mix with a little emulsion first, and ensure that you do not add more than 1 tablespoon of stainer to 5 tablespoons of emulsion, or the paint may not dry properly. Add this mixture to the emulsion, stirring thoroughly to mix the colour evenly.

Tinting transparent oil glaze

When choosing a colour to tint oil glaze, bear in mind that the glaze will begin to yellow slightly three to four months after it has been applied. Red, for example, will become more orange and pale blue will turn green. For this reason, try to avoid tinting glaze with light colours, or choose a water-based paint instead of glaze. A way of impeding the yellow cast of glaze or varnish is to add a drop or two of white eggshell paint to the glaze when colouring them. The quantities given below may vary depending on the staining power of the colour (see the table on pp.324–7).

What you need

Approx 7–10 centimetres (3–4 inches) artists' oil paints squeezed from the tube
Turpentine
0.5 litre (1 pint) oil glaze

Squeeze the paint into a container. Add a small amount of turpentine to thin it out, and stir well with a brush to make a smooth mixture. Add the glaze, mixing carefully to distribute the colour evenly. Tiny dots of undissolved colour turn into garish streaks when brushed out.

Tinting varnish/eggshell/gloss

Follow the method for tinting transparent oil glaze, above, substituting the oil glaze with varnish (polyurethane or oil-based), eggshell or gloss paint.

Tinting plaster

White plaster powder can be mixed dry with powder colours before it is applied to walls. Some pigments are not alkali-resistant, and the lime content of plaster will cause them to fade completely within a couple of months. Choose only alkali-resistant pigments (see the table on pp.324–7). For a pleasant parchment colour mix approximately ½–1 cup of raw sienna powder colour into a bucket of white plaster. Then, following the manufacturer's instructions, mix the coloured plaster powder with water.

Hints & Tips

SOME OF the materials in this book may be familiar to you, others may not. Here is some general advice on how to buy and store materials, and some special tips on varnishing paint finishes.

Protecting paint finishes

Varnish can be used to protect any decorative paint finish but it is particularly useful for glazework and water-based washes, which become damaged easily. Take into account the role the surface has to perform as well as the sort of paint you are protecting when selecting a varnish (the table that appears on pp.328–31 gives a handy summary of the uses and properties of different types of varnish).

General purpose oil-based varnishes and polyurethane varnish are the toughest wearing and most waterproof. They are suitable for protecting paint finishes in bathrooms, kitchens and areas likely to be subject to scuffing from children and animals.

Transparent oil glazes will only accept oil-based varnishes but water-based paints such as emulsion, or home-made washes can be protected with oil- or water-based varnishes, including diluted PVA (this is protective but not waterproof) and acrylic varnish.

BUYING & STORING MATERIALS

Buying in bulk is usually cheapest and most products have a shelf-life of many months, if not years, if correctly stored. Some materials have special storage requirements but as a general rule keep them in dry conditions away from light or extremes of temperature. Avoid keeping materials anywhere freezing temperatures may occur, such as in a shed. Below are some special tips.

Gelatin-based glue

Gelatin-based glues such as rabbit-skin glue and bone glue are available in quantities ranging from ¹/₂-kilo (1-pound) to 5-kilo (10-pound) bags. They have an unlimited shelf-life providing they are kept in their powder or granule form and away from damp or insects. Once mixed with water they begin to rot after only a few days. For this reason make up only the quantity you need at any given time.

Gold leaf and metallic powders

The cost of real gold leaf varies according to the carat of the gold. Pure 22-carat gold will never tarnish but Dutch metal (this is not real gold) will dull, even in the book it comes in, over a number of years. Once Dutch metal has been applied, protect it with varnish to prevent oxidation and subsequent dulling of the finish. Metallic powders are available in containers ranging from small jars to ¹/₂-kilo (1-pound) bags. They

should be varnished to prevent the finish becoming dull. See the entry for powder colours for storage tips.

Paint and varnish

Replace the lids of paint and varnish tins firmly and providing that the lid seal is not damaged, store the tins upside-down. This ensures that any skin effectively forms at the bottom of the container. Before re-using paints, remove the skin and then stir or shake thoroughly. Do not shake any type of varnish as this introduces air bubbles, which show when the varnish is brushed out. Keep some brushes specifically for varnishing as varnish can loosen dried paint in brushes, spoiling the finish.

Plaster

It is important to keep plaster dry, but no matter how careful you are, it has a limited shelf-life of only a few months, after which it begins to absorb moisture and go gritty, which makes it unusable. Plaster's drying time increases after only several weeks of storage.

Powder colours (including whiting)

Small quantities are sold in jars, larger quantities of about ¹/₂ kilo (1 pound) upwards usually come in bags. Keep powder colours and metallic powders in airtight jars with screw-top lids and store them in a dry place. Because they are toxic and should never be inhaled, always

spoon them out carefully (never pour them) and avoid jars with flip-top lids, which tend to jerk the powder around on opening.

Shellac

This is available in bottles ranging from 250 millilitres (¹/₂ pint) to 5 litres (1¹/₄ gallons). Shellac has a shelf-life of about a year. As shellac contains methylated spirits, which evaporates at low temperatures, it tends to thicken over several hours of exposure to air. It can be thinned with methylated spirits.

Stencils

Stencils are best stored flat, each layer covered with paper to prevent the patterns from catching each other and ripping.

Transparent oil glaze

This is sold in tins in the same quantity as paint: ¹/₂ litre (1 pint) upwards. Different brands look a slightly different colour in the container but this will not affect the colour when used. Glaze has a shelf-life of about a year or so.

Waxes

Waxes and wax polishes sometimes harden in the tin, even if never opened. You can revitalize them by placing the tin in a *bain-marie* (double boiler) and heating it very gently until the wax is soft; then mix in a little fresh turpentine.

Obtaining perfect results

To give varnished paintwork a perfect, smooth finish apply several coats of varnish, lightly sanding with 220 grit paper between coats.

When the last coat is thoroughly dry, use 0000 grade wire wool, dipped in beeswax furniture polish, and buff the surface as though you were polishing a piece of furniture. This will remove any small imperfections and pieces of grit in the surface and give a beautifully silky and reflective surface, free of pits, bumps and all the little particles of dust and grit that usually seem to settle on varnish as it dries. Ten minutes later buff with a duster. This method of finishing is particularly useful for special effects where the material imitated is shiny, for example marble.

Redecorating surfaces

Standard manufactured paints, like gloss and emulsion, can be sanded or washed down as appropriate and repainted. With varnished finishes you can either key the surface with sandpaper or use a proprietary stripper to remove the varnish completely. Wax finishes such as liming and antiquing can, with patience, be removed and redecorated with paint. Rub the surface with turpentine, followed by detergent and water, and then sand to provide a key for the paint.

Transparent oil glaze can be sanded down and painted with an oil-based undercoat prior to being redecorated with oil- or water-based paint or glaze. This is hard work and time consuming, so is only suitable for furniture or small areas, like dados. (You should not expect to achieve a perfectly smooth finish.) If you are planning to glaze whole walls, consider putting up lining paper. This can simply be stripped off prior to redecorating.

Green decorating

Virtually every area of decorating touches on one or another environmental issue. There are pros and cons for both animal-based products and chemically produced ones. Though some people object to using products with animal glues in, for example, the argument for them is that they are biodegradable. Synthetic glues, like PVA, on the other hand, are not animal-based but they do contain chemicals that do not biodegrade.

Not all aerosol paints contain CFCs but many release other harmful solvents into the air. Look out for and try to buy only those that are labelled CFC-free on the container and are indicated as being environmentally friendly.

Some types of brush are made from animal bristles. Badger-hair brushes are made from badger bristle imported from China and the Far East. Badgers are a protected species in many countries. For softening glazework, I use a lily-bristle softener instead of a badger-hair softener. Only in softening watercolour work does a badger-hair softener give a superior finish to any other brush.

Paint and solvent disposal

Many paints and solvents do not break down in the water treatment system so it is important not to dispose of solvents (except for methylated spirits or water) and paints containing solvents down the drain. Instead, pour them into old, empty paint containers, carefully marking the outside with the type of solvent or paint.

Never mix different types of solvent and avoid using old food containers as not only may the contents be mistaken but some solvents may dissolve the container – with disastrous results. Always secure the lids of the containers tightly and keep out of the reach of children.

Check with your local authority to see if they offer facilities for the disposal of waste products such as these. If they do not, the liquid wastes will have to go out with the rest of the household rubbish and either be burned or buried at the local municipal dump.

QUANTITIES

It is impossible to be exact because coverage will depend on how liberally you apply the material, the absorbency of the surface being decorated and the weather (if it is warm paint evaporates and you need to apply more). The quantities in the table below will give you an idea of how much paint or varnish you would need for one coat on the walls of an average size room with a floor area of 4.5 × 4.5 metres and a height of 3 metres (15 × 15 × 10 feet). This gives a wall area of 60 square metres (67 square yards). The amount of wash you need depends on how thin you make it.

Paint type	Number of litres	Number of gallons
Primers	7½	1½
Undercoat	7½	1½
Emulsion	7½	1½
Varnish	5	1
Eggshell	7½	1½
Gloss	7½	1½
Glaze	2	½
Wash	1–2	¼–½
Distemper	7½	1½

Pastes and powders are used in special finishes for tiny decorative objects, furniture and panelling.

ANTIQUING WAX For an average size chest of drawers: a 500-gram (1-pound 1-ounce) tin of beeswax furniture polish, about 250 grams (8 ounces) of powder to mix with the wax (either powder colour, fuller's earth or rottenstone).

LIMING WAX For an average size chest of drawers: one 500-gram (1-pound 1-ounce) tin of beeswax furniture polish and not more than 500 grams (1 pound 1 ounce) of titanium white powder colour.

METALLIC POWDER 100 grams (3½ ounces) is enough to gild an average lamp base.

A LIST OF TERMS & NAMES

Adam, Robert (1728–92) Scottish architect and designer, a leading figure in the neo-Classical movement in British domestic architecture.

ageing variety of abrasive techniques for simulating the effect of time and wear on new paint, wood, plastic, or plasterwork.

aniline dye synthetic pigment found in some paints and varnishes.

anthemion honeysuckle or lotus flower motif or fan-shaped leaf design.

Anthemion in lily-leaf frame

antiquing decorative process that imparts painted surfaces with a false sense of age, so mimicking the discolouration caused by dust and dirt.

arabesque surface decoration, originally found on Arabic paintings, consisting of intertwining leaf, flower or animal forms, or rhythmic designs.

architrave moulded frame that surrounds a doorway, arch, window or wall panel.

armillary sphere a model of the celestial sphere.

armoire large cupboard, usually decorated and with two doors.

Art Deco design style of the inter-war years (named after the 1925 *Exposition des Arts Décoratifs* in Paris) that was heavily influenced by Cubist art and contemporary mechanical forms.

Art Nouveau late nineteenth-century style of art and architecture, opposed to the Classicism of the immediate past.

Arts and Crafts movement late Victorian group of artists who advocated a revival of traditional craftmanship and pre-industrial values.

Aztec characteristic of the art and culture of the Aztecs, an ancient Mexican Indian civilization.

bain-marie double boiler designed for heating substances slowly in cookery and useful for making gesso.

Bakelite the first entirely synthetic industrial plastic, patented in 1907.

Baroque rich European style of architecture and decoration, popular during the seventeenth and eighteenth centuries, chiefly characterized by its floral lines, confidence, theatrical use of ornamentation and grandeur.

bas-relief sculpture that projects slightly from the background but is not detached from it.

Bauhaus design school based in Germany during the 1920s that sought to dismantle the barriers that separate decorative art and engineering.

beading moulding originally designed to resemble a string of beads and used for edging and ornamentation.

Biedermeier style of interior decoration and design that is a version of early nineteenth-century Classical revival styles, such as Empire. The name is that of a German fictional character.

Boucher, François (1703–70) French Rococo artist and designer whose work is typical of eighteenth-century French courtly art.

Brescia city in Lombardy, Italy, known for the red-brown marble that is quarried locally.

brocade heavy, opulent silk with raised patterns, originally worked in gold or silver thread.

butter muslin unbleached muslin, cream in colour.

Byzantine art style that flourished during the sixth century, and, later, from the ninth to the eleventh century, in Byzantium (later Constantinople), and which combined elements from ancient Greece, Oriental culture and Christianity.

cabriole S-shaped design of furniture leg, widely used on early eighteenth-century chairs.

cachepot literally "pot-hider". An ornamental container used to house flowerpots.

calico plain, coarse woven cotton originally from India.

Carrara town in Tuscany, renowned for its white, grey-veined marble.

cartouche panel bearing inscriptions or emblems, often in *trompe l'oeil*.

caryatid sculptured female figure or bust, usually used to support a ceiling, or the architrave, cornice and frieze above a door or fireplace.

castellation resemblance to a castle wall created by the inclusion of battlement- and turret-like patterns.

censer vessel in which incense is burnt over charcoal during ecclesiastical ceremonies.

Cézanne, Paul (1839–1906) leading French post-impressionist painter whose work is characterized by the careful placing of textured brushstrokes in rich tones of colour.

CFC abbreviated form of chlorofluorocarbon, an environment-threatening substance used in the manufacture of some aerosol sprays.

cheesecloth loosely woven cotton fabric, originally used to cover cheese.

chevron regular zigzag line, often used in medieval heraldic designs.

Chinoiserie term for Chinese pieces of decorative art of the seventeenth- and eighteenth-century Western style that coupled contemporary European forms with Oriental motifs.

chintz closely woven, medium-weight cotton fabric, usually glazed and traditionally printed with a colourful floral design on a light background.

chisel head shape of the bristles of a decorating brush which have worn down obliquely at the side with use, thus improving their performance.

clair bois literally, "pale wood". A technique used to imitate the polished finishes of light-coloured woods.

Classical architectural or decorative stylistic motifs prevalent in the designs of Greek or Roman antiquity.

Cliff, Clarice (1899–1972) English pottery designer, associated with the Art Deco movement.

colourwashing simple water-based paint technique used to produce a softly textured, patchy finish, achieved by applying several layers of thin paint.

combination gilding method of gilding where two or more techniques are used together to give the impression that the finer technique alone has been used.

combing technique in which the teeth of a decorator's comb are scraped through a surface glaze.

Castellation

complementary colours any pair of colours that, when placed on a colour wheel, occupy opposing positions. The complementary of any primary colour (red, yellow, blue) is the secondary colour made by mixing the other two.

composition paste of rosin, glue and whiting used for producing mouldings.

Cooper, Susie (b.1902) British ceramicist of the Twenties and Thirties.

corbel projecting architectural bracket, often of stone or brick, that supports a cornice or beam.

cornice external feature projecting from the upper wall, or a moulding used to conceal the joint between the top of a wall and the ceiling.

crackleglaze see *craquelure*.

craquelure decorative glaze finish developed in eighteenth-century France to reproduce the fine network of cracks on Eastern lacquerwork and pottery. Also known as crackleglaze.

creamware earthenware that possesses a deep cream colour.

dado lower part of a wall, between the dado rail and the floor.

dado rail projected horizontal moulding traditionally running at waist-height along a wall, dividing the dado from the upper wall.

damask silk or linen fabric, with a lavish textural pattern.

découpage method of decorating walls and objects with paper cutouts.

Delftware tin-glazed earthenware from the Netherlands, traditionally in a blue and white colour combination.

Della Robbia fifteenth-century Renaissance Florentine family of sculptors who used a glazed ceramic medium for decorative sculpture, usually depicting a religious subject framed by a floral wreath.

dentil ornamental moulding; one of a repeat of rectangular, evenly spaced blocks, usually placed underneath a Classical cornice.

distemper group of paints formed by mixing pigments with water, bound with casein, glue or egg, which were widely used before the introduction of emulsion paints.

distressing process of artificially abrading a new surface to create the appearance of old age.

dragging technique of pulling a long-haired brush through wet transparent oil glaze, or distemper, to produce a series of fine lines on walls or furniture.

dry-brushing paint technique that keeps the bristle surface of a brush relatively dry in order to build up a cloudy effect, or to touch with paint the highlights of a textured surface.

dryers chemicals added to decorating materials to speed up their drying rate.

earth colours oxide pigments, such as raw umber, that are made from refined clays and minerals dug from the ground. Available as powders or liquids, they have a natural, timeless quality that makes them ideal for tinting, dulling and antiquing.

ebonized treated with colour to look like ebony.

egg-and-dart pattern, often found on carved architectural mouldings, comprising a row of oval shapes interspersed with arrows.

Empire grandiose French style, that mixed Classical decorative devices with Egyptian and Napoleonic imagery.

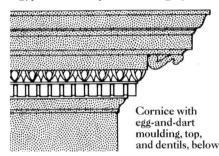

Cornice with egg-and-dart moulding, top, and dentils, below

faience European decorated style of tin-glazed earthenware.

faux **effects** literally, "false" effects. Finishes created to imitate another material, such as marble (*faux marbre*) or wood (*faux bois*).

ferrule metal brace on a paintbrush, used to strengthen the handle and grip the bristles.

filigree delicate ornamentation or tracery, often produced with fine wires of gold or silver.

finial terminal part of any ornamental projection, in the form of a spire or vase, for example, that crowns buildings or furniture.

flagged bristles pig bristles that are naturally split at the end. Brushes with "flags" give a superior finish.

flat finish matt, non-greasy finish.

fleur-de-lys old French motif that takes the form of a stylized lily or iris flower.

fly-spotting finish created by spattering paint, coloured glaze, varnish or ink on to a surface to convey a feeling of age.

fossilstone marble marble in which fossilized animal and plant forms create a mottled pattern.

French polishing treatment of a wooden surface with French polish to give a highly reflective, smooth finish.

fresco durable painting, usually found on walls and ceilings, created by incorporating watercolours directly into wet plaster surfaces; the technique was perfected in Renaissance Italy.

frieze broad horizontal band on the upper part of a wall that is decorated separately from the rest of the room with stencils, paintings, wallpaper or plasterwork.

gilding method of colouring surfaces gold, either by the application of gold leaf or gold paint.

Gill, Eric (1882–1940) English sculptor, engraver and typographer.

gingham checked or striped textile, usually woven from two differently coloured yarns.

Gothic architectural style, of twelfth-century French origin, widely adopted throughout Western Europe until displaced by the Classical influences of the Renaissance.

Gothic arch pointed arch, characteristic of medieval Gothic architecture.

Gothic Revival robust Gothic style of the mid-nineteenth century, noted for its sombre authenticity and display of medieval pomp.

Gothick early- to mid-eighteenth-century decorative style that celebrated the more exuberant elements of the medieval Gothic style, interpreting them in a contemporary setting.

gouache opaque water-based paint, in which the pigments are bound with glue or gum arabic.

grisaille visual trick that harnesses monochrome shades of paint to represent areas of light and shade and thus create, on a flat surface, the illusion of a three-dimensional ornament or an architectural feature.

Gropius, Walter (1883–1969) German architect and designer, Director of the Bauhaus school, from 1919 to 1928.

gypsum plaster standard plaster for interior walls, for patching surfaces and for producing mouldings.

half tone any colour tint judged to be halfway in tone between a given hue and white.

hemp scrim open-weave fabric made from the hemp plant.

hessian plain, coarse fabric, woven from rough fibre and used to make upholstery canvas.

icon Byzantine type of oil painting, with a prescribed set of religious images executed on a wooden panel.

inlay form of decoration on flat surfaces, such as furniture, made with a pattern of holes filled with materials, such as coloured woods, metals or mother-of-pearl.

Kandinsky, Wassily (1866–1944) Russian-born expressionist painter who pioneered a purely abstract style of art. He taught at the Bauhaus until it was closed.

kelim flat-woven tapestry rug, manufactured in the Middle East, typified by the use of brilliant colours and bold patterns.

Klee, Paul (1879–1940) Swiss painter and etcher whose work harmonized formal and imaginative elements.

lacquerwork Oriental decoration that is lacquered in order to provide a strong, high-gloss surface.

Lalique, René (1860–1945) French designer and craftsman, renowned for his Art Nouveau glass pieces.

Landseer, Sir Edwin Henry (1802–73) English realist painter, famous for his studies of animals in landscapes.

Langley, Batty (1697–1751) architect, furniture designer and author, partly responsible for the revival of interest in ogive arches and rosettes that marked the Gothick style.

lapis lazuli blue mineral, used both as a gem stone and as the pigment known as ultramarine blue.

limewash substance composed of slaked lime and water that is used for whitening exterior walls. Also known as whitewash.

liming decorative technique that harnesses liming wax to leave a white pigment in the grain of bare wood, creating a mellow finish.

lincrusta patented nineteenth-century type of cast plastic.

linenfold panelling a style of panel, which is moulded or carved in a design intended to mimic the pattern created by folded cloth.

Lloyd Loom furniture machine-made, closely-woven furniture (especially chairs), patented by the American, Marshall Lloyd.

low relief see *bas-relief*.

Mackintosh, Charles Rennie (1868–1928) Scottish artist, architect and furniture designer, allied to the Art Nouveau movement.

majolica style of earthenware with a thick, white glaze coloured with pigments.

marbling variety of paint techniques designed to recreate artificially the appearance of marble.

marquetry decorative veneer composed of inlaid shapes of exotic woods, bone, metal or ivory.

mask cut-out card shape used to cover a surface and so provide a barrier against a layer of paint.

matchboarding form of cladding in which long wooden boards are held together with tongue-and-groove joints.

Mayan characteristic of the art and architecture of the so-called ancient American Indian civilization.

memento mori (Latin) "remember that you must die": object that serves as a reminder of human mortality.

milk paint primer paint, at one time applied to furniture, based on a protein found in milk.

mitre joint right-angle corner formed when two strips of material, especially wood, each with an edge sloping at a 45° angle, are joined together.

Modernism a style which developed in the fine and applied arts in the early part of the twentieth century, based on a rejection of traditional approaches in favour of more industrial, unorna-mented genres.

Moorish associated with the art, architecture and culture of the Moors, who established dominance in North Africa and in southern Spain in the eighth century.

Morris, William (1834–96) major English designer, painter, poet and exponent of the decorative arts. A leading figure in the Arts and Crafts movement, he was also an important influence on the Pre-Raphaelites.

mosaic decorative design produced from the assembly of small pieces of stone, marble or glass.

muslin fine, woven cotton fabric used for curtains, hangings, etc.

mutton cloth variable-weave cotton cloth (also known as stockinette).

neo-Classical relating to the eighteenth-century European movement, inspired by the architectural forms of Classicism and characterized by a sense of proportion and harmony.

New Bauhaus design school formed in Chicago following the close of the Bauhaus by the Nazis in 1933.

obelisk square or rectangular stone monument, tapering to a pyramidal point at the top.

Odeon wall lamp Art Deco shell-shaped glass lamp, once installed in Odeon cinemas in Britain.

ogee decorative S-shaped moulding.

ogive arch characteristic Gothic arch, with ogee-shaped sides; popular in eighteenth-century Gothick design.

onyx ornamental marbled stone.

Orientalist a member of a Victorian movement of designers and artists, typified by an interest in Oriental design and motifs.

ormolu ornament of cast-metal alloy, that is gilded industrially.

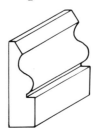

Moulding with ogee section

panel moulding moulding consisting of small, plain surfaces, that are either inlaid or raised.

papier-mâché layers of paper, or paper pulp, mixed with paste, which dry to form a light but tough material.

parquetry type of inlay of flooring where wooden tiles are laid to form geometrical patterns.

patina colour and texture that appears on the surface of a material as a result of age or atmospheric corrosion.

pelmet structure used to conceal the top edge of a curtain or blind.

pickled another word for woods that have been limed.

picture rail moulding running along the top of a wall to take the hooks from which framed pictures hang.

pietra serena type of stone widely used in Florentine Renaissance architecture.

pilaster shallow, rectangular section of a pillar, added to the face of a wall for ornamental interest.

Piranesi, Giovanni Battista (1720–78) Italian designer, engraver and architect whose major works include the series of etchings named *Le antichitá Romane*.

porphyry purplish rock embedded with crystals of feldspar, which can be simulated with spattered paint.

portico interior and exterior canopy supported on columns or brackets above a doorway or entrance.

post-impressionist term referring to certain artists operating after the Impressionist movement of art in nineteenth-century France.

Pre-Raphaelite brotherhood association of mid-nineteenth century English artists who sought to represent the religious earnestness of painting before Raphael in works of art which tend to be symbolic and literary.

primary colours in painting terms, red, yellow and blue, from which all other colours can be produced.

quoin-stone stone delineating the external corner in the wall of a building.

ragging paint technique that employs a crumpled piece of rag to create decorative broken-colour finishes.

Raku moulded Japanese earthenware, first produced in the fifteenth century.

rattan palm giving its name to the wickerwork produced from its stems.

Regency English decorative style that absorbed a wide range of contemporary Continental influences. Popular during the early nineteenth century.

Rococo exuberant early eighteenth-century European decorative style characterized by its scalloped curves, elaborate scrolls and pastel colours.

Rustic frivolous eighteenth-century style of decoration applied to both roughly-hewn outdoor furniture and interior plasterwork.

saltglaze slightly pitted glaze applied to stoneware by throwing salt on to the fire of the kiln in which the pots are being baked.

sanguine red chalk containing ferric oxide, used in drawing.

satinwood expensive, hard, pale wood with a satiny grain.

sconce wall-fixed bracket used for holding a candle or light.

scrubbed limewash paint technique that gives walls the appearance of well-scrubbed limewash, which was employed to paint exterior walls.

serpentine marble dark-green or brown patterned stone with veining.

Sèvres porcelain porcelain produced in Sèvres, France, which led European ceramic fashions from 1760 to 1815.

shagreen material created from the dried skins of fish; used in inlays.

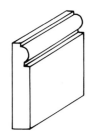

Torus moulding on skirting board

Shaker name of an American sect founded in 1747. The title derives from the excited state of their worship. Their furniture is typified by its functional design and lack of ornament.

shellac varnishing highly skilled sister technique of French polishing.

Siena marble yellow-coloured marble with veining, originating from Siena, a city in Tuscany.

sienna yellowish-brown pigment. The term is a variant of the name of the town, Siena.

sisal robust fibre, used in the manufacture of flooring and rope.

Soane, Sir John (1753–1837) English architect whose approach to interior decor was influenced by Roman and Byzantine architecture.

spattering decorative technique in which a brush, dipped in paint, ink, glaze or varnish, is knocked to spray dots of colour on to a surface.

spectrum colours colours of the rainbow, formed when light is split into its component parts.

spongeware ceramics decorated with colours that are applied with a sponge to give a blotchy effect.

sponging painting technique that uses a damp sponge to produce a mottled, patchy effect.

stencil card stout oiled manila card or thick cartridge paper, from which shapes are cut in order to make stencils.

stencilling method of decoration in which paint is applied through a cut-out design to create images on a surface.

stippling painting or texturing a surface with a fine, mottled pattern, using a stippler or stiff-bristled brush.

stock widest section of the handle of a paintbrush.

stucco fine plaster-type material used both to cover exterior brickwork and to decorate internal walls and ceilings.

sugarsoap alkaline compound used for cleaning or stripping paint.

swag festoon motif, usually representing a line of drapery or a chain of leaves, flowers or fruit.

swatch small piece of material or card used as a sample.

template shape made from paper or card, that acts as a fixed guide for cutting out the same shapes from a variety of other materials.

terracotta literally "cooked earth". High-quality, unglazed fired clay.

terra verde earth colour: Italian for green earth.

ticking stout cotton fabric with a distinctive pattern of narrow stripes.

tie back length of ribbon or cord, or a metal bracket, used to pin a curtain to the side of a window.

tongue-and-groove joint made between two boards by means of a tongue projecting from the edge of one board that slots into a groove along the edge of the other.

torus convex moulding that is semi-circular in cross-section, found on

skirting boards, mouldings, beading and the base of Classical columns.

trefoil arch decorative arch with three arcs arranged in a circle, found in Gothic architecture.

trompe l'oeil any of a variety of optical illusions, such as *grisaille* that are designed, literally, "to trick the eye".

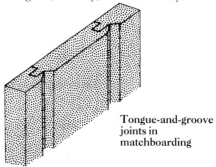

Tongue-and-groove joints in matchboarding

uplighter lamp, often attached to walls, that throws light upwards on to the upper part of walls and the ceiling.

verdigris green colour, produced as a result of naturally-occurring corrosion on copper, bronze and brass.

Victorian Eclectic person who subscribes to the belief that art and interior decoration should draw from a range of different styles.

vignette small illustration that is not contained within a border.

Voysey, Charles Francis (1857–1941) English designer influenced by William Morris, but with a lighter style.

wainscotting lining – usually wood panelling – used to cover the lower wall.

wash thin, home-made paint or diluted, proprietary paint, such as emulsion. Traditionally known as colourwash since it was made by adding colour to limewash.

whitewash see *limewash*.

wickerwork slender, flexible twigs that have been woven together.

window casement window containing frames that are hinged on one side or at the top or bottom.

woodblock block of wood from which a design has been cut. Used for printing an image on to walls or furniture.

woodgraining technique used to imitate the characteristic markings of a variety of natural woodgrains.

Wright, Frank Lloyd (1867–1959) American architect and furniture designer, who cultivated a modern taste for dynamic, angular forms.

ziggurat architectural pyramidal style with castellated edges, popularly adapted into Art Deco.

GUIDE TO SUPPLIERS

General note As well as Crown Berger and F.A. Heffer (listed under Decorating Tools and Materials), suppliers listed on pages 342–5 kindly lent items for photography. Companies that operate a mail order service are indicated ✉

Decorating Tools and Materials

J. W. Bollom
13 Theobald's Road
London WC1X 8FN

SHOWROOM
314–6 Old Brompton Road
London SW5 9JH
General painting supplies, manufacturers of Pervalac crackle medium, range of palette colour emulsions.

C. Brewer
327 Putney Bridge Road
London SW15 2PG
General painting supplies. Branches throughout SE England.

Brodie and Middleton Ltd. ✉
68 Drury Lane
London WC2B 5SP
Decorating brushes, French enamel varnish, glues, metallic powders, paints, pigments and powder colours.

Cornelissen and Son Ltd. ✉
105 Great Russell Street
London WC1B 3RY
Bone glue, brushes, gilding materials, gum arabic, pigments and rabbit-skin glue.

Craig & Rose plc.
172 Leith Walk
Edinburgh EH6 5EB
Extra pale dead-flat varnish, gold leaf, goldsize, specialist brushes and transparent oil glaze. Paint manufacturers; stockists nationwide.

Crown Berger Europe Ltd.
P.O. Box 37
Crown House
Hollins Road
Darwen
Lancashire BB3 0BG
Range of over 600 colours of paint in a choice of finishes for both interior and exterior surfaces.

GENERAL SOURCES

Artists' suppliers The following materials are usually available from good artists' suppliers: artists' acrylics, artists' acrylic varnishes, artists' inks, artists' oil paints, artists' paintbrushes, bone glue, craft knives, goldsize, gouache, gum arabic, metallic paints, modellers' enamel paints, palette knives, poster paints, rabbit-skin glue, scalpels, school powders (non-toxic but not as intense as powder colours), shellac, spray paints, stencil or manila card, universal stainers, wax crayons, writing inks.

DIY stores The following materials, which are used in this book, are usually available from good DIY stores: beeswax furniture polish, button polish, dust mask (paper), dusting brushes, eggshell paint, emulsion paint, EVA, filler, goldsize, hammer-finish enamel paint, knotting, masking tape, mutton cloth, oil-based varnishes, paint buckets, painter's mates, plaster, polyurethane varnish, primers, protective gloves and goggles, PVA, respiratory mask, sand, sanding sealer, sandpaper, scrapers, self-adhesive lead, shellac, smooth-texture coating, solvents, sponges, spray paints, trowels, white polish, wire brushes, wire wool.

Chemists Chemist shops often sell fuller's earth and natural sponges.

Daler-Rowney Ltd. ✉
12 Percy Street
London W1A 2BP
Artists' materials including acetate, acrylic gesso, artists' acrylics, artists' oil paints, gouache, powder colours, stencil card and transfer metal leaf.

Green & Stone ✉
259 King's Road
London SW3 5ER

19 West Market Place ✉
Cirencester
Gloucestershire GL7 2AE
Artists' materials including acrylic varnish, specialist brushes, casein paints, crackle varnish, gesso and gesso paints, gum arabic, linseed oil, powder colours, shellac, stencilling materials and transparent oil glaze.

W. Habberley Meadows Ltd.
5 Saxon Way
Chelmsley Wood
Birmingham B37 5AY
Artists' brushes, paints and materials.

F. A. Heffer & Sons Ltd.
24 The Pavement
London SW4 0JA
Specialist brushes.

John T. Keep & Sons Ltd. ✉
15 Theobald's Road
London WC1X 8FN
Crackle medium, powder colours, shellac, specialist brushes, transparent oil glaze and universal stainers.

Lyn Le Grice Stencil Design Ltd.
Bread Street
Penzance TR18 2EQ
Stencil books, kits and materials. Stencilling courses.

E. Milner Oxford Ltd.
Clanville Road
Cowley
Oxford OX4 2DB
General painting supplies including crackle varnish, specialist brushes, transparent oil glaze and universal stainers.

John Myland ✉
80 Norwood High Street
London SE27 9NW
Artists' brushes, bone glue, French enamel varnish, liming wax, oil-based varnish, palette-colour emulsions (including earth colours), pigments, powder colours, rabbit-skin glue, rottenstone, shellac, transparent oil glaze and universal stainers.

The Paint Service Co. Ltd.
19 Eccleston Street
London SW1 9LX
*Specialist brushes, transparent oil glaze
and varnishes.*

Paper and Paints ✉
4 Park Walk
London SW10 0AD
*Suppliers of many specialist paints and
decorating materials and a range of
"historic" colours. Colourmatching
service available.*

E. Ploton (Sundries) Ltd. ✉
273 Archway Road
London N6 5AA
*Artists' materials including acetate,
acrylic gesso, acrylic varnish, artists'
acrylics, artists' oil paints, crackle
varnish, gouache, gum arabic, metallic
powders, specialist brushes and transfer
metal leaf.*

Potmolen Paint
27 Woodcock Industrial Estate
Warminster
Wiltshire BA12 9DX
*Specialist paint suppliers including
distempers, gilding materials and
traditional materials.*

J. H. Ratcliffe & Co. (Paints) Ltd. ✉
135a Linaker Street
Southport PR8 5DF
*Brushes and tools for graining, and
transparent oil glaze.*

Robertson and Co. Ltd.
1a Hercules Street
London N7 6AT
*Artists' oil paints, bronze powders, inks,
varnishes and watercolours.*

Simpsons Paints Ltd.
122–4 Broadley Street
London NW8 8BB
*Gold leaf, specialist brushes and
transparent oil glaze.*

Stuart R. Stevenson
68 Clerkenwell Road
London EC1M 5QA
Artists' and gilding materials.

Lewis Ward & Co.
128 Fortune Green Road
London NW6 1DN
*Specialist brushes including Omega,
Whistler and foreign brands.*

Architectural salvage

The following are an excellent
source of reclaimed period fittings,
old furniture and unusual
"one-offs".

Architectural Antiques
Savoy Showrooms
New Road
South Molton
Devon EX36 4BH
*Baths and bathroom furniture, fireplaces
and surrounds, pub interiors, panelling
and staircases.*

Architectural Heritage
Taddington Manor
Taddington
Near Cutsdean
Cheltenham
Gloucestershire GL54 5RY
*Fireplaces and surrounds, period
panelling produced in a range of woods
and stained glass.*

Bailey's Architectural Antiques
The Engine Shed
Ashburton Industrial Estate
Ross-on-Wye
Herefordshire HR9 7BW
*Carved marble, fireplaces, hand-painted
tiles, pews, stained glass and bathrooms.*

**Cantabrian Antiques and
Architectural Furnishings**
16 Park Street
Lynton
North Devon EX35 6BY
*Baths and bathroom fittings, beams, door
furniture, fireplaces, marble surrounds
and wood panelling. Unusual items.*

Havenplan Ltd.
The Old Station
Station Road
Killamarsh
Sheffield S31 8EN
*Architectural furniture, including church
furnishings, doors, fireplaces and
panelling.*

The House Hospital
68 Battersea High Street
London SW11 3HX
*Baths and bathroom furniture, brass
fittings, cast iron radiators, doors,
fireplaces and spindles.*

**London Architectural Salvage
Company**
St. Michael and All Angels
Mark Street
London EC2A 4ER
*Bathroom and kitchen furniture and
fittings, ceramics, doors, shutters,
flooring, lighting, metalware, door
furniture, panelling and carved
woodwork, staircases and spindles.*

REFERENCE BOOKS

The Dover Bookshop ✉
18 Earlham Street, London WC2H 9LN
Reference and stencil books

The Dover Pictorial Archive Series
Decorative Frames and Borders E. V. Gillon Jnr.
Cartouches and Decorative Small Frames E. V. Gillon Jnr.
Pugin's Gothic Ornament A. C. Pugin
Florid Victorian Ornament K. Klimsch
Art Deco Spot Illustrations W. Rowe
Scroll Ornaments of the Early Victorian Period F. Knight
Rustic Vignettes for Artists and Craftsmen W. H. Pyne
Historic Ornament, a Pictorial Archive C. B. Griesbach
Découpage Eleanor Hasbrouck Rawlings

OTHER USEFUL WORKS
History of the English House Nathaniel Lloyd
    Architectural Press Facsimile reprint 1983
Period Houses and their Details Colin Amery
    Architectural Press 1974
A Grammar of Ornament Owen Jones
    Omega Facsimile reprint 1989
Ornament Stuart Durant
    Macdonald 1986
Authentic Decor Peter Thornton
    Weidenfeld and Nicolson 1984

Robertson and Partners
Jodrell Street
Nuneaton
Warwickshire CV11 5EH
*Doors, flooring and staircases salvaged
from old houses.*

Solopark
The Old Railway Station
Station Road
Pampisford
Cambridge CB2 4HB
*Architectural antiques, stripped pine doors
and flooring tiles.*

**Andy Thornton Architectural
Antiques Ltd.**
Ainleys Industrial Estate
Elland
West Yorkshire HX5 9JP
*Cast iron baths, doors, fireplaces, pews
and revolving doors.*

Walcot Reclamation Ltd.
108 Walcot Street
Bath
Avon BA1 5BG
Traditional architectural antiques.

Fabrics and wallpapers

Joanna Booth
247 King's Road
London SW3 5EL
*Antique textiles including tapestries,
cushions and curtains. Also wood
carvings, early oak furniture and old
drawings.*

Colefax and Fowler
39 Brook Street
London W1Y 2JE
*Reproduction 18th and 19th century
fabrics and wallpapers, upholstered
furniture and decorative accessories.*

The Design Archives
79 Walton Street
London SW3 2HP
*Curtain material, upholstery fabric and
wallpapers produced from original 17th,
18th and 19th century designs.*

**Gallery of Antique Costume &
Textiles**
2 Church Street
London NW8 8ED
*Antique textiles including costumes,
curtains, furnishings, hangings,
needlework, quilts, religious vestments
and tapestries.*

Judy Greenwood Antiques
657 Fulham Road
London SW6 5PY
*Antique textiles including paisley and 19th
century French curtains and quilts.*

Danielle Hartwright
Antique Textiles
Liberty's of Regent Street
Regent Street
London W1R 6AH
Antique Aubusson curtains and pelmets.

Karls ✉
6 Cheval Place
London SW7 1EF
*Swedish reproduction fabrics and
wallpapers. Supply trade only: write for
list of retail outlets.*

Laura Ashley
Customer Services
Braywick House
Braywick Road
Maidenhead
Berkshire SL6 1DW
*Range of period design and country fabrics
and wallpapers. Outlets nationwide.*

Ornamenta Ltd.
PO Box No 784
London SW7 2TG
*Trompe l'oeil and hand-printed
wallpaper decorations, come ready-cut.*

Osborne & Little
304–308 King's Road
London SW3 5UH

39 Queen Street
Edinburgh EH2 3NH
*Wide range of original, contemporary and
Classical fabrics, wallpapers and
trimmings. For list of stockists write to
Head Office, Osborne & Little, 49
Temperley Road, London SW12 3QE.*

Rare Carpets Gallery
45 Fernshaw Road
London SW10

496 King's Road
London SW10 0LE
*Hand-made antique and contemporary
carpets, antique furniture and textiles.*

Arthur Sanderson & Sons Ltd.
52 Berners Street
London W1P 3AD
*Hand-printed wallpapers, co-ordinating
ranges of wallpapers, borders, fabrics and
voiles. Bed linen, carpets and paints.*

Souleiado
171 Fulham Road
London SW3 6JW
*Provençal prints on cotton and objects
made from cotton fabrics, bed linen and
tablecloths.*

Stothert & Miles Ltd.
8 Holbein Place
London SW1W 8NL
*Reproduction textiles and fabrics of 18th
and 19th century country house styles.*

Bernard Thorp
6 Burnsall Street
London SW3 3SR
*Hand screen-printers and weavers,
specializing in custom coloured designs
printed on a range of fabrics.*

Timney Fowler
388 King's Road
London SW3 5UZ
*Contemporary range of black and white
furnishing fabrics, wallpapers and
borders in a neo-Classical style.*

Warner Fabrics plc.
7–11 Noel Street
London W1V 4AL
*Traditional and contemporary printed
and woven fabrics and wallcoverings.*

Watts & Co.
7 Tufton Street
London SW1P 3QE
*Reproduction 18th and 19th century fabric
designs including gold cloth. Also hand-
printed wallpapers, tassels, tiebacks and
trimmings. Write for list of stockists.*

Flooring

Amtico
17 St. George Street
London W1R 9DE
*Manufacturers of quality vinyl tiles for
flooring within the home or commercially.
See pages 37, 41, 63 and 141 for
examples. Write for details of outlets and
flooring contractors.*

Castlenau Tiles
15 Church Road
London SW13 9HR
Ceramic and terracotta tiles.

Fired Earth
Middle Aston
Oxfordshire OX5 3PX
Hand-made floor and wall tiles.

Paris Ceramics
543 Battersea Park Road
London SW11 3BL
European traditional ceramics including antique terracotta (reclaimed from French country houses) and stone floors.

Furniture and accessories

Antique, reproduction and contemporary merchandise.

David Alexander Antiques
102 Waterford Road
London SW6 2HA
16th–18th century furniture and accessories, and architectural items.

Nick Allen Consultancy
Ground Floor Studio
80b Battersea Rise
London SW11 1EH
Versatile range of steel furniture. Works to commission. Studio collection also available at The Studio, 6 Cale Street, London SW3 3QU.

Philip Allison Antiques & Decorative Arts
The Furniture Cave
533 King's Road
London SW10 0TZ
Antique and reproduction oak and mahogany furniture and accessories.

Maria Andipa Icon Gallery
162 Walton Street
London SW3 2JL
Icons from around the world, country furniture and oil lamps.

Antiquarius
(Banjarah Tent, Chelsea Clocks and Antiques, Persiflage)
131–141 King's Road
London SW3 5ST
Antique furniture, decorative accessories and clocks.

Antique Designs Ltd.
277 Lillie Road
London SW6 7PN
Reproduction furniture in various European styles ranging from Biedermeier to Art Deco.

Antiquus
90–92 Pimlico Road
London SW1W 8PL
Objects, paintings and furniture from the antique world to the 19th century.

K. Armelin Antiques
592 King's Road
London SW6 2DX
English and French 18th and early 19th century furniture.

BDI
The Furniture Cave,
533 King's Road
London SW10 0TZ
Decorative English and continental furniture. Also architectural fitments, sculpture and antique furnishing fabrics.

Mary Bellis Antiques
Charnham Close
Hungerford
Berkshire RG17 0EJ
Quality 16th and 17th century oak furniture and works of art.

Jean Brown
The Furniture Cave
533 King's Road
London SW10 0TZ
Mainly 19th century French decorative furniture, objets d'art and small architectural pieces.

Browns
The Furniture Cave
533 King's Road
London SW10 0TZ
Georgian, Victorian and Edwardian furniture, mirrors, prints and other decorative items.

Carless and Gray
608 King's Road
London SW6 2DZ
Unusual antique and reproduction decorative furniture and accessories.

Decorative Living
55 New King's Road
London SW6 4SE
Antique and Colonial design furniture. Also unusual decorative accessories including lighting.

The Dining Room Shop
62–4 White Hart Lane
London SW13 0PZ
Everything for the dining room, including furniture, china and glass.

Charles Edwards
582 King's Road
London SW6 2DY
Decorative antique furniture, pictures and lighting fixtures.

Five Five Six Antiques
556 King's Road
London SW6 2DZ
Beautiful and unusual objects, furniture and paintings. Antique and contemporary.

Robin Gage
Unit 7
The Talina Centre
23a Bagleys Lane
London SW6 2BW
Reproductions of 18th and 19th century French, Italian and neo-Classical decorative accessories.

The General Trading Company Ltd.
144 Sloane Street
London SW1X 9BL
Household furnishings, china, glass, linen and stationery from all over the world, including antiques and Oriental items.

Graham & Green
4 & 7 Elgin Crescent
London W11 2JA
Antique, reproduction and contemporary decorative and useful accessories. Also furniture, ceramics, glass, textiles and lighting. Brochure available.

Elizabeth Griffiths
Clockwork Studios
38 Southwell Road
London SE5 9PG
Fine artist making papier-mâché vessels.

Hirst Antiques
59 Pembridge Road
London W11 3HN
Four-poster and half-tester antique beds, decorative furniture and objects.

Lacquer Chest
71 & 75 Kensington Church Street
London W8 4BG
Extensive range of esoteric antique objects, including furniture, glasswork, paintings and pottery.

Ligne Roset
132 Shaftesbury Avenue
London W1V 7DN
Extensive range of contemporary upholstery and cabinet systems, with complementary accessories and lighting.

Michael Marriott Ltd.
588 Fulham Road
London SW6 5NT
18th and 19th century furniture and decorative antique prints.

Michael Midgley and Carolyn Cusk Ltd.
13 Hewer Street
London W10 6DU
Hand-painted reproduction 18th and 19th century furniture and accessories.

Richard Miles Antiques
8 Holbein Place
London SW1W 8NL
Antique furniture and decorative accessories from Regency "Gothic" to Colonial Anglo-Indian in exotic woods.

M.S.M. Antiques
The Furniture Cave
533 King's Road
London SW10 0TZ
Antique and reproduction furniture, decorative accessories, fabrics, fireplaces and lighting from all periods.

Neal Street East
5 Neal Street
London WC2H 9PU
Homeware, cookware, lighting, textiles and books from the Orient.

Oggetti
101 Jermyn Street
London SW1Y 6EE
A wide range of contemporary objects and accessories of high-quality design.

Old Pine
594 King's Road
London SW6 2DX
Individually painted antique furniture of French and English origin.

Barrie Quinn Antiques
3–4 Broxholme House
New King's Road
London SW6 4AA
Range of antique furniture, mirrors, decorative accessories and ceramic jardinières.

Rogier Antiques
20a Pimlico Road
London SW1W 8LJ
European antique and reproduction objects, specializing in Provençal style. Also painted, gilded and lacquered work.

Edward Russell Decorative Accessories Ltd.
18–20 Scrutton Street
London EC2A 4RJ
Manufacturers of decorative accessories and lamps.

Santa Fe Trading Post
334 Bruton Place
London W1X 7AA
Traditionally crafted contemporary pine washstands, hand-painted candlesticks.

David Savage Furnituremakers
21 Westcombe
Bideford
North Devon EX39 3JQ
Contemporary hand-crafted furniture made from European hardwoods, polished with natural oils and waxes.

Serena Stapleton Antiques
75 Lower Richmond Road
London SW15 1ET
18th and 19th century decorative furniture, pictures and objets d'art.

Themes and Variations
231 Westbourne Grove
London W11 2SE
Contemporary furniture, decorative accessories and lighting.

Tobias & the Angel
68 White Hart Lane
London SW13 0PZ
Contemporary and antique (country and Victorian) decorative accessories, furniture, garden accessories, kitchenware, lighting and fabrics.

David Weston Ltd.
44 Duke Street
London SW1Y 6DD
Globes, scientific instruments and various marine antiques.

Mark Wilkinson
27 High Street
Bromham
Chippenham
Wiltshire SN15 2HA
Bespoke furniture designers and manufacturers of kitchens, bedrooms and bathrooms. Write for other outlets.

Oscar Woollens Ltd.
81–85 Hampstead Road
London NW1 2PL
Modern furniture from the world's top European and American designers.

Robert Young
68 Battersea Bridge Road
London SW11 3AG
English and European antique country furniture, decorative accessories and stocks of naive and folk art.

Glass and ceramics

Beverly
30 Church Street
London NW8
Antique and contemporary glass and ceramics, specializing in Art Nouveau and Art Deco pieces. Also metalwork.

Isobel Dennis
Clockwork Studios
38 Southwell Road
London SE5 9PG
Bright, contemporary, hand-finished ceramic bowls and dishes with a fruit and floral theme.

Jonathan Horne (Antiques) Ltd.
66c Kensington Church Street
London W8 4BY
Specialists in early English pottery from 17th–19th century including large stocks of 18th century tiles.

Lalique
24 Mount Street
London W1Y 5RB
Importers and distributors of Lalique crystal and Christofle silverware.

The Perfect Glass Shop
5 Park Walk
Fulham Road
London SW10 0AJ
Modern, traditional and antique glassware. Engraving and repairs.

Phillips West Two
10 Salem Road
London W2 4DL
Fine art auctioneers with 44 branches.

Putnams Collections Ltd.
29 Short's Gardens
London WC2H 9AP
Large collection of Staffordshire transfer printed china circa 1800–1930. Also fabrics with designs taken from china.

Lighting

Fergus Cochrane Antiques
570 King's Road
London SW6 2DY
Antique lighting: wall-lights, sconces, chandeliers, candlesticks and lamp bases.

Jack Casimir Ltd.
23 Pembridge Road
London W11 3HG
16th–19th century antique lighting, fireplace accessories and metalware.

Jones Antique Lighting
194 Westbourne Grove
London W11 2RH
Antique lighting 1860–1960. Table, wall and ceiling lights and glass shades.

Lumineres Ltd.
at Remember Antiques
68 Stanhope Road
St Albans
Hertfordshire AL1 5BL
Reproduction brass wall lamps and Griffin table lamps.

Edward Russell Decorative Accessories
18–20 Scrutton Street
London EC2A 4RJ
Hand-made lampshades and wooden lamp bases. Faux painting, trompe l'oeil and watercoloured items.

Tempus Stet Ltd.
Trinity Business Centre
305–309 Rotherhithe Street
London SE16 1EY
Reproduction lighting and mirrors in a range of finishes. Write for local stockists.

Christopher Wray's Lighting Emporium
600 King's Road
London SW6 2DX
Antique and reproduction lighting. Write for details of other outlets.

Metalwork
Freud
198 Shaftesbury Avenue
London WC2H 8JL
Contemporary steel candlesticks and a range of metal furniture.

Ikon Corporation
B5L Metropolitan Wharf
Wapping Wall
London E1 9SS
Contemporary accessories in aluminium.

The Light Shop
34–48 Turnham Green Terrace
London W4 4PL
Contemporary metal candlesticks.

Peter Place Antiques
636 King's Road
London SW6 2DU
Antique and reproduction iron chandeliers and wall sconces. Also 19th century ceramics and decorative country artefacts.

McCloud & Co. Ltd. ✉
61 Hillier Road
London SW11 6AX
Decorative metalwork, reproduction and contemporary designs for furniture and lighting in patinated steel and other media.

Mouldings and timber
Daler-Rowney Ltd. ✉
12 Percy Street
London W1A 2BP
Manufacturers of lincrusta friezes and dados.

E. J. Harmer & Co. Ltd.
19a Birbeck Hill
London SE21 8JS
Able to reproduce all periods of plasterwork.

George Jackson & Sons
Unit 19
Mitcham Industrial Estate
Streatham Road
Mitcham
Surrey CR4 2AJ
Plasterwork and composition details from 18th century mouldings.

Locker & Riley Ltd.
Capital House
Bruce Grove
Wickford
Essex SS11 8DB
Manufacturers and installers of fibrous plasterwork designs of all periods.

The Newson Group
190 Ebury Street
London SW1 8UP
Wide range of materials for decoration including timber, mouldings, doors and windows, fireplaces and accessories, flooring, plasterwork, plumbing and decorating tools, materials and accessories. Catalogue available. Examples of materials used: dado rail, skirting board and door on page 77; pierced screen on page 49; cornice, panelling and banister on page 87; dado rail on page 159.

Oakleaf Reproductions Ltd. ✉
Ling Bob Mills
Main Street
Wilsden
Bradford
Yorkshire BD15 0JP
Quality hand-stained mouldings in rigid polyurethane foam of highly ornate and detailed woodwork. For examples see chest, panelling, beams and corbels on page 115, panelling on page 119, frieze on page 141.

Thames Moulding Company
16b Whytecliffe Road
Purley
Surrey CR2 2AU
Historically accurate period mouldings.

Paintings and prints
ARC Prints and Frames
26 North Street
London SW4 0HB
Decorative 17th–19th century reproduction prints, specializing in architecture. Expert framing service.

Norman Blackburn
32 Ledbury Road
London W11 2AB
Interesting old prints (1600–1860) in period frames.

Corporate Fine Art
24 Cale Street
Chelsea Green
London SW3 3QU
Fine antique prints and maps, specializing in London items.

Crane Gallery
171a Sloane Street
London SW1X 9QG
High-quality American and British folk art.

Stern Art Dealers
46 Ledbury Road
London W11 2AB
Large stock of 19th and early 20th century English and European oil paintings.

Plumbing fitments
C. P. Hart & Sons Ltd.
Newnham Terrace
Hercules Road
London SE1 7DR
High-quality bath and kitchen products in traditional and contemporary styles.

Sitting Pretty Ltd.
131 Dawes Road
London SW6 7EA
Traditional and classical bathrooms, accessories including bathracks, towels and hand-painted mirrors.

INDEX

ACKNOWLEDGMENTS

Stylist (furnishings and accessories)
Lucinda Egerton

Decorative painters
led by *Erin Sorensen:*
Jane Higginbottom
Julia Last
Sophie Lightfoot
Sarah Mander

Author's acknowledgments
I would like to thank Michael Crockett for his patience and understanding and the editorial team at Dorling Kindersley who have given their all to this project for one and a half years: Rosie, Steve, Mark and Sarah. Also, thanks to Simon Kenny for his supervision of site work while I was working on this book, and especially to my Editor, David Lamb, for developing the idea for this book and for smoothing the path at every stage. Finally, I owe a debt of gratitude to my wife for her patience, help and understanding.

Dorling Kindersley would like to thank the following people: Katherine Townshend for her help with the photography; Crown Paints for supplying paint; The Newson Group for timber and other materials; Brian's Props & Locations for transport; and Sarah Whelan, and The Stylists for additional styling. Also, Hilary Bird for the index; Liza Bruml, Josephine Buchanan, Ruth Carim, Heather Dewhurst, Lesley Ellis, Claire Mitchison and Roger Smoothy for their help with the text; and Michel Blake and Teresa Solomon for production.